Kings Over the Water

Kings Over the Water

The Saga of the Stuart Pretenders

Theo Aronson

This edition published in 2014 by:

Thistle Publishing
36 Great Smith Street
London
SW1P 3BU

www.thistlepublishing.co.uk

ISBN-13: 978-1-910198-07-0

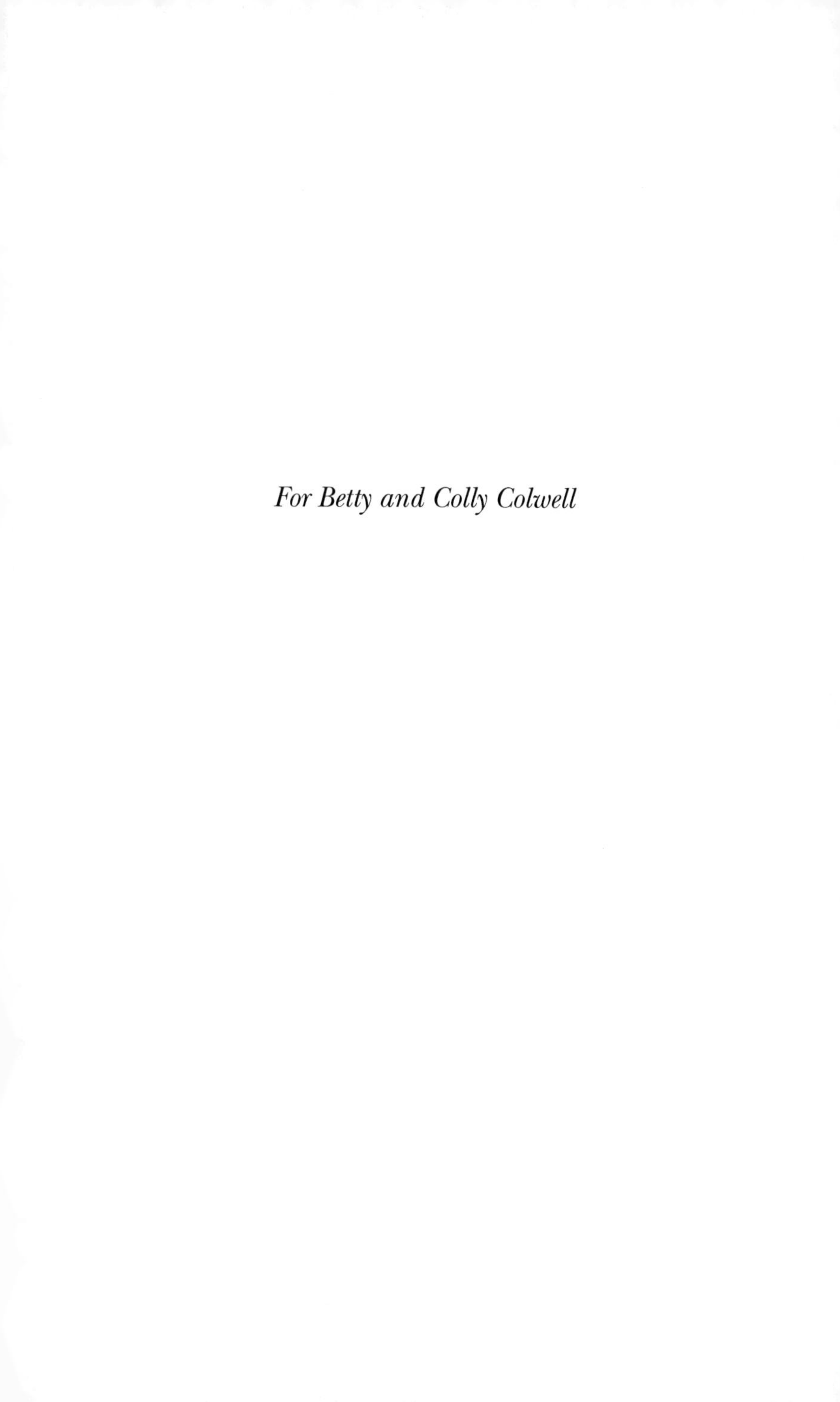

For Betty and Colly Colwell

CONTENTS

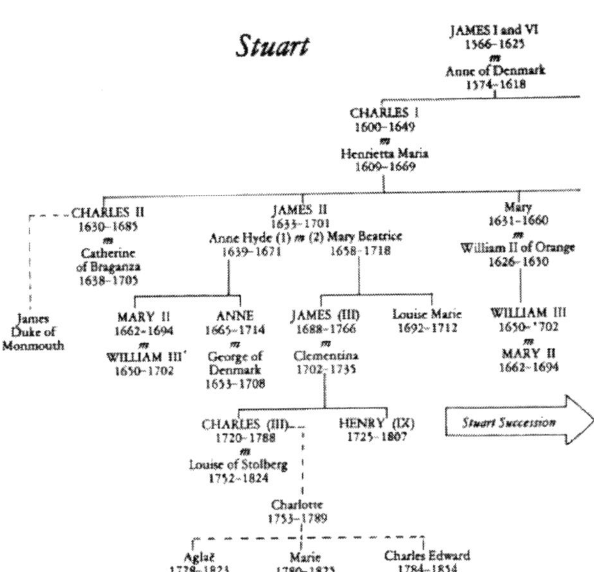

A simplified genealogical table showing the Stuart and Hanoverian successions

Hanover

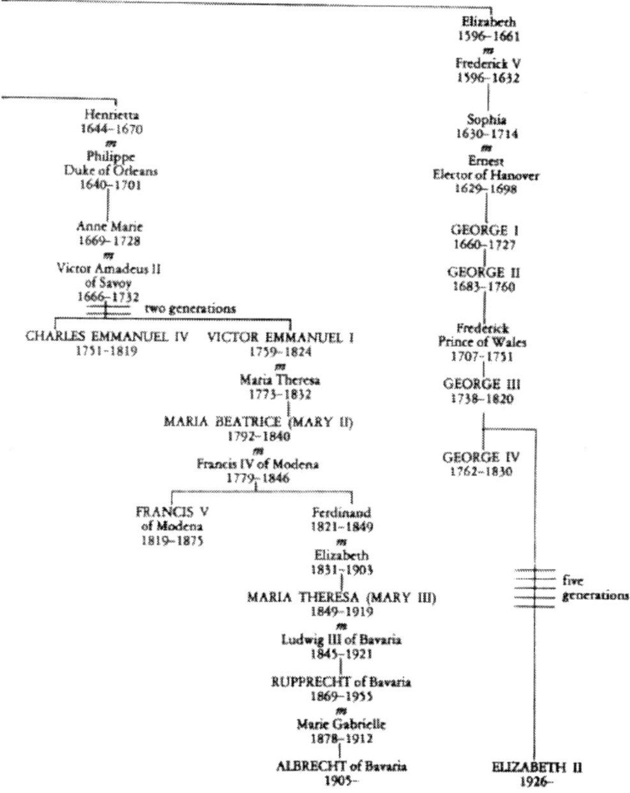

Elizabeth
1596–1661
m
Frederick V
1596–1632
Sophia
1630–1714
m
Ernest
Elector of Hanover
1629–1698
GEORGE I
1660–1727
GEORGE II
1683–1760
Frederick
Prince of Wales
1707–1751
GEORGE III
1738–1820
GEORGE IV
1762–1830
five
generations
ELIZABETH II
1926–
Henrietta
1644–1670
m
Philippe
Duke of Orleans
1640–1701
Anne Marie
1669–1728
m
Victor Amadeus II
of Savoy
1666–1732
two generations
CHARLES EMMANUEL IV
1751–1819
VICTOR EMMANUEL I
1759–1824
m
Maria Theresa
1773–1832
MARIA BEATRICE (MARY II)
1792–1840
m
Francis IV of Modena
1779–1846
FRANCIS V
of Modena
1819–1875
Ferdinand
1821–1849
m
Elizabeth
1831–1903
MARIA THERESA (MARY III)
1849–1919
m
Ludwig III of Bavaria
1845–1921
RUPPRECHT of Bavaria
1869–1955
m
Marie Gabrielle
1878–1912
ALBRECHT of Bavaria
1905–

Part One

The Catholic King

Chapter One

1

'Nobody,' King Charles II used to say, 'will kill me to make James King.' And nobody did. The Merry Monarch may have had his faults but they were preferable, reckoned the majority of his subjects, to those of his brother James, Duke of York.

On the other hand, nobody could prevent the King from dying a natural death. Charles II might have taken 'an unconscionable time a-dying' but die he eventually did. And on his death, on 6 February 1685, his brother succeeded to the thrones of the three kingdoms of England, Scotland and Ireland as King James II.

Whatever his other shortcomings, James II certainly looked like a king. Fifty-one at the time of his accession, his air was undeniably regal. He was tall, stiff-backed, well-proportioned. His long, sad, Stuart face was framed by a fair and sumptuously curled periwig. The gaze from his dark blue eyes was suitably imperious. He wore his clothes with great authority.

Whether in dully-gleaming, intricately-fashioned armour or in taffeta, lace and velvet, James II cut an impressive figure. And his manner matched his looks. Like all the Stuart kings, James II had an aloof, somewhat withdrawn quality. He moved with great dignity; he spoke with great authority.

This kingly bearing was backed up by yet another of those Stuart legacies—an unquestioning belief in the Divine Right of Kings. *Non desideriis hominum sed voluntate Dei*—not by the desires of men but by the will of God—was the Stuart motto. Not for a moment did James II believe that monarchs were accountable to anyone other than God and themselves. Authoritarian, legitimist, James II ascended the throne with the firm intention of enforcing the Royal Prerogative. His subjects, who had chopped off the head of his father, Charles I, must not be given the opportunity of trying anything like that again. 'I know the English,' he once declared. 'One must not show them at the start that one is afraid of them.'

If the new King was not exactly afraid of his English subjects, he had good reason to be wary of them. The disruption of a great part of his life had been due to their unpredictability. As it was, he had precious little English blood in his veins. His father, the *triste,* romantic, obstinate Charles I, had been Scots; his mother, the elegant and devoutly Catholic Henrietta Maria, had been part-French, part-Italian. Born in St James's Palace on 4 October 1633, James had been only seven when his father first crossed swords with his English

Parliament. For the following half a dozen or so years, the young Duke of York had been buffeted by the winds of the Civil War. Together with his mother and his elder brother Charles, he was already in exile in France when he heard that his father had been executed. The news could hardly have endeared the English to the impressionable, fifteen-year-old Prince.

James spent the following twelve years in exile; or on what his elder brother Charles, in his wry fashion, used to call his 'travels'. To free himself from the discordant, dejected, intrigue-ridden atmosphere of his brother's court in exile, James took to soldiering. He joined, first the French and then—switching sides with the bland inconsequence of the period—the Spanish army. These years of campaigning were to be the happiest he would ever know. They also intensified what was already a distinctly military mind: by his late twenties James was the fearless, honest, methodical, uncomplicated, uncompromising man that he was to remain throughout his life.

The restoration of the monarchy in 1660 released a sunburst of royal splendour to a Britain grown grey with puritanism. And as the marriage of James's brother, Charles II, to Catherine of Braganza was childless, James remained the heir to this dazzling crown. A greater contrast between the Duke of York and his charming, easy-going, supple-minded and cynical brother would have been difficult to imagine. 'Dismal Jimmy' was Nell Gwyn's nickname for the humourless James.

In one way only did the heir resemble the monarch and this was in his licentiousness. Indeed, in the number and variety of his sexual adventures, the Duke of York outstripped even his notoriously dissolute brother. 'I do not believe there are two men who love women more than you and I do,' Charles II once remarked to a French ambassador, 'but my brother loves them more.' Demanding a high standard of neither beauty nor hygiene, James satisfied his lusts how and wherever he could. Yet even his frequent lovemaking was a singularly unromantic. A certain Miss Hamilton, on being taken to bed by the lecherous Prince, complained of his love talk being confined to 'the cunning of foxes and the mettle of horses; giving her accounts of broken legs and arms, dislocated shoulders and other curious and diverting adventures' of the hunting field. With James, foxhunting was almost as important as fornication.

James's sexual activities would have been of minor importance had they not affected the succession to the crown. For no sooner had the monarchy been restored in 1660 than the Duke of York found himself in a dilemma. His current mistress—a blond, big-breasted girl by the name of Anne Hyde—was pregnant. There was nothing remarkable about this except that James appears to have given her a solemn promise that, in the event of her finding herself with child, he would marry her. There was even said to have been a meticulously drawn up contract to this effect. The agreement, made during the last, seemingly hopeless days of exile (Anne

Hyde's father had been one of Charles II's companions in exile) suddenly took on all the importance of a matter of state. Should the heir to the throne honour his promise? Some thought not. Why should a Prince of the Blood ally himself to this thrusting, unattractive girl whose father had started public life as a mere lawyer?

Chief amongst the opponents to the match was James's mother, Henrietta Maria. Threatening that 'whenever that woman shall be brought into Whitehall by one door, she would instantly quit by another,' Henrietta Maria set about finding a way by which she could avoid having to enact this particular bit of Restoration comedy. She spread rumours to the effect that James was far from being Anne Hyde's only lover. The child, she claimed, could have been fathered by any number of men. The Queen even found one such man—Tom Killigrew—ready to back up her theory. Killigrew gamely declared that 'he had had the honour of being upon the most intimate terms with her. He affirmed that he had found the critical minute in a certain closet built over the water, for a purpose very different from that of giving ease to the pain of love.'

Surely, argued Henrietta Maria, James was not prepared to saddle himself with such a strumpet?

But saddle himself with her he did. Whatever his other failings, the Duke of York was a man of his word. On the night of 3 September 1660, James and Anne Hyde were married. Seven weeks later their first child was born. Anne Hyde was to bear James seven more children, only two of whom survived childhood. Both these girls were destined to become queens of England: the elder became Queen Mary II, the younger became Queen Anne.

The marriage was happy enough. More intelligent than her husband, Anne quickly developed into a domineering wife, leading him, as that ubiquitous chronicler of the period, Samuel Pepys, put it, by the nose in all things 'but his cod-piece'. For whatever effect Anne's nagging might have had on her husband's mental attitudes, it had none whatsoever on his sexual promiscuity. The number of his mistresses was outstripped only by the number of his illegitimate children.

To compensate for her husband's infidelity, Anne took to eating. 'It was really an edifying sight to see her at table,' wrote the admiring Due de Gramont. 'The Duke on the contrary, giving way to new caprices, exhausted himself by his inconstancy and was gradually wasting away whilst the poor Duchess, gratifying her good appetite, grew so fat and plump that it was a blessing to see her.'

And the fatter she grew, the more imperious she became. Given her autocratic and haughty manner, one would have imagined that Anne Hyde had been born to the purple.

For the first half a dozen or so years after the Restoration James's countrymen were well enough pleased with the prospect of him as the probable heir. After all, no one expected the male members of a royal house to be especially intelligent or abstemious or amusing. And there was no denying that, in his capacity as Lord High Admiral, the Duke of York was taking his office very seriously indeed; he was doing sterling work in building up the Navy and he showed great courage in the course of a couple of naval battles against the Dutch. Upright and unyielding, James soon established himself as the darling of conservatism and Anglicanism.

But gradually, for one reason or another, dissatisfaction against him began to mount. It reached a climax during the late 1660s. For it was then that James took what the majority of his countrymen considered to be an unforgivable step: he was convened to the Roman Catholic faith.

From this conversion stemmed almost a century of turbulence for the Stuart dynasty.

2

Thus far the three Stuart Kings of England—James I, Charles I and Charles II—had been Protestants. Any yearnings they might have had towards the religion of their Scottish predecessors, including that most romantic of figures Mary Queen of Scots, had been kept firmly private. Even the marriage of Charles I to the Catholic Henrietta Maria had not affected the religion of the reigning House; with the exception of the youngest daughter, all their children had been Anglicans.

Throughout those long years of Continental exile, when James had been fighting with the Catholic armies of France and Spain, he had shown little sign of wishing to change his religion. Indeed, when his mother, the then exiled and widowed Henrietta Maria, had tried to talk his younger brother Henry into becoming a Catholic, James had been firmly opposed to the scheme. The chances of a restoration had seemed slim enough; neither Charles nor James wanted them jeopardised by the raising of any Catholic bogies. They fully appreciated that the majority of Englishmen were resolutely, almost fanatically, anti-papist. The infamous fires of Smithfield were seldom out of the minds of a great many Protestants.

And James was no less appreciative of this when he was convened to the Catholic faith. It is some measure of his honesty that not for a moment did he allow this consideration to deter him. That his position, his popularity, even his chances of succeeding to the throne would be threatened by this step, did not prevent him from taking it. As honourable, as obstinate and as uncompromising as ever, James fastened the rope about his own neck.

The precise reasons for his conversion remain obscure. No doubt the Duke of York was encouraged by his strong-willed wife, for Anne was converted before him. Or perhaps, as a dedicated monarchist, he was attracted to the hierarchical structure of the Roman Catholic Church, and to the unquestioning obedience of its congregation. After all, was not Protestantism the creed of rebels and republicans? James himself used to claim that his conversion was due to extensive reading, discussion and contemplation of the subject.

But whatever the reasons, having undergone his conversion, James adhered to it with all the rigidity of his nature. For the first few years, on the insistence of his less scrupulous brother Charles II, he was obliged to attend Anglican services, but once his Catholicism had been made public, nothing would induce James to soft-pedal it. When a body of Anglican bishops once asked him merely to appear beside the King in the Anglican Chapel Royal, James refused. 'My principles do not allow me to dissimulate my religion after this fashion,' he replied haughtily.

Having made one unpopular move, James made another. Early in the year 1671 his wife Anne died. James promptly set about finding a new wife. After all, with Charles II's marriage to Catherine of Braganza continuing childless and with James having only two female children, Mary and Anne, it was important that he do something about producing a male heir. An envoy was duly instructed to 'provide the Duke of York with a young and lovely wife, capable of attracting him away from illicit love affairs which cause him great heart-searching; he desires a bride who will satisfy his taste for the fair sex, and so quiet his conscience and his spirit.'

It was not an easy assignment. Beautiful young Catholic princesses were not exactly thick on the ground that season. But a scouring of the courts of Europe resulted in the choice of Mary Beatrice, Princess d'Este, or Mary of Modena as she was generally known. That Mary Beatrice, at fourteen, was less than half James's age, that she was set on becoming a nun, that she cried for forty-eight hours on being told that she was to marry a strange prince in a strange, immoral, heretical kingdom, mattered not at all. The bewildered girl was packed off to England. She arrived there on 21 November 1673 and on seeing her tall, solemn-faced, forty-year-old husband for the first time, burst into fresh tears. This did not stop James from marrying her and bedding her on the very night of her arrival. He had always had a strong sense of duty.

Had Mary Beatrice been a Protestant, her husband's countrymen would have found very little fault with her. In addition to her Italianate beauty, she was tall and slender with great charm of manner and a lively mind. But, as a Catholic, she immediately aroused suspicion. Already an agitated Parliament had protested to Charles II against the match; it predicted 'divers misfortunes and inconveniences' and feared that the new Duchess of York would 'further Papistical intrigues'. Amongst the more gullible, Mary Beatrice was believed to be the Pope's illegitimate daughter; the very dagger by which he planned to strike at the Protestant heart of England.

With this marriage, public feeling against James continued to mount. Even before the arrival of Mary Beatrice with her train of Italian ladies and Catholic priests, Parliament had begun its campaign against the newly converted Duke. The Test Act, by which only members of the Anglican Church could hold public office, was aimed directly at James and forced him to resign all his offices. The wild story of a 'Popish plot', in which Charles was to be assassinated and James put on the throne, was generally believed, and enabled the Whigs in three successive parliaments to try and prevent him from inheriting the crown. If Charles II died without issue, read the terms of these Whig Exclusion Bills, the crown must pass to the next Protestant in line of succession. For three years, during the heated discussion of the Exclusion Bills, James and Mary Beatrice were obliged to live in exile, first in Flanders and then in Scotland.

Throughout these years of banishment James held firm to his beliefs. The air over London might be thick with talk of yet more papist plots, and ranting members of Parliament might declare that they 'would not have so much as a Popish Man nor a Popish Woman to remain here, nor so much as a Popish Dog or a Popish Bitch, no, not so much as a Popish Cat that should purr and mew about the King,' but nothing would induce James to trim his sails to the Protestant wind. He would neither give up his rights to the crown nor change his religion. When Anglican friends implored him to return to the Established Church he refused.

'Never say anything to me again of turning Protestant,' ran his uncompromising reply; 'do not expect it or flatter yourself that I shall ever be it; I never shall; and if occasion were, I hope God would give me grace to suffer death for the true religion ...'

He could hardly have put it more clearly than that.

And gradually, with the inevitability of the changing tide, public opinion began to turn in James's favour. By the year 1682 the Tories were in the ascendant and, whether he be Catholic or not, no one could deny that James seemed the very personification of Toryism. A traditionalist, a disciplinarian, a conservative, he would surely prove to be a more trustworthy King than his affable but double-dealing brother. So James returned in something like triumph from his exile and for the last three years of his brother's life, James was King in all but name.

One thing only spoiled James's prospects; he had no Catholic heir. Charles II had seen to it that the two daughters of James's first marriage had been raised as Protestants and although James had plenty of illegitimate children, there seemed little likelihood that Mary Beatrice would bear him an heir. Her eight pregnancies had resulted in four miscarriages, three children who had not survived infancy and a fourth who died at the age of four. In her native Modena, there was no doubt whatsoever that these children had been poisoned by the Protestants.

Be that as it may, it seemed that it would need a miracle, or something very like a miracle, to secure the Catholic succession.

Charles II died on 6 February 1685 at the age of fifty-four. But not before he too had revealed his leanings towards the Catholic faith. A priest was smuggled up a secret stairway into the royal bedchamber at Whitehall Palace and there the dying King was given extreme unction according to the rites of the Roman Catholic Church.

He had hedged his last bet.

The Duke of York, at fifty-one, now succeeded to the thrones of the three kingdoms as James II. To some, there seemed to be no reason why he should not become the most powerful of the Stuart monarchs. He was believed to be strong-minded, he had the support of the Anglican Tories, he had promised to preserve the government 'in Church and State as it is now by law established'. One contemporary had even gone so far as to describe him as 'the darling of the Nation'.

But Charles, apparently, had always thought otherwise. If James ever became King, he once predicted, 'he would never be able to hold it out four years to an end.'

Charles II, who could be wrong about some things, was right about this.

3

Two other couples were about to play their parts in the unfolding Stuart family drama. One was James's eldest daughter Mary with her husband Prince William of Orange. The other was his second daughter Anne with her husband Prince George of Denmark.

Of the two daughters, Mary was the more appealing. Twenty-two at the time of her father's accession, she had been born on 30 April 1662. Her sister Anne was some three years younger. As, first her mother, Anne Hyde, and then her father, the Duke of York, began their slow but sure drift towards Rome, so did her uncle, Charles II, ensure that she and her sister Anne were brought up as Protestants. In fact, on the death of their mother, Charles II removed them from their father's Catholic influence entirely. He set the two girls up at Richmond House. Here they were taught, if not much else, that Catholicism was just about the wickedest thing in the world. Not even the charm of their father's new wife, the fifteen-year-old Mary Beatrice ('I have provided you with a playfellow,' was James's way of introducing his daughters to their stepmother) could reconcile Mary and Anne to their father's religion.

Yet it seems that both girls were falling prey to influences which many would have considered far more dangerous than Catholicism. The air at Richmond House might have been free of any taint of religious or political controversy but it was not entirely healthy. The half-dozen or so girls who were being brought up with the two princesses created about them an unnatural, highly emotional atmosphere, unrelieved by any contact with young male company. Before long, the adolescent Mary had fallen violently in love with an older girl by the name of Frances Apsley. Letters to her adored 'husband' poured forth in a turbulent stream. She swung between bliss when her 'dear dearest loving kind charming obliging sweet dear' Frances declared her equally fervent love, and black despair when Frances seemed to be showing indifference.

In the meantime Princess Anne was conducting a no less passionate correspondence with a Mistress Cornwallis. When this was intercepted and Mistress Cornwallis was sent packing, Anne fell under the influence of another of the girls, the handsome and masterful Sarah Jennings. The influence of Mistress Jennings would far outlast these feverish schooldays for, as Sarah, Duchess of Marlborough, she would continue to play a dominant role in Anne's life.

One way to put an end to these adolescent moonings was, of course, marriage. But this was hardly the reason why, when Mary was fifteen, she was told that she must marry her cousin, Prince William of Orange. In this case, sexual attraction was the very last consideration.

The twenty-seven-year-old William of Orange, Stadtholder of Holland, was nephew to Charles and James, the only son of their late sister Mary. He was therefore half Stuart. Anyone less like a Stuart, however, would have been difficult to imagine. For one thing, Prince William was singularly unattractive. Small, hunched, hook-nosed, hollow-cheeked, he looked like some pallid bird of prey. Although those luxuriant and flattering periwigs had been in fashion for over ten years, William still sported his own, rather lank hair. In his dark, simply-cut clothes he cut an almost sinister figure beside his tall, stylishly dressed uncles.

Nor did he have their voracious sexual appetites. In fact, women seemed to interest William not at all. Throughout his life, there were to be whispers of his homosexual tendencies. 'He had no vice but of one sort,' claimed Bishop Gilbert Burnet, 'in which he was very cautious and secret.' Although Burnet's revelation may, or may not, have referred to William's homosexuality, there was no doubt that he was always attracted to dashing and handsome young men. At the time of his marriage to Mary, William's closest companion was a red-headed young man by the name of Hans Willem Bentinck. Bentinck had joined William's service as a page and since then the two of them had been inseparable. When William was thought to be dying of smallpox in 1675 and the doctors decided that the only cure was for a young man of his own age to lie in bed with him, the twenty-five-year-old Bentinck unhesitatingly volunteered for the dangerous mission. The warmth of Bentinck's body induced the sweat that helped cure William.

But whether William was fully alive to the homosexual nature of his relationships with men like Bentinck is doubtful. It is more likely that William was simply happier in the company of men; he had neither the taste nor the talent for gallantry. A sternly Calvinistic upbringing had rendered him abstemious, priggish and parsimonious. 'His behaviour', says Bishop Burnet, 'was solemn and serious, seldom cheerful and but with a few. He spoke little and very shortly and most commonly with a disgusting dryness, which was his character at all times.' All in all, there was something distinctly chilling about the Prince of Orange.

Such then, was the real husband who was about to replace Princess Mary's make-believe husband, Frances Apsley. It was no wonder that the poor girl 'wept all that afternoon and the following day' on being told the news.

Everyone else, though, seemed happy enough. The English were delighted that the Princess who might one day be their Queen was marrying a man who was both Protestant and anti-French (William was dedicated to the destruction of French power) and even James had enough sense to realise that his countrymen would never tolerate a Catholic marriage. Happiest of all was William. Not only would the English match strengthen his hand against Louis XIV's France but it would move him several steps closer to the British throne. If James and Mary Beatrice did not provide the country with a Catholic heir, William and Mary might well provide it with a Protestant one.

These were certainly the thoughts of Charles II. On the wedding night, 4 November 1677, the genially drunken Charles saw the couple safely into bed and, drawing the curtains, embarrassed the strait-laced William by the loudly-voiced injunction: 'Now, nephew, to your work! St George for England!'

William's work,' alas, turned out to be no more successful than the work of either Charles or James.

No more than Charles's Catherine nor James's Mary Beatrice could Mary of Orange produce an heir. Her pregnancies simply ended in miscarriages.

Yet her marriage had its compensations. Once the couple had settled in Holland, Mary found herself becoming very fond of her husband. She realised that he was not nearly as cold a fish as his critics imagined and there was something about the flat, orderly Dutch landscape that suited both their temperaments. Naturally diligent, discreet and temperate, Mary came to admire these same qualities in William. She soon adjusted her submissive personality to his more dominant one. Her considerable charm acted as a foil to his bluntness; the sweetness of her temper softened the moroseness of his. With each passing year her loyalty to William increased.

It would never, of course, have occurred to Mary that there was anything untoward in William's intimate male friendships but when he became involved with one of her ladies, Elizabeth Villiers, she was very upset. She had little cause to be. Elizabeth Villiers—'Squinting Betty'—was no beauty; in fact, William's association with this forthright, intelligent, independent and arrogant woman of the world, who was a good eight years older than his wife, could even have been platonic. William admired Betty for her mind, not her body. But it took the conventional Mary many years to accustom herself to her husband's always discreetly conducted friendship.

Mary's other great loyalty was to the Protestant cause. Extremely devout, Mary gradually came to look upon herself as the instrument of God's—a Protestant God's—will. With each of Mary Beatrice's miscarriages, Mary's position as Protestant heiress presumptive to the British throne was more securely entrenched. It was simply a question of biding one's time.

Whether William of Orange was prepared to exercise the same patience was quite another matter. By now this ambitious Prince had his eyes fixed firmly on the throne of the three kingdoms. On James II's accession he sent his father-in-law a resoundingly worded pledge of loyalty. 'I shall be, to the last breath of my life,' he promised, 'yours, with zeal and fidelity.'

But it is doubtful that even the guileless James was taken in.

4

Very different from the elegant and good-natured Mary was her sister Anne. Born on 6 February 1665, Princess Anne was very much Anne Hyde's daughter. She was a fair; fat, graceless young woman with a commonplace mind and a malicious tongue. Her interests were mainly confined to clothes, cards and gossip. Her closest companion remained Sarah Jennings, who had by now married John Churchill—the brother of one of James II's mistresses.

Anne, too, was married. On 28 July 1683, at the age of eighteen, she was married to Prince George of Denmark, whose only advantage, it was generally agreed, was that he was a Protestant. 'I have tried him drunk and I have tried him sober,' runs Charles II's famous summing up of his niece's husband, 'but there is nothing in him.' 'Prince George was obliged to breathe deeply,' quipped another observer, 'lest people took him for dead and buried him.' In short, the Prince of Denmark was an amiable nonentity.

As such, he suited Princess Anne very well. She was not one to mind—or indeed, even to notice—his stupidity, his lumpishness, his corpulence or his amazing capacity for hard liquor. When he grumbled that 'We talk here of going to tea, of going to Winchester, and everything else except sitting still all summer, which is the height of my ambition,' Anne could appreciate his feelings. She also was happiest when doing nothing. Anne could only be grateful that, in marked contrast to the rest of the men in her family, Prince George was such a faithful husband.

But alas, the fact that he fathered no illegitimate children did not mean that he was successful in fathering any legitimate ones. Try as they might (and the fact that Anne experienced seventeen pregnancies in seventeen years shows how hard they did try) the couple were able to produce only one child that survived infancy. And he was to die at the age of eleven. At the time of James II's accession, however, this son had not yet been born.

So, no less than the Catholic succession, it seemed, was the Protestant succession in need of a miracle.

5

Whatever shortage there might have been of legitimate children to the Stuart dynasty, there was none whatsoever of illegitimate ones. Charles II alone had fourteen bastards. And it was one of these who emerged as the final family member to be involved in the approaching whirlwind of dynastic rivalry. He was James, the dashing Duke of Monmouth.

Monmouth's mother had been Lucy Walter, a 'brown, bold and beautiful' creature who had either seduced, or been seduced by, the amorous young Charles in the confused days of his Continental exile. To anyone who cared to listen—and a great many did—Lucy Walter always maintained that Charles had married her. Their son James, she said, was legitimate. In the early days Charles, who was extremely fond of his good-looking son, neither confirmed nor denied Lucy's story. And after the Restoration, by which time Lucy had conveniently died, Charles owned the eleven-year-old boy as his illegitimate son and created him Duke of Monmouth.

He was, by all appearances, a son to be proud of. The gods had certainly smiled on the young Monmouth: he was devastatingly handsome, beautifully mannered, exceptionally brave. Women adored him, courtiers flattered him, statesmen deferred to him and his father spoiled him outrageously. At the age of fourteen he was married to the twelve-year-old daughter of the wealthy Earl of Buccleuch; although, as Charles put it, 'they are both too young to lie all night together.'

But if Monmouth was too young for some things, he was quite old enough for others. Already, by that time, he had become a significant political figure. Because Charles II's brother Henry had died in 1660 and his brother James had been converted to the Catholic faith eight years later, Monmouth had become an important contender for the throne. Gradually, encouraged by certain Whigs, Monmouth began to think of himself as Charles's heir. Surely, as a Protestant, he would be more acceptable than his Catholic uncle, James? His doting father appointed him Captain-General of the English army and in a campaign against the rebellious Covenanters in Scotland, Monmouth showed a considerable degree of military skill.

This increased, even further, Monmouth's popularity. The London mob adored the dazzling young man. 'The Duke of Monmouth was feasted yesterday ...' reported the English envoy at The Hague to William of Orange. 'As he returned home he had the usual acclamations from one end of the City to the other.'

Such admiration turned Monmouth's vainglorious head. For, in spite of all his surface attractions,

Monmouth was a stupid young man, conceited and easily influenced. Nell Gwyn, with her talent for nicknames, always referred to him as 'Prince Perkin'. Now, as he travelled the country in semi-royal state and heard himself toasted as Prince of Wales, Monmouth came to believe that nothing could stop him from becoming King. He had every qualification, he imagined, bar one: he remained a bastard.

But this was something which his supporters were hoping to disprove. During the last decade or so of Charles's reign, they began spreading the story of the 'Black Box'. In this mysterious black box, which no one ever actually seems to have seen, was alleged to lie the marriage contract between Charles II and Lucy Walter. If such a document existed, there would be no doubt whatsoever that the Duke of Monmouth must succeed his father as King. But try as they might, Monmouth's champions could produce neither box nor marriage contract and, in the summer of 1680, Charles was obliged to publish a solemn declaration that 'on the word of a King and Faith of a Christian' he had married no woman other than Catherine of Braganza, his Queen.

Yet the rumour persisted. Almost.exactly two centuries later, in 1879, the controversial marriage certificate was said to have been discovered at Montagu House. With the words 'that might cause a lot of trouble,' the then Duke of Buccleuch very sensibly destroyed the document; Queen Victoria would hardly have relished this proof that Lucy Walter's descendants had a better right to the throne than she.

Undismayed by Charles's public denial of his legitimacy, Monmouth continued to dream his dreams. And not only to dream them but to try and transform them into reality. His intrigues against his father and his uncle became more persistent with each passing year. Eventually the long-suffering Charles had to banish him, not only once but twice.

On each occasion, Monmouth made for the Netherlands. His warm welcome by Prince William convinced James that the two of them were in league. 'The Duke of York remains of the opinion that the Prince of Orange and the Duke of Monmouth flatter themselves with the hope of being able to bring about a rising in one of the three kingdoms,' reported the French ambassador to Versailles.

Monmouth was still enjoying William's hospitality when, in February 1685, he heard that his father had died, and that James was now King.

Chapter Two

1

King James II has gone down in history as something of a monster: a tyrannical, despotic, unpatriotic bigot, determined to force the Catholic religion on his unhappy English subjects. It has been rightly claimed that the only English king to suffer a worse reputation is the controversial Richard III.

Yet, at the time of his accession, James seemed set fair for a successful reign. An agreeably Tory, Anglican and royalist Parliament voted him an unprecedently large income and it was generally assumed that, in time, it would agree to the removal of some of the restrictions on Catholic worship. The country seemed quite content for the King to reign as an absolute monarch.

Within a matter of months the storm clouds were beginning to gather. That James was in some measure responsible for this rapid disintegration is true, but it was not because of his iron-handedness that it came about; it was due, rather, to his weakness. For James

II, who at first glance appeared so strong, so authoritarian and so masterful was nothing of the sort. On the contrary, he was a born second-in-command, entirely lacking in any qualities of leadership. What looked like strength of character was really weakness. He was direct where he should have been subtle, unyielding where he should have been dextrous, headstrong where he should have been patient. Only on his accession to a position of supreme power were these failings fully revealed.

That is why the accusations levelled against James II are exaggerations. He was not a tyrant: it was simply that he lived in daily fear of rebellion by his turbulent subjects. He was not a despot: rather he had a vision of himself as a firmly impartial, God-anointed father figure. He was not unpatriotic: instead he was the most English of the Stuart kings, anxious to see his country free of continental influence. He was not bigoted: he was mainly concerned with the removal of the restrictions on Catholics and the introduction of religious toleration. James's intentions were good enough; it was his blunt, unimaginative, ham-handed approach that was so unfortunate.

Never short of enemies, James II was in many ways his own worst enemy.

2

James's wife, Mary Beatrice, was twenty-six when she became Queen. The. new King could hardly have wished for a more decorative and accomplished consort. Her looks—her cascading, jet-black hair, her creamy skin, her lustrous eyes, her sensuous mouth—were set off by the gracefulness of her bearing and the elegance of her clothes. Being tall and slim, she could wear with ease the elaborate fashions of the late seventeenth century: the stiff, elongated bodices, the panniered skirts, the lace ruffles, the roped pearls, the flashing embroideries, the cinnamon-coloured velvets and satins and taffetas.

In court circles Mary Beatrice was very popular. Beside her dour, didactic, intellectually limited husband, she appeared witty, good-humoured and intelligent. Her charm was exceptional. Even the occasional flashes of her Italian temper served to enhance her vivacity.

But beyond the limits of the court, Mary Beatrice had few admirers. She might carry out her public duties with considerable style but she could never win the hearts of her adopted countrymen. To the majority of her husband's subjects she remained the very symbol of the two things for which he was distrusted most: his allegiance to Rome and his friendship with France.

As James allowed her to play no active part in affairs of state, Mary Beatrice dedicated herself to domestic matters. Until becoming Queen, she had spent most of her married life in St James's Palace. Mary Beatrice had always enjoyed the peace of this pink brick residence with its views across the trees and water to Westminster Abbey. Now she was obliged to move to Whitehall Palace; to what she described as 'one of the largest and most uncomfortable houses in the world'. In fact, it was not a palace at all, but a bewildering conglomeration of buildings containing over two thousand rooms. Some of the apartments, like the Banqueting Hall with its ceiling by Rubens, were magnificent; others were dingy and inconvenient. James had commissioned Sir Christopher Wren to design new apartments for the Queen, so it was not until the beginning of 1687 that Mary Beatrice was settled in her suite with its marble mantelpieces, painted ceilings, panelled walls, taffeta curtains, incomparable Grinling Gibbons carvings and towering, elaborately canopied state bed.

The King had also ordered the building of a new Roman Catholic chapel at Whitehall. This meant that the devout Mary Beatrice, who had had to make do with a private oratory in her apartments at St James's, now had two chapels: the new one at Whitehall and the Queen's Chapel at St James's, which had until then been reserved for the use of Charles II's Catholic Queen.

But there were many who considered this public flaunting of the royal couple's religion to be extremely ill-advised. A leading Duke, carrying the Sword of State before the Sovereign to the first midnight Mass in the Chapel Royal, even refused to enter the building.

'My Lord,' chided the King, 'your father would have gone further.'

'Your Majesty's father was the better man,' came the deft reply, 'and he would not have gone so far.'

The diarist John Evelyn was equally disapproving ('I could not have believed that I should ever have seen such things in the King of England's palace, after it had pleased God to enlighten this nation' ran his shocked comment) but he had to admit to the beauty of the building. The marble work was 'magnificent', the carving 'exquisite', the thrones for the King and Queen 'glorious', the richly embroidered copes of the priests 'sumptuous'.

This same theatrical sumptuousness marked the Coronation on 23 April 1685. 'No coronation of any preceding King of England had been so well conducted,' noted Mary Beatrice, 'and all the arrangements had been made under the especial superintendence of King James ...' Indeed, the combination of James's belief in the Divine Right of Kings with his obsession with detail ensured the success of the occasion. The Queen looked particularly resplendent. Her dress was of white and silver brocade lavishly sewn with diamonds; her train of purple velvet was edged with gold lace and lined with ermine and white silk; she wore three crowns during the course of the day and the third was so thickly encrusted with jewels that no gold could be seen. Her bearing throughout the day's tiring ceremonies was faultless. It was noticed that she conducted herself with more composure, grace and devotion than did the King.

One thing only, she afterwards noted, marred the occasion. 'There was a presage that struck us and everyone who noticed it. They could not make the crown stay firmly on the King's head; it appeared always on the point of falling, however carefully they fixed it.'

In that superstitious age, the incident appeared highly significant.

For all the brilliance of her new position, Mary Beatrice was not happy. Her private life was far from serene. Only fifteen when she married James, Mary Beatrice had the misfortune to fall in love with him. 'I became very fond of my husband and my affection for him increased with every year that we lived together,' she admitted in later life. But, she went on to say, it must have been sinful to love anyone as much as she loved him for 'the fault brought its own punishment in the pain I suffered on discovering that I was not the exclusive object of his regard.'

She was certainly not that. It would have needed more than Mary Beatrice's combination of beauty, youth and charm to keep James at home. 'Of all the vices,' sighed the King, 'the forbidden love of women is the most bewitching, and harder to be mastered if it be not crushed in the very bud.' And, as he had not crushed it in the very bud, he surrendered himself entirely to its fascination.

Among the host of rivals with whom the naturally jealous Mary Beatrice had to contend (the secret stairway to James's bedroom was always a-rustle with skirts) were two long-standing mistresses. The first was a pale, scrawny creature named Arabella Churchill. James, whose other great physical passion was hunting, fell in love with Arabella Churchill when she tumbled from her horse on the hunting field to reveal sprawled limbs of 'exquisite beauty'. She was his mistress for some twelve years (and this in spite of the fact that his marriage to Mary Beatrice took place half way through this period) and their association had two significant consequences. Arabella's brother, John, entered James's service and so began his rise to eventual fame as the first Duke of Marlborough; and her eldest son by James became an equally distinguished soldier, James, Duke of Berwick, Marshal of France.

Arabella Churchill was succeeded by Catherine Sedley. She, too, was a plain, forthright young woman who professed herself astonished at James's infatuation with her. 'It cannot be my beauty because I haven't any,' she shrugged, 'and it cannot be my wit because he hasn't enough of it himself to know that I have any.' What it was, of course, was her rampant sexuality. Like Arabella, Catherine bore her royal lover several children and in spite of James's resolution to have done with her as soon as he became King, she was soon reinstated.

The presence of these two graceless but fruitful women had always been distressing to the beautiful but childless Queen. She was more distressed still when, not long after the Coronation, Arabella Churchill's two sons were publicly received at court. This was followed, a few months later, by the granting of the titles of Baroness Darlington and Countess of Dorchester to Catherine Sedley. This, notes one observer, 'the Queen took very grievously, so as for two dinners ... she hardly ate one morsel, nor spoke one word to the King or to any about her ... though other times she used to be extremely pleasant, full of discourse and good humour.'

In fact, her companions found that the Queen was becoming quieter, sadder and more withdrawn by the day. 'She has no other amusement whatsoever,' reported one sympathiser, 'save that of playing basset every evening—except on Sundays and the eve of days on which she receives communion.' More and more she immersed herself in her religion. Yet she could not always control her Latin pride or her Latin temper. On one occasion, having filled the room with priests, she sent for her husband and publicly berated him. She was determined, she exclaimed, 'to witness her own degradation and his disregard of the most sacred obligations no longer.' Either she or his mistress would have to go.

A contrite James packed Catherine Sedley off to Ireland. But not permanently. She was back in six months and before long the King was again visiting her at her house in St James's Square.

The one subject on which the King and Queen agreed was, of course, their shared religion. Although they were not as bigoted as their enemies implied, both husband and wife were dedicated to the advancement of the Roman Catholic faith. They saw this as their *raison d'être*. Mary Beatrice took pride in the public fashion in which her husband heard Mass, she delighted in his establishment of a papal nuncio in England, she approved of his promotion of Catholics to positions of power, she encouraged him in his efforts to remove the restrictions on Catholics. And she was no less disappointed than he was by the fact that there was still no Catholic heir.

In the first summer of the reign, husband and wife had good reason to stand together. In June 1685 they heard that James's nephew—James, Duke of Monmouth—had landed in the West Country to launch a rebellion. Monmouth, convinced of his own popularity, egged on by his supporters, misled by the half-promises of certain Whigs and overestimating the public feeling against James, had decided that his hour had struck: he must win the crown for Protestantism.

3

Monmouth had himself proclaimed King in the market place at Taunton, in Somerset. As he could hardly style himself King James II, he settled for the somewhat bizarre title of King Monmouth. With his dazzling looks, his personal magnetism and his reputation for bravery, the thirty-six-year-old Monmouth had very little trouble in arousing local enthusiasm for his cause. The motley band of 150 supporters with which he had landed at Lyme in Dorset had rapidly grown to six thousand. In the face of this enthusiastic, if ill-armed throng, the county militia of Devon and Somerset hung back; indeed, some of them deserted to join the swashbuckling new monarch. Already Monmouth had issued a proclamation denouncing James II as 'a usurper, murderer, traitor and tyrant,' accusing him, among other things, of having started the Great Fire of London and of poisoning King Charles II. He even, in a grandiloquent gesture, put a price on the King's head.

But King Monmouth's moment of glory was short-lived. A week after landing he received some disastrous news. His fellow rebel, the Earl of Argyll, who had launched a simultaneous rebellion in Scotland, had failed dismally. The combined forces of Argyll's own clan, the Campbells, and the Convenanters, proved no match for James II's Scottish army. Argyll was captured and beheaded.

Whether Monmouth imagined that he would get any help from his cousins, William and Mary of Orange, is uncertain. In the past, and in spite of outraged protests from James, they had both shown him great kindness. Mary was particularly taken with the decorative young man. Both Monmouth and Argyll had mounted their expeditions under the very nose of Prince William, and at no stage had the Stadtholder shown any sign of disapproval. But William was no fool. He realised that the headstrong Monmouth had precious little hope of success. Monmouth's failure would suit William very well: it would rid him of his main Protestant rival for the throne.

So once Monmouth had set sail, William dispatched six regiments to help his uncle put down the rebellion. Not only was William not prepared to help Monmouth win the crown for Protestantism, he was actively opposing him.

More distressing for Monmouth was the fact that very few of the Whig gentry of the West Country, on whom he had been relying for support, seemed prepared to declare in his favour. Nor, as the royal army marched closer, did any of its commanders desert to his side. As Monmouth's tatterdemalion force tramped bravely on towards Bristol, James's army closed in behind, retaking both Lyme, where Monmouth had landed, and Taunton, where he had been proclaimed King.

The end came on 5 July 1685. In one last valiant gesture, Monmouth launched a night attack on the royal forces encamped on Sedgemoor. Everything went wrong. Monmouth's force was routed and he went galloping off the field. Two days later he was discovered cowering among the ferns in the New Forest. Legend has it that his pursuers were led to the spot by Monmouth's faithful dog who had picked up his scent. Monmouth 'trembled exceedingly all over, not able to speak,' noted one of his captors.

As well he might. Having proclaimed himself King and having accused James of a host of atrocities, Monmouth could expect very little mercy. Nevertheless he sent James a contrite letter, begging for an audience. The King saw him at Whitehall for half an hour. The rumour that a triumphant Mary Beatrice had taunted the Protestant Monmouth as he crawled about the floor with his hands tied behind his back is quite unfounded: a couple of Secretaries of State were the only others in the room with the King.

When, from the Tower, Monmouth wrote to Mary Beatrice begging her to plead for his life, she answered that 'had he offended against herself alone, she would gladly have forgiven him, but since he was a traitor to both King and country, she could not and ought not to interfere'.

From James, Monmouth could not even hope for pardon. The King was polite but unforgiving. With his exaggerated notion of the mystique of monarchy—even assumed monarchy—the stiff-backed James considered Monmouth's abject attitude distasteful. 'He did behave himself not so well as I expected, not so as one ought to have expected from one who had taken it upon himself to be a King,' James afterwards remarked. As a Bill of Attainder had been passed on Monmouth at the time of his landing, there was no need for a trial: he must automatically be executed for high treason.

A firm believer in charms and spells and soothsayers, Monmouth was convinced of the truth of a prophecy that if he lived until St Swithin's Day—15 July—he would one day be a great man in the world. He tried, in vain, to have the day of execution postponed until after that date, but it was on St Swithin's

Day itself that he was beheaded. The executioner took no less than five blows of his axe to chop off that beautiful head. Only under guard could he be got away to safety from the angry crowd.

'Thus ended this quondam duke,' noted Evelyn, 'darling of his father and the ladies, being extremely handsome and adroit ... debauched by lusts, seduced by crafty knaves. He failed and perished.'

CHAPTER THREE

1

In keeping his crown safe from Monmouth, James II was encouraged in the very attitudes which would lead to his losing it to someone else.

On the one hand, even the limited support given to Monmouth and Argyll increased James's long-standing distrust of his subjects. The rebels were ruthlessly punished (the merciless commission of inquiry came to be known as the 'Bloody Assizes') and the army enlarged. On the other hand, the fact that the rebellion had been unsuccessful gave him confidence to carry out his plans to move forward faster and more assertively than he might otherwise have done.

His chief concern, of course, was for the Catholic religion. But contrary to what his critics have claimed, not even James could have imagined mat he would be able to convert the entire British population to Catholicism. Nor would he have been able to force it on them. Estimates vary, but it is said that at the time only one in seven of his subjects was a Roman Catholic; the fear of some sort of papist takeover was thus certainly exaggerated. 'This is a project so difficult—not to say impossible—to carry out,' noted the French Ambassador, 'that sensible men do not fear it.'

But sensible men were few and far between. In England, Catholicism could still conjure up visions of plots, burnings, bloody persecutions, bigoted Jesuits and the Spanish Inquisition. And at least some of this English fear of popery was plain xenophobia; an understandable distrust of the might of Louis.XIV's France. A great many Englishmen were convinced that a Catholic King on the British throne would offer no resistance to the territorial ambitions of the Catholic King on the French throne. Their apprehensions were amply backed up, in October 1685, by Louis XIV's infamous revocation of the Edict of Nantes, which resulted in a stream of Huguenot refugees to England. The influx of these persecuted Protestants was hardly guaranteed to reconcile Englishmen to James's Catholic schemes. Many were convinced that the army which James was busily building up on Hounslow Heath was to be used—as Louis XIV's dragoons had been used—against the Protestants.

But James's schemes were not anything like as sinister as the majority of his subjects imagined. In fact James seems to have had no clear, long-term objective. His immediate concern was for the removal of the unfair restrictions on Catholics and for the establishment of religious toleration. Even as explained to the sympathetic French Ambassador, James's ambitions seem eminently moderate. His ultimate goal was to grant Catholics 'entire liberty of conscience and the free exercise of their religion.'

In this apparently laudable endeavour, James came up against the Anglican Church; and against a stubbornness and an intolerance far stronger than that of which he is usually accused. Yet, instead of handling these Anglican Tories (who were, after all, his most loyal supporters) with tact and patience and subtlety; James pressed on with characteristic pigheadedness.

Each step proved more unpopular than the last. He celebrated Mass in public; he established new Catholic chapels; he granted regiments in his enlarged army to Catholic officers; a hand-picked bench of judges sanctioned his plan to admit Catholics to high offices of state; an equally complaisant ecclesiastical commission set about forcing a Catholic president on Magdalen College, Oxford; he had a papal nuncio accredited to his court; he issued a Declaration of Indulgence whereby almost all penal laws against religion were suspended; and finally, he dissolved Parliament, which had proved consistently hostile to his romanising zeal.

Yet all this need not have cost James his crown. After all, his frantic activity was winning very few converts to Rome, and his subjects took comfort from the fact that he could not live for ever. By contemporary standards James was an old man, and across the

North Sea was waiting a young heiress presumptive—the devoutly Protestant Mary of Orange with her no less devoutly Protestant husband, William. As James had no Catholic heir to continue his proselytising, his subjects were prepared to put up with him.

But in the autumn of 1687 James set in train what he hoped would be his most spectacular achievement for the Catholic cause yet. He and Mary Beatrice paid a visit to the West Country. While the Queen wallowed in the hot springs of Bath, the King was busily tackling the question of her continuing childlessness in a less matter-of-fact fashion. He paid a visit to the shrine of St Winifred at Holywell in Wales. The well, which had been a place of pilgrimage in the days before the Reformation (Henry VIII 's Queen, Catherine of Aragon, is reputed to have prayed there) had since been closed. James ordered it to be unsealed and, kneeling before it, prayed for a son.

Within two months his subjects were astonished to hear that the Queen, who had not been pregnant for five years, was with child.

2

The news of Mary Beatrice's 'great belly' caused a flurry of alarm and suspicion among james's Protestant subjects. And nowhere was the alarm and suspicion keener than in the breast of his second daughter, Princess Anne of Denmark. 'Words cannot express the fury of the Princess ... at the Queen's condition,' reported the Venetian Ambassador, 'she can conceal it from no one.'

Princess Anne's allegiance to the Protestant faith was in no doubt. Her father's occasional attempts at conversion had always proved fruitless. 'I abhor the principles of the Church of Rome ...' she assured her approving sister Mary, 'and there is the greatest reason in the world to do so, for the doctrine of the Church of Rome is wicked and dangerous, and directly contrary to the Scriptures.'

But it is unlikely that Anne's ardently expressed Protestantism was the chief reason for her fury at her step-mother's condition. So plain and lumpish herself, Anne had never really liked the graceful Mary Beatrice; she was always quick to claim that the Queen 'is the most hated in the world of all sorts of people'. Much of the scandal about Mary Beatrice that surged through the confusion of courts and stairways at Whitehall could be traced back to Princess Anne's household in the Cockpit. An additional cause for Anne's jealousy was the fact that two of her baby daughters had died early in 1687 and that in the spring of the following year she miscarried again. Anne thus remained childless, with very little likelihood of ever producing a healthy heir.

From the very first she was sceptical about the Queen's pregnancy. There was something very odd, she wrote to Mary, about the fact that their stepmother should have conceived on the very first occasion that she and the King slept together after his pilgrimage to Holywell. And how could they be so certain that the child would be a son? Already the jubilant Catholics were talking about 'a miracle'. It all seemed a little too opportune.

Mary was inclined to agree. The letter from her father, in which he told her that Mary Beatrice was pregnant, seemed far too confident; 'and that at a time when no woman could have been certain, as to give rise to some slight suspicion'.

To her husband, Prince George, when he was sober enough to take it in, Princess Anne complained about the fact that her stepmother never allowed her to see, let alone touch, her belly. Anne 'had sometimes stayed by her even indecently long in the mornings to see her rise, and to give her her shift; but she never did either'. It would never have occurred to Anne that the more fastidious Mary Beatrice was embarrassed.

'Whenever one talks of her being with child, she looks as if she was afraid one should touch her,' reported Anne to Mary. 'And whenever I have happened to be in the room as she has been undressing, she has always gone into the next room to put on her smock. These things give me so much cause of suspicion, that I believe, when she is brought to bed, nobody will be convinced 'tis her child, except it prove a daughter. For my part, I declare I shall not, except I see the child and she parted.'

Yet as the time drew near for mother and child to be 'parted,' Anne took herself off to Bath. This was odd. Anne knew that the Queen tended to give birth prematurely. Did she reckon that if she did not actually witness the birth, she would later be in a better position to deny its authenticity? And when there was a suggestion that William and Mary come over for the great occasion, Anne lost no time in warning them against any such move. 'I should be frightened out of my wits for fear any harm should happen to either of you,' she wrote.

Anne was not, of course, the only one to be sowing doubts and spreading rumours. The country was seething with gossip. On the one hand it was being claimed that the Queen had already miscarried or that the pregnancy was fictitious (caricatures showed her pinning on a cushion) and, on the other, that the child had been fathered by either the papal nuncio or a Jesuit priest. When a priest at Chester was challenged to explain how he could be so certain that the child would be a boy, he answered that as St Winifred was known to grant all or nothing, the baby would undoubtedly be a prince.

Mary Beatrice was extremely upset by all these slanders. Twice she almost miscarried. Yet any hope of getting away from the venomous atmosphere was impossible. She had wanted to go to Windsor for her confinement but James realised that this would simply add weight to the suspicion that they were planning some sort of deception. As Whitehall was full of the dust and clamour of building, it was agreed that Mary Beatrice would move to St James's Palace for the confinement. Late in the evening of 9 June 1688, the Queen was carried in her sedan chair across the park. That night she and the King slept together in their huge, elaborately canopied and curtained bed. Before eight the following morning, James returned to his own apartments.

There now took place what must be the best documented, yet least credited, royal birth in history.

On that morning of Sunday 10 June, James had only just begun dressing in his rooms when Mary Beatrice sent him an urgent message. She was about to give birth. He was to summon witnesses immediately. Much was made afterwards of the fact that all the Queen's Protestant ladies were in church at the time but, as it happened, it was one of these same Protestant ladies—Mrs Dawson, a woman of the bedchamber—who was the first to arrive. She found the Queen, attended only by her old Italian nurse and a midwife, sitting on a stool beside her towering bed. Mary Beatrice asked for a bed to be made up in the ante-chamber to allow for the public viewing but as the room had not been aired, Mrs Dawson suggested that she return to her own bed. But first, a large warming pan—in which Mrs Dawson saw live coals—was used to warm the bed.

It was in this warming pan, James II's enemies were ever after to swear, that a live baby was smuggled into the Queen's bed.

Gradually the bedchamber began to fill up, not only with the Protestant ladies but with all the people, Protestant and Catholic, that the King had summoned. By the time that the Queen was about to give birth—almost two hours after the bed had been warmed—there were sixty-seven people crowded into the room. Although the curtains across the foot of the bed had been drawn, those at the sides were open. In addition to the King, who held the Queen throughout her ordeal, and, of course, the midwife, the proceedings were closely watched by two of the Queen's ladies, the Lord Chamberlain and the rest of the Privy Councillors. When the pain was too acute, Mary Beatrice begged the King to shield her face behind his tumbling periwig: 'she said she could not be brought to bed and have so many men look on her.'

Just before ten o'clock the Queen cried out, 'Oh, I die! You kill me, you kill me.' Soon after this the baby was delivered.

'I don't hear the child cry,' she whispered, but her answer was a lusty yelling from the baby. James, who still had no idea of the sex of the child, asked the nurse what it was.

'What your Majesty desires,' she answered.

The King was exultant. As the infant was carried by the nurse through the throng into the ante-chamber, one of the gentlemen cried out, 'Room for the Prince of Wales!'

The child was named James Francis Edward. He might have become one of Britain's greatest kings, but he was to go down in history as the Old Pretender.

3

Side by side with the Queen's controversial pregnancy went an acceleration of the King's romanising policies. Quite clearly, the prospect of an heir had given James fresh impetus. In May 1688—about a month before the birth of his son—the King ordered his reissued Declaration of Indulgence to be read aloud in churches throughout the kingdom. This Declaration, by which the religious toleration enjoyed by Anglicans was to be extended to all religious groups, was apparently too bitter a pill for the Anglican clergy to swallow. The Archbishop of Canterbury, accompanied by six of his bishops, petitioned James to withdraw the order. He refused. And not only did he refuse but he had the seven bishops arrested and packed off to the Tower to await trial.

It was an extremely foolish move. As the barges carrying the bishops floated down the Thames from Whitehall to the Tower, the people lining the banks and crowding the overlooking windows cheered them on their way. The more ardent among them went plunging into the muddy water to be blessed and even the guards knelt down in prayer beside their prisoners.

Just over a fortnight after the birth of the Prince of Wales, the bishops were tried. The trial, in Westminster Hall, was a triumph for the accused. All day long crowds surged about the building, cheering the defiant bishops and questioning the legitimacy of the King's son. When the bishops were acquitted, the scenes became more tumultuous still. Bonfires—expressly forbidden by the King—blazed throughout the city and an effigy of the Pope was burnt at the very doors of St James's Palace. It was no wonder that the terrified papal nuncio described the rejoicing as 'a scene of unspeakable horror, displaying, in all its rancour, the malignity of this heretical people against the Church.'

On the very day—30 June 1688—that the seven bishops were acquitted, another seven Englishmen were making history. This 'Immortal Seven'—the Earls of Danby, Shrewsbury and Devonshire, Lord Lumley, Henry Sydney, Edward Russell and the Bishop of London—wrote a letter to Prince William of Orange. In it, they invited him to come to England with an army, to re-establish a free parliament and to investigate the legitimacy of the Prince of Wales.

4

From the summer palace of Honselaersdyck—that severely classical grey stone house close to the flat Dutch coastline—Princess Mary was following the tumultuous events in her father's kingdom. Although more philosophic and less malicious than her sister Anne, Mary could hardly welcome the arrival of her new half-brother. It was not that she hankered after the crown; it was simply that she could not stomach the prospect of a continuing Catholic dynasty.

The attitude of her husband, the astute William of Orange, was more positive. If he did not exactly hanker after the throne of the three kingdoms, Prince William was more than ready to ascend it. As a half-Stuart, married to a Stuart, he felt that he had a right to it. As a Protestant, he felt that he had a duty towards it. As a dedicated enemy of France, he needed it to strengthen his hand in international affairs.

But, as a cautious, almost fatalistic man, William was not prepared to emulate his cousin Monmouth by staging some premature rebellion. He wanted to be the spider, not the fly.

Not even the unwelcome birth of a Catholic heir encouraged him into any over-hasty reaction. When a triumphant James wrote to announce his good tidings (he made a point of telling William that his son was 'a very strong boy') William answered by sending an envoy to offer his congratulations. He even sanctioned the public saying of prayers for the infant. But it was not long before rumours of a mystery surrounding the birth came filtering into Holland. William's envoy returned with the news that very few Englishmen believed that the child was the Queen's; the whole business was alleged to have been a Jesuit trick.

This was certainly Princess Anne's opinion. All a-tremble with indignation, she dashed off a letter to Mary. Why, she demanded, after all that 'great bustle' about the Queen going to Windsor for her confinement, had she suddenly gone to St James's? Could it be because this rambling old palace (there were four doors and precious little light in Mary Beatrice's bedchamber) was 'the properest place to act such a cheat in' ? And how strange that the Queen should give birth just two days after hearing that Princess Anne was due to return to town from Bath. Why should Mary Beatrice claim that the child 'was come at the full time' when by her own reckoning it had not been due until a month later? 'After all this,' scribbled Anne, ' 'tis possible it may be her child; but where one believes it, a *thousand* do not.'

She was right about this. Stories about a faked birth were widespread.

And the fact that one variation contradicted another made not the slightest difference to the eagerness with which the stories were believed. The Queen, they said, had not been pregnant at all; she had miscarried; she had given birth to a dead child; she had given birth to a girl; the baby had been one of several bought by 'a popish woman' for a thousand pounds each; the real mother was Irish, specially brought over to give birth in a room in St James's Palace.

But whichever of these versions one cared to believe, all agreed that a live male child had been smuggled into the Queen's bed in a warming pan.

And no sooner had the child been born than there were rumours that he had died, to be replaced by another. The original baby was said to have had a round face and black eyes; the substitute baby had a long face and blue eyes. A surgeon claimed to have made a cautery on the baby's neck and then to have been shown a baby without any such mark. An aide, sent by the agitated Princess Anne, swore to having seen a dead baby in the nursery and, a few hours later, to having been shown a healthy baby.

This torrent of speculation disturbed Princess Mary profoundly. While her calculating husband was quite ready to believe the warming pan story, she was not entirely convinced. She had known nothing but kindness from her young stepmother ('I love her as if she were my own daughter,' Mary Beatrice had once exclaimed) and she did not know how to answer the Queen's ecstatic letters. In desperation she wrote to Anne, sending her a long list of questions concerning the baby's birth. No detail—from the identity of the people present to the cutting of the cord—was to be left undescribed. Although admitting that she was 'generally lazy,' Anne applied herseif to Mary's formidable questionnaire. Her string of replies gleaned, for the most part, from Mrs Dawson, were hardly conclusive. Nevertheless they seem to have satisfied Mary that the birth had been faked. Perhaps she really believed this; perhaps it was simply what, in the depths of her Protestant soul, she wanted to believe.

Essentially honest, Mary could not keep her disapproval hidden from her father and stepmother. Mary Beatrice noticed the change in her attitude immediately. Twice she wrote to Mary, complaining of the fact that she seemed to be showing no interest in her half-brother. Why, asked the worried Mary Beatrice, was Mary so indifferent to the child?

Mary's reply was adroit. 'All the King's children will have as much affection and kindness from me as can be expected from children of the same father,' she wrote.

So, having convinced herself that the child was not the true heir to the throne, Mary was ready to listen to the plea from the 'Immortal Seven' for her husband to come over and save the situation. Her Protestant duty, as she now saw it, was to support her husband in the dethroning of her Catholic father.

Chapter Four

1

The infant Prince of Wales was formally baptised on 15 October 1688. The ceremony, in the Queen's Chapel at St-James's, was conducted with full Catholic rites; the godparents were the Pope, represented by the nuncio, and the Queen Dowager, Catherine of Braganza. Yet, despite the brilliance of the occasion, it lacked joyousness. If the bad fairy was not there in person, she was certainly present in the minds of every member of that sumptuously dressed assembly, for everyone knew that Prince William of Orange intended invading England. Even the stolid James had woken up to the fact that the worst was about to happen. At his levee the following day he told the Earl of Clarendon the disturbing news that he had had no word of congratulation from his daughter Mary.

And then he said a significant thing: 'You will find the Prince of Orange a worse man than Cromwell,' he warned.

During the past few weeks James had been making frantic efforts to undo some of his own damage. Revealing the weakness behind that stony façade, he began making panicky concessions; recently appointed Catholics were dismissed from various high offices and Anglicans reinstated, a deputation of bishops was received and appeased, a general pardon was granted to all political offenders. He dashed off effusive letters to his daughter Mary. 'And although I know you are a good wife and ought to be so,' he wrote, 'yet for the same reason, I must believe you will be still as good a daughter to a father that has always loved you so tenderly, and that has never done the least thing to make you doubt it.'

His appeals were echoed by Mary Beatrice. The Queen wrote to say that she refused to believe that William was planning an invasion or that Mary would accompany him. 'I don't believe you could have such a thought against the worst of fathers, much less against the best, that has always been kind to you and loved you better than all the rest of his children.'

It was no wonder that Mary's lustrous Stuart eyes were so often filled with tears.

As the question of the Prince of Wales's legitimacy seemed to be the chief bone of contention, the desperate King decided to institute a public inquiry into the circumstances of the birth. A host of witnesses, ranging from the Queen Dowager to a laundress, gave evidence under oath. Much of this gynaecological information was considered to be 'obscene to a degree of horror' and 'put all the ladies to the blush.'

Nevertheless it served to prove, conclusively, that it was the Queen who had given birth to the baby.

'The unprejudiced were left in no shadow of doubt,' observed one Englishman, 'but the number of unprejudiced in England was small.'

It was indeed. The mass of the public simply refused to believe the truth, including Princess Anne. When Lord Clarendon (he was her uncle, the late Anne Hyde's brother) arrived to tell her the result, he was deeply shocked, both by her incredulity and by her bawdy comments. When her father sent the entire Privy Council to back up Clarendon's testimony, Anne changed her tune. Their visit, she assured them sanctimoniously, was quite unnecessary; the King's word was quite good enough for her.

There was nothing much left for James to do other than wait for his son-in-law's invasion. Having very wisely refused any help from Louis XIV, he deployed his own forces as best he could. How loyal they would prove to be, he did not know. Regiments were brought in from Ireland and Scotland, coastal garrisons were strengthened, the bulk of the army was massed at Hounslow and the fleet was concentrated along the most likely area of attack—the east coast. Everything now depended on an east wind to swell the Dutch sails.

From the windows of his apartments at Whitehall, James II could see the weathercock on the roof of the Banqueting House. All he had to do was to watch for the first sign of what his hopeful subjects were now calling the 'Protestant wind'.

2

The wind shifted towards the end of October. But it did not remain in the east long enough for William's invasion fleet to get very far. The Dutch were forced back to shore. James was not at all surprised by this show of Divine intervention; 'the Host', he explained, 'has been exposed these several days.'

The King was being too sanguine by half. Within a few days the Protestant wind was once more blowing at full force and William's vast armada was sailing down the east coast of England. Huge banners, proclaiming 'The liberty of England and the Protestant religion,' fluttered from the mastheads. But instead of landing, as expected, along the east coast, the invasion fleet moved boldly southward through the Straits of Dover and then westward along the English Channel as far as Torbay in Devon. Unchallenged, William landed his great army on 5 November 1688.

The 'Glorious Revolution' was under way.

Yet, from first to last, it was a singularly inglorious affair. There was no fervent upsurge of national feeling to support William in his crusade against James. The greater part of the nation had no strong feelings either way; it was quite content to leave matters in the hands of a few noblemen. Nor was William prepared to march resolutely against James; on the contrary, he was hoping to avoid a direct confrontation altogether. If his uncle chose to flee rather than fight, that would suit him very well. Having issued a proclamation to the effect that he had come to establish, among other things, a free parliament, religious toleration and the truth about the Prince of Wales's parentage, Prince William inched his way towards London.

James's behaviour was equally lack-lustre. Even less than William did he want any confrontation. If the Prince of Orange had landed any closer to London, James might well have been able to rouse some of his countrymen into an immediate repulsion of the foreign invader, but he was finding William's long, slow advance unnerving. He remained in London, reluctant either to fight or to negotiate. 'The Virgin Mary,' quipped one irreverent observer, 'is to do all.'

As the days went by, William moved deeper and deeper into the country and one by one various noblemen and officers deserted James. Not until William had been in the country for over a fortnight did James bestir himself. On 19 November, he joined the royal army in Salisbury. His arrival proved to be anything but a rallying call to his already dispirited forces; his nose started bleeding, and with this loss of blood went a loss of all resolve. When Lord Churchill, brother of James's onetime mistress Arabella Churchill and his second-in-command, led a wholesale desertion, the King could take no more. He returned to London.

But there were still more betrayals to be faced. On the way back to the capital James's other son-in-law, the oafish Prince George of Denmark disappeared. During the course of the last few days George had greeted the news of each fresh desertion with an amazed *'Est-il possible?'* Now, on being told of his son-in-law's own desertion, James could manage the wry remark, 'So! *Est-il possible* gone too?' Quite frankly, the King had suffered worse losses; the defection of 'a stout trooper', he said, would have been more serious. He minded only because George was 'the husband of my dearest child.'

But George had made no sudden decision. Even before accompanying James to Salisbury, he had made up his mind. James's 'dearest child,' Princess Anne, writing secretly to Prince William, had wished him every success in 'this so just undertaking' and had assured him that her husband would be joining him 'as soon as his friends thought it proper.'

Anne herself was the next to go. Early one morning, still wearing her dressing gown and accompanied by her adored Sarah Churchill, she slipped out of the Cockpit at Whitehall by a back stairway and headed towards Nottingham. She left behind a letter for the Queen. In honeyed phrases she explained that the shock of her husband's unexpected desertion, coupled with the prospect of the King's displeasure, had been too much for her to bear. 'Never was anyone in such an unhappy condition,' she gushed, 'so divided between duty and affection to a father and a husband.'

This professed divided loyalty did not prevent Anne, on reaching Leicester, from forming an association 'to destroy all the papists in England in case the Prince of Orange should be murdered by any of them.'

Anne's desertion finished James. Her betrayal came as a final blow to his already reeling nervous system. 'God help me!' he cried out. 'My own children have forsaken me!' It now seemed to him as though there was no one he could trust; no one to whom he could turn for help and advice. Every hour brought news of yet another defection or of yet another great officer of state slipping across to France. 'So many fugitives are named,' noted the Tuscan envoy, 'that it would appear there is no one left to flee now except the King and Queen.'

Rejected, bewildered, hopelessly out of his depth, James decided on the one course of action best suited to William's plans. He fled. It is tempting to speculate on what might have happened if James had remained to negotiate with the invader. After all, no one had offered William the crown; nor had he yet laid claim to it. The Prince could hardly have elbowed a *de facto* King off his own throne, let alone imprison or behead him; and the notoriously fickle and insular public might well have come to resent any manhandling of an English King by a Dutchman. But by deciding on flight, James played right into William's hands. The Prince of Orange, it was said, 'was very cheerful and could not conceal his satisfaction at the King's being gone.'

James was to leave behind an empty throne which William, together with the complaisant Mary, was only too happy to fill.

3

Throughout these turbulent weeks, Mary Beatrice had remained at Whitehall. For the thirty-year-old Queen, this was a frightening and lonely period. Not only had the King gone off to Salisbury for a time but he had insisted that their infant son be sent away to safety. The boy had been taken to Portsmouth by Lord and Lady Powis. Alone in her splendid new apartments at Whitehall, Mary Beatrice did her best to show calm in the face of an increasingly dangerous situation. The mobs were out in the streets, burning Roman Catholic chapels and harassing priests. The air was thick with talk of betrayals, packings-up and flight. Even in her own bedchamber the Queen could not feel safe. One day, on drawing on her glove, she felt something in it: it was a pamphlet carrying a scurrilous story about the birth of her son.

The return of James from Salisbury brought no comfort. In fact, the presence of the demoralised King made matters worse. 'The confusion at the English court could not be greater,' noted the Tuscan envoy. 'When the King arrived in the Queen's room, he abandoned himself to despair, telling her that all was lost, for he saw himself betrayed and deserted by his most dear and trusted servants.' James's only coherent thought was for the safety of his family. His son must be kept out of the hands of the Protestants. He gave orders for the infant Prince to be taken from

Portsmouth across the Channel to France; the Queen would set out from Dover on the same day.

But it was already too late. Lord Dartmouth, in charge of the arrangements at Portsmouth, refused to comply with the King's wishes. So the Prince was sent back to London by road. For twenty-four hours an anguished Mary Beatrice had no idea of the whereabouts of her son. Perhaps it was just as well, for the Powis coach, carrying the heir back to London, had a hair-raising journey. The little party lost its way in a forest, it narrowly escaped capture by a detachment of Protestant cavalry, it was forced to take shelter in a shabby house on the outskirts of Guildford and, just before reaching Whitehall at three in the morning, it was attacked by an angry crowd in Southwark. The only consolation was that the Prince of Wales had slept soundly through all these vicissitudes.

The King decided that the Queen and their son were to make their escape to France in the early hours of Monday 10 December. A distraught Mary Beatrice begged to be allowed to stay with her husband; loving James so deeply, she was quite prepared for the infant Prince to be sent to France in the care of someone else. But, for the one time in this confused period, James was firm. She must go. He would follow her later.

The night sky was still aglow with the flames of the buildings set alight by the mob some hours before, when Mary Beatrice slipped out of the Palace. She was disguised as an Italian laundress, in a black dress, a cloth cloak and a muffler. With her were her baby, the French Comte de Lauzun, an Italian servant named Francesco Riva and two nurses. It was a night of bitter cold and driving rain. A coach, waiting at the gate of the privy garden took the little group to Horseferry Stairs on the river. They clambered down into an open boat and, in torrential rain, rowed across to Lambeth Stairs. Here they discovered that the horses had not yet been put into the waiting coach; so for something like an hour the Queen huddled against the wall of St Mary's Church. Across the black and storm-tossed river, Mary Beatrice would have been able to make out, for the last time, the lights of Whitehall.

There was a spine-chilling moment when a lantern-carrying stranger, intrigued by the little group, came towards them. The resourceful Riva tripped him up as though by accident and the man, accepting Riva's profuse apologies, disappeared into a nearby inn. When the coach was finally ready, the Queen with her baby and the women, climbed aboard and set out, through the wild night.

At Gravesend the party was rowed out to a specially hired yacht. To prevent the captain from suspecting the identity of the bedraggled group, one of the women conspirators, already aboard the vessel, shouted reproaches at her 'sister' for keeping them waiting. Once safely aboard, Mary Beatrice was hustled into the hold. The crossing was frightful. Always a bad sailor, Mary Beatrice was violently seasick and even the normally placid Prince of Wales was fractious. At one stage they passed so close to two English frigates that they could hear the bells ringing for prayers: they must have felt certain of capture.

The yacht reached Calais on the morning of 11 December 1688. As the Continental calendar was different, the date in France was 21 December. The Queen was welcomed by the surprised Governor of the town and accommodated in the comfortable home of the Procureur du Roi. From here she wrote to Louis XIV in order, as she put it, 'to seek consolation and refuge with the greatest and most generous monarch on earth.' She wished to entrust to his care her most precious treasure: her son, the future King of England.

4

The Queen's flight had been dramatic; the King's was merely muddled. In the early hours of the very day—11 December 1688—that Mary Beatrice arrived in France, James crept out of his apartments in Whitehall. As a disguise, he wore a black wig. Accompanied by a gentleman and a page, the King, like the Queen the morning before, was rowed across the dark and swirling Thames to Lambeth. In midstream he dropped the Great Seal overboard. It may have been an accident but perhaps James imagined that without the Great Seal no parliament could be called.

From Lambeth the little party rode hell-for-leather along the slippery Kentish lanes and by ten that morning they were at Elmley Ferry on the Swale. Here they boarded a specially hired customs boat. But while waiting for the tide, the boat was boarded by a rowdy party of seamen on the lookout for escaping papists. Their leader, not recognising the most important escaping papist of all, suggested that James hand over his valuables; his men, he explained, were a rough bunch. The King obliged but managed to save his Coronation ring by pushing it into his drawers. Presumably he imagined that, just as no parliament could be called without the Great Seal, no usurper could reign as King without the Coronation ring. When neither jewels nor a bribe of fifty guineas shook the anti-papist convictions of the leader of the seamen, James was arrested, brought ashore and held captive in an inn at Faversham. Its' name, ironically enough, was 'The Arms of England'.

These English arms proved anything but comforting. Once James's true identity had become known (some of his subjects had a maddening tendency to sink to their knees at the unexpected sight of him) the highly gratified seamen were more convinced than ever that so valuable a prize must not be allowed to slip away. To local officialdom, on the other hand, the illustrious captive was a source of acute embarrassment. What was to be done with him? After several days of dithering, and much to William's discomfort, it was decided that the King must be taken back to London. He arrived there on Sunday, 16 December.

And then an extraordinary thing happened. To James's astonishment, his entry into his capital was triumphant. The crowd, whose capariousness James had always distrusted, proved never more fickle than now. His coach could hardly pass through the press of excited people. They waved, they cheered, they lit bonfires, they clanged bells. It was all very strange. James, in his ponderous fashion, decided that his subject's previous dissatisfaction must have been 'not at his person but at his religion.'

But James had no intention of being diverted by this sudden show of popularity. After all, nothing had changed. William was already at Windsor and James was no more anxious to become his prisoner than he had ever been. He was still set on escape.

And William was just as set on letting him escape. Subtly, the Prince began to put pressure on the demoralised King. He ignored James's suggestion that they meet. He replaced the loyal guard at Whitehall with Dutch soldiers. He sent a deputation to tell James—in the early hours of the morning—that 'for the safety of his person,' he must get out of London as soon as possible. And in case the implications of this message were not clear enough, a member of the deputation warned the King that Prince William intended imprisoning him.

So the frightened James moved, under guard, to Rochester. Here he discovered—as William intended that he should—that although the front of the house in which he was being held was guarded, the back garden, which ran down to the banks of the Medway, was not. There was nothing to prevent him from getting away and James slipped out of the house one midnight and boarded a waiting pinnace. It carried him, in the teeth of an icy wind, towards the yacht that would take him to France. On Christmas Eve 1688, the *Henrietta* set sail and at three the following morning, exactly a fortnight after he had started his escape, James landed at Ambleteuse on the French coast.

5

The Glorious Revolution of Whig mythology was over. Within six weeks of James's arrival in France, William and Mary were proclaimed King and Queen. William had not been prepared to settle for anything less. Those who had imagined that he would be content with the role of Regent or Prince Consort were soon disillusioned: indeed, according to an indiscretion on the part of William's close friend Bentinck, the Prince would have preferred to wear the crown alone, with Mary as a mere Queen Consort. But in the end, husband and wife agreed to reign jointly as William III and Mary II. And as Mary had not the slightest desire to wield power, it was William alone who ruled.

But not everyone was prepared to accept him. The crowds that had cheered the bewildered James on his forced return to London had given an indication of a reaction in his favour. He had been right in assuming that it was his papistry, not his person, that had been so bitterly resented. There was a widespread feeling that there should merely have been some clipping of James's wings; that it was wrong for an anointed king to be driven out, like some latter-day Lear, by his own daughters.

With an exiled monarch often having more appeal than a reigning one, the grass on the other side of the Channel suddenly seemed much greener. If James had now turned Protestant, declared Sir George Halifax a few months after the King's flight, 'he could not be kept out four months.'

James had hardly landed in France before a movement in his favour—a Jacobite movement, taking its name from the Latin for James—began to gather force. Composed mainly of conscience-stricken English Tories, Irish Catholics, and Scotsmen whose hearts could still beat faster for the Scottish House of Stuart, the Jacobites looked to James as their true sovereign. Even some of William's ministers were known to 'look one way and row another'. Throughout the three kingdoms certain gentlemen, raising their glasses to toast the monarch, would pass their lace-cuffed hands over the water decanter: in this way, they would be drinking the health, not of King William III, but of the 'King over the Water'.

It was the dawn of that most romantic of legends; the Jacobite saga, in which men would scheme and fight and die in the hope of restoring three generations of exiled Stuarts to the British throne.

Part Two

The Jacobite King

Chapter Five

1

Whatever James's former subjects might have thought, Louis XIV had no doubt whatsoever that his royal guest was still the King of England, Scotland and Ireland. There were several reasons for the Sun King's attitude. A practising Catholic, he would always have preferred a Catholic to a Protestant monarch; an unquestioning legitimist, he could hardly approve of the dethronement of an anointed king; an astute politician, he appreciated the value of James II in his almost continuous battle against William of Orange. The two monarchs, moreover, were first cousins: James's mother, Henrietta Maria, had been the sister of Louis's father, Louis XIII.

It was as a fellow sovereign then, that Louis XIV welcomed James and Mary Beatrice to France. He lost no time in establishing them in a palace which was second only to Versailles in splendour: the Chateau of St Germain-en-Laye. Rising high above the Seine, some twelve miles west of Paris, St Germain was to be the centre of the Jacobite movement for the following quarter of a century. It was a magnificent palace—immense, sombre, sprawling, set above a formal terrace designed by Le Notre and stretching for a mile and a half along the river. Its park and gardens were superb. The palace had been hastily but lavishly decorated for its royal guests. The King's suite had been painted in dark green and gold, the Queen's oratory in white and gold. Thirty-one porcelain vases had been brought in for the flowers in the Queen's apartments; the orangery was ablaze with two hundred pots of flowering shrubs. On the Queen's dressing table was a toilet set in silver-gilt. The choice of her bedroom tapestries was less happy. When Mary Beatrice recoiled at the scenes of the family of Darius cringing at the feet of the all-conquering Alexander, her tactful host had them replaced by a less appropriate set.

To enable his guests to live in a style befitting so opulent a palace, the French King not only let them have it rent-free but provided them with a monthly pension equivalent to some £3,000. He had already presented Mary Beatrice with a casket containing the welcome gift of gold *louis* to the value of about £10,000; as the Queen had managed to save some of her personal jewellery and as the King had smuggled out some three thousand guineas, it was assumed that they would be able to maintain a suitably impressive court.

At first the household at St Germain was almost entirely French but gradually, in dribs and drabs, the faithful followers arrived from across the Channel. Within a month, except for a handful of Italians, the court had taken on an exclusively British character. This brought its own complications. As many new posts had to be created to employ all these loyalists, and as very few of them could afford to live outside the palace, it was soon crammed to capacity. And it was not long before St Germain took on the inward-looking, impecunious air of most courts in exile.

What made things still more difficult was the fact that the exiles were up against the most brilliant, extravagant and formal court in Europe. Before long, James and Mary Beatrice had become enmeshed in a web of protocol, the intricacies of which they had never before experienced.

Mary Beatrice made her first mistake with the Sun King's brother—the Duke of Orleans, always known as Monsieur. The small, scented, rouged, braceleted, bejewelled and beribboned Monsieur was a specialist in etiquette. When the Queen of England neglected to kiss him on their first meeting he was furious. Taking peevishly to his bed, he refused to meet the Queen again until the matter of kissing had been cleared up.

'Tell me what you wish me to do;' begged the bewildered Mary Beatrice of Louis XIV, 'I will salute whosoever you think proper; but in England I would kiss no man.'

Her second mistake was with Louis's daughter-in-law, the Dauphine. This ugly Bavarian princess was no less obsessed than Monsieur with matters of precedence. She bitterly resented the fact that this princess from Modena was now a queen whereas she was still a princess. When Mary Beatrice sent Lord Powis to give her compliments to the Dauphine, she, like Monsieur, took to her bed and refused to see the English Queen's envoy. Lord Powis, she grumbled, was not nearly illustrious enough: he was merely a marquis, not a duke. Obligingly, James made Powis a duke. But this was still not enough. So the good-natured Mary Beatrice, overlooking the fact that the Dauphine should have called on her first, went in person to pay her respects.

The English Queen took every care to be correctly dressed for the occasion. In her dress of black velvet over an elegant petticoat, and with her dark hair elaborately styled, she could not be faulted. Louis led her to the door of the Dauphine's apartments (the Princess was still feigning illness) but would not enter: the presence of the monarch would mean that the Dauphine could not occupy an armchair—only a chair without arms—and this indignity the Dauphine was determined to avoid. Mary Beatrice was not going to be seated more importantly than she.

The Queen, imagining that the Dauphine would be in bed, was delighted to find her up and dressed.

'Madame,' explained the Dauphine sweetly, 'I wished to get up to receive such an honour as your Majesty does me.'

But she took care, it was noticed by her hawk-eyed ladies, to seat the Queen in an armchair on her left, and not as protocol demanded, on the right.

There was more trouble when the rest of the Princesses of the Blood trooped in to pay their respects to Mary Beatrice. Although highly gratified to receive her kisses, they resented the fact that only the tomboyish wife of the ladylike Monsieur should be given an armchair while they were relegated to stools. But these had been the French King's instructions.

It was no wonder that one of Mary Beatrice's ladies, in attempting to describe these royal jostlings to an eager aunt in Ireland, contented herself with sending a passage torn out of a devotional book: 'The Lord said unto my Lord, sit thou on my right hand until I make thine enemies my footstool.'

On less touchy observers, Mary Beatrice was making an excellent impression. Madame de Sévigné was in raptures about her smooth complexion, her dark eyes, her generous mouth, her flawless teeth, her graceful figure, her quick wit. 'That is what a Queen should be like,' announced Louis XIV; she possessed 'such high qualities, such graceful and majestic manners, and above all, such piety and virtue' that he was delighted to be able to help her.

In fact, the fifty-year-old Sun King was so enthusiastic about the thirty-year-old Mary Beatrice that there was a suspicion that he might be falling in love with her. But Madame de Maintenon, whom the King had married secretly some years before, had no cause for jealousy: much to the astonishment of the French court, Mary Beatrice was clearly in love with her elderly husband.

The Queen's devotion to the King, bizarre enough in a court where marital affection was 'a thing gone right out of fashion,' was still more inexplicable as James became better known. At Versailles they had been expecting a proud, forceful, authoritarian monarch; what they saw was a vague, irresolute and unimpressive old man with a tendency to gabble on and on about his misfortunes. 'To tell the truth,' declared the robust Duchess of Orleans, 'our dear King James is good and honest, but the silliest man I have ever seen in my life ... Piety makes people incredibly stupid.' Indeed, James's excessive devotion to the Catholic Church seemed faintly idiotic to the worldly French court. Even members of his own circle complained about the number of priests in the entourage at St Germain. 'There goes a good man;' shrugged the Archbishop of Rheims, 'he has renounced three kingdoms for a Mass.'

Madame de Sévigné was even more dismissive. 'When one listens to him,' she sighed, 'one realises why he is here.'

2

Having seated herself on her father's throne, Queen Mary II proceeded to astonish observers by her apparent lack of remorse. Even her closest adherents professed themselves shocked by her insouciance. She arrived at Whitehall in the highest spirits, laughing and talking, and moved among the bowing courtiers and curtseying ladies as though she were at a wedding. That night she slept in Mary Beatrice's bed. Up at first light the following day, and still in her dressing-gown, she darted from room to room—opening cupboards, peering through doors, turning down quilts. Such light-hearted behaviour, decided Sarah Churchill, was 'very strange and unbecoming'.

'For, whatever necessity there was of deposing King James,' continued Lady Churchill, 'he was still her father, who had been so lately driven from that chamber, and that bed; and, if she felt no tenderness, I thought she should at least have looked grave, or even pensively sad, at so melancholy a reverse of fortune.'

But poor Mary was merely acting a part. On instructions from William, who was determined that they should show no sign of guilty conscience, she was putting on a brave face. Alone, she was much less cheerful.

'Many people have the fortune to be able to talk of things about which I have to be silent,' she confided to a friend. 'You must not doubt the sincerity of my feelings when I say that I cannot forget my father, and I. grieve for his misfortune.'

Every day seemed to bring another reminder of her treachery. When only one bishop came to pay her his respects, she sent her chaplain to ask the Archbishop of Canterbury—whom James had once imprisoned—for his blessing. His Grace's reply cut like a whiplash. 'She must first ask her father's [blessing]' ran his message, 'for his would not otherwise be heard in Heaven.'

And when the prudish Mary lefused to acknowledge James's one-time mistress, Catherine Sedley, she soon felt the edge of Catherine's famously sharp tongue. 'Why so haughty, madam?' she demanded. 'I have not sinned more notoriously in breaking the seventh commandment *with* your father, than you have done in breaking the fifth *against* him.'

Two days before the Coronation—which took place on 11 April 1689 and at which the Archbishop of Canterbury refused to officiate—Mary received a letter from her father. It left her in no doubt as to his feelings towards her. If she were crowned while he and the Prince of Wales were still living, he threatened 'the curse of an outraged father would light upon her, as well as that of God who had commanded duty to parents.'

In a last minute attempt to clear her conscience before attending the Coronation ceremony, Mary's sister Anne again called in Mrs Dawson to question her about the birth of the Prince of Wales. The old lady's answer gave her no cause for comfort. 'He is, madam,' she swore, 'as surely your brother, the son of King James and of his Queen, as you are the daughter of the late Duchess of York.'

Although William had already dropped all pretence of not believing in the legitimacy of the Prince of Wales ('The King [William III] in his heart never doubted of that birth,' wrote Lord Ailesbury), Princess Anne had good reason to be concerned about it. As usual, she was pregnant. A couple of months after the Coronation she gave birth to a son. As he was a strong boy, who showed every sign of surviving infancy, there was much rejoicing at court. Here surely, was a sign of Divine approval—and Divine forgiveness. With William and Mary, unlikely to produce an heir, and with Anne the heir presumptive, the line would now be continued through Anne's son. The boy was named William, after the King.

But instead of strengthening the bonds between William, Mary and Anne, the birth of an heir in the next generation subjected them to greater strain. For the truth was that Princess Anne's attachment to her sister and brother-in-law had barely outlasted the Glorious Revolution. The days when she had flaunted her fat figure, all bedecked with orange ribbons, had long since passed. Always jealous, Anne resented the ruling whereby, in the event of Mary's death, William would continue to reign, and that she would have to wait until his death before inheriting the throne. To her circle, William now became 'the monster'.

For her part, Mary could not help resenting the fact that Anne had given birth to a son. She became more resentful still when her sister's domineering friend Sarah Churchill, now Lady Marlborough, began to encourage Anne to act independently of William. Without a word to either William or Mary,

Lady Marlborough arranged for Parliament to debate the question of an increase in Anne's allowance. Mary was furious. On tackling her sister about the rumours of this debate, Mary was told, in Anne's maddeningly off-hand fashion, that 'some of her friends' were hoping to improve her settlement.

'Pray,' asked Mary imperiously, 'what friends have you but the King and me?'

But Mary knew well enough. Both she and William had always disapproved of Lady Marlborough. They disapproved of her still more when they learnt that the Commons had granted Anne an annual sum of £50,000 for life.

The family atmosphere became even more poisonous when Anne asked for the lodgings at Whitehall which had recently been vacated by one of the late Charles II's mistresses. Mary refused. Her sister would have to wait until the Earl of Devonshire had decided whether or not he wanted the lodgings. In that case, snapped Anne, she would remain where she was, she 'would not have my Lord Devonshire's leavings.'

Nor would Mary allow Anne to use the vacant Richmond House. Here, Anne's annoyance was understandable. After all, William and Mary were busily refurbishing both Hampton Court and Kensington Palace for their own use; surely she, who now had a royal heir to raise, was also entitled to a country residence? But Mary remained obdurate and Anne slammed out of the room.

It was no wonder that the Jacobites could talk gleefully about thieves falling out and that they should begin thinking of ways whereby the turbulent family situation could be turned to their advantage. The father's curse might yet split the daughters asunder.

3

If James II was prepared to sit back and wait for the tide to turn in his favour, Louis XIV was not. James had been in France for little more than a fortnight when the French King invited him to his elegant little house at Marly. Over a private supper Louis talked James into setting out for Ireland to launch a campaign against William. The English King felt honour bound to agree. Although the idea of an undemanding exile had its appeal, so deeply ingrained was James's sense of royal obligation and so dedicated his commitment to the Catholic cause, that he could not refuse. Louis XIV might only be interested in using James as a means of keeping William pinned down in Ireland, but for James the adventure promised a greater prize.

Certain that the road to London lay through Dublin, James was about to make the first of the many Stuart attempts to win back the crown.

Ireland had been the obvious choice for such a campaign. Except for a number of Protestants in the north, this green and misty land was fervently Catholic. If the kingdom of England was happy enough to accept William and Mary, the kingdom of Ireland was not. Lord Tyrconnel, whom James had previously appointed Lieutenant-General of the Irish army, was urging him to come over and take advantage of this strong Catholic force. 'Sir,' prompted Tyrconnel, 'I beg of you to consider whether you can with honour continue where you are, when you possess a kingdom of your own, plentiful in all things for human life.'

Prodded by the shrewd Louis XIV and encouraged by the fiery Tyrconnel, James made ready for an Irish campaign. And as Scotland was hardly more reconciled to the new régime, it was agreed to stage a Scottish rebellion to coincide with the campaign in Ireland. Displaying the romantic naivete which was to typify so many Jacobite undertakings, the King and Queen wrote off to their fellow Catholics for help. Surely the Catholic powers would be only too ready to support this anti-Protestant crusade? But whether it be from Rome, Modena, Florence, Turin, Venice or Vienna, there was no help forthcoming. The fact that the days of religious wars were over was unappreciated by the simple-minded James and the devout Mary Beatrice. The powers of Europe, whether Catholic or not, were only interested in keeping France in check. William III was their ally against Louis XIV; why should they undermine him?

But France proved generous enough. James was given ships, arms, money and men. For the English King's own use, Louis provided carriages, horses, canteens of cultery, a dinner service, a bed and linen.

When James sailed from Brest early in March 1689, the French King was there to see him off. Presenting him with his own jewelled sword, Louis delivered a touching farewell. 'I hope I may never see you again,' he declared, 'but if Fate wills we should meet once more, you will find me unchanged.'

Madame de Sévigné's parting pronouncement was far more trenchant. 'He is now where he ought to be,' she announced, 'he has a good cause; he defends the true religion; being a courageous man, he must conquer or die.'

4

Having landed at Kinsale in southern Ireland on 12 March 1689, James entered Dublin twelve days later. He was rapturously received. In a black slouch hat, a snuff-coloured, silver-laced suit and the blue Garter ribbon, James looked the very picture of a stylish Stuart King. With Tyrconnel riding before him carrying the sword of state, the King passed through the acclaiming streets. Young girls flung flowers at his feet, cheers rang in his ears, tapestries billowed from house fronts. At the gates of Dublin Casde, James was greeted by four gorgeously robed bishops carrying the Host. Dismounting, he knelt down on the cobbles. At the Cathedral, he attended a Te Deum. Before long, he had established a court and summoned a parliament; Dublin had become, if not the most colourful, certainly the most frenetic capital in

Europe. Never had this small Irish city known such scenes of debauchery. Indeed, the purpose of the campaign seemed lost in an orgy of drinking and gambling and fornication.

Not that the purpose had ever been very clear. James saw the campaign as a means of clearing the path first to Scotland and then to England. The Irish, headed by Tyrconnel, saw it as a way of establishing an independent Ireland. The French saw it as a method of keeping William's mind, and troops, off the Continent. But however one happened to see it soon became quite irrelevant; the campaign .just never seemed to get under way. The combination of James's dithering, his advisers' bickering, the ill-trained, ill-disciplined and ill-armed troops, the shortage of supplies, the lack of funds, the drenching rain, all worked against any hope of success.

'It is a chaos like that before the creation,' wrote one exasperated French general. Only no creation emerged from this particular chaos. Month followed month and still James could make no headway against the firmly entrenched, if no more adventurous, forces that had come over from England. The situation remained one of stalemate.

The only institution to make any progress was the newly convened Irish parliament. And here the progress was frantic. In no time at all it had passed a series of vindictive measures against the Protestant English. The members made it quite plain that their sole interest in James's campaign was to get their own back on their English oppressors. This, not unnaturally, alienated James's English and Scottish sympathisers. Already the campaign in Ireland was being regarded as a war between Protestants and Catholics. None of this was likely to further James's cause.

If the Jacobites had been bogged down in Ireland, in Scotland they were proving to be much more lively. The Duke of Gordon, refusing to recognise William and Mary as King and Queen of Scotland, had been holding Edinburgh Castle in the name of James II. When the Castle fell to the Orangists, Viscount Dundee ('Butcher' to his enemies and 'Bonny' to his friends) carried on the fight by raising the clans against William. On 17 July 1689, Dundee led his fearsome Highlanders down from the craggy heights of Killiecrankie onto William's advancing troops. Although the bloody day went to the Jacobites, Dundee was mortally wounded. He died the following day. With him, for the moment, died Jacobite hopes in Scotland. Leaderless, the clans dispersed.

In the summer of 1690, after James had been in Ireland for well over a year, William landed at Carrickfergus to take personal command of his forces. He was determined to breathe new life into the campaign. He was as good as his word. From then on, things moved swiftly to a climax. On 1 July, uncle and nephew met in battle on the River Boyne. For James, the Battle of the Boyne was an inglorious affair. Throughout the day's fighting he remained as irresolute as ever. Although his forces occupied the more advantageous position, he hesitated to attack. William, on the other hand, was determined to give battle. Boldly crossing the river, he forced James to defend himself. But it was hopeless. By evening James was leading his army in its flight from the battlefield.

With the Battle of the Boyne, James lost Catholic Ireland, and Protestant Ireland gained one of its greatest anniversaries.

Arriving at Dublin Castle, James was met by the Duchess of Tyrconnel. To his dry complaint that the Irish had certainly run well that day, the Duchess gave an even drier rejoinder: he seemed, she said, to have beaten them. Her opinion was echoed throughout Ireland. And on James announcing that he intended leaving the country, most Irishmen decided that he was deserting them. They could not forgive him. And they have not forgiven him yet.

James sailed from Kinsale and on 20 July 1690 he landed at Brest. Contrary to Madame de Sévigné's ringing prediction, he had neither conquered nor died.

'We are utterly astonished ...' she now declared, 'at the return of the poor King of England.'

5

As the Jacobites had anticipated, the coolness between Queen Mary and Princess Anne was beginning to work to their advantage. Disenchanted with her morose brother-in-law, Anne was having second thoughts about her betrayal of her father. One day, in a fit of remorse, she wrote asking James to forgive her: 'if wishes could recall what is past,' she gushed, 'I had long since redeemed my fault.'

In her double-dealing, Anne was being egged on by Sarah Marlborough. In fact by now both Lord and Lady Marlborough were up to their necks in Jacobite plotting. Marlborough who, as Lord Churchill, had broken James's spirit by defecting to William in 1688, was now thinking of defecting to James. In an abject letter to St Germain, he assured his previous sovereign that 'he could neither sleep nor eat in peace for the remembrances of his crimes against him.' He promised, moreover, to bring Princess Anne 'back to her duty'. As Anne was putty in the hands of her beloved Lady Marlborough, it did not take long to convince her in which direction her duty lay.

For the well-intentioned Mary, all this was extremely upsetting. She had troubles enough without Anne turning traitor. Nothing could still her own guilty conscience about her father. During the Irish campaign her sympathies had been cruelly torn. 'I have every reason to be in distress for a husband ...' she admitted, 'but I am a daughter as well, and I do not even know what wishes I ought to make for a father.'

The Jacobites were delighted to hear about Mary's embarrassment at the theatre when she was obliged to sit through such lines as 'she usurps the throne, keeps the old King in prison and at the same time is praying for a blessing on the army.' Only her highly developed sense of dignity kept Mary from leaving her box.

With William so often away on Continental campaigns (the Irish campaign had merely been one of many) Mary was left to cope, not only with open defiance to the new régime on the part of certain peers and clergymen, but with a tangle of Jacobite conspiracies. Many taverns and coffee-houses were hives of sedition; no number of regulations or arrests seemed able to stem the flood of treasonable cross-Channel correspondence. Things became all the more alarming, then, as Mary came to suspect that Anne was being drawn into these intrigues; that she was gradually being converted into a figurehead for Jacobite opposition.

When Anne's husband, the empty-headed Prince George of Denmark, suddenly stowed his luggage aboard a ship at Portsmouth and announced that he was going to serve his adopted country as an ordinary naval officer, it was generally believed that he was trying to focus attention on Anne in her role as rival to Mary. Annoyed, Mary refused to allow George to do any such thing. He must remove his luggage and leave Portsmouth at once. On George complaining that he would cut a sorry figure if, after his patriotic gesture, he were to pick up his bags and slink off", Mary remained firm. George complied, and the family rift deepened.

Convinced that the Marlboroughs were behind all this suspicious behaviour, Mary decided to tackle

Anne on the subject. The sisters met at Kensington Palace, to which William and Mary had recently moved. There was something about this formal, unpretentious, well-designed house that had far more appeal for the sovereigns than the jumble of Whitehall; they might almost be back in their beloved Holland. Now, amongst the damasks, velvets, tapestries and blue and white porcelain with which Mary had furnished her new home, a violent scene was played out between James II 's daughters.

Mary started by asking Anne to break with Sarah Marlborough. Whether Mary, or even Anne herself, fully appreciated the sexual nature of the friendship between Anne and Sarah is unlikely; in any case, Mary was concerned only with its political aspect. But Anne refused to make the break. When Mary lost her temper, Anne lost hers. When the Queen accused her sister of throwing away public money—part of her parliamentary grant—on a favourite whose husband was suspected of treachery against the Crown, Anne stormed out of the Palace.

The following day—1 May 1692—William dismissed Marlborough from all his offices. Although William had other, very good, reasons for getting rid of Marlborough (he was quite right in suspecting that Marlborough was in touch with James) very few believed that it was not the result of Mary's quarrel with Anne. But the stubborn Princess was not to be beaten. She continued to bring Sarah to court. When Mary objected, Anne wrote her such an insulting letter that her emissary refused to deliver it. But delivered it was, and Mary answered it by forbidding Lady Marlborough to live in Anne's Whitehall apartments—the Cockpit—any longer. In high fury, Anne and Sarah left the Cockpit and set themselves up at Sion House.

The break between the royal sisters was complete.

On only one more occasion during their lifetimes did the two sisters speak to each other. While still living at Sion House, Anne gave birth to yet another stillborn child. Mary came to pay a visit of sympathy but, in her self-righteous fashion, tackled Anne again on the question of Lady Marlborough's dismissal. There was another violent scene. This time it was Mary who slammed out. Matching her sister's vindictiveness, Mary set about subjecting Anne to various petty humiliations. The royal guards were removed from her household; she was denied certain royal privileges; she was no longer accorded a royal salute.

A few weeks later Marlborough was arrested and sent to the Tower on a warrant 'that he was charged with high treason and for abetting and adhering to their Majesties' enemies.' Anne was appalled. She was more appalled still when Sarah announced that she intended leaving Sion in order to be nearer her imprisoned husband. 'If you should ever do so cruel a thing as to leave me,' cried out the distraught Anne, 'and should you do it without my consent (which if I ever give you, may I never see the face of heaven) I will shut myself up and never see the world more ...'

Mary and Anne had one final encounter. One day, in the autumn of that same year, Princess Anne and Prince George were driving through Kensington. As they swayed along the road towards London, their coach was overtaken by another. In it sat Queen Mary. Hurriedly, each sister turned her head away and stared in the opposite direction. The Queen's coach clattered by and disappeared down the road. It was the last that James II's daughters ever saw of one another.

No wonder that the pious Mary should regard the whole wretched business in terms of Divine judgement. 'In all this,' she sighed, 'I see the hand of God, and look upon our disagreeing as a punishment upon us for the irregularity by us committed upon the Revolution.'

6

In the spring of 1692, James set out on his second attempt to win back his crown. The time had never seemed more favourable. Marlborough had not been the only one to show signs of turning his coat. The Jacobite party was stronger than ever, and James was assured, by the army of spies and agents, that large areas of the country were ready to rally to his banner. William, moreover, was campaigning in Flanders.

James's optimism was shared by Louis XIV. Always ready to strike a blow at William of Orange, the French King assembled a large invasion fleet and organised a combined French, English and Irish army, numbering over ten thousand men. An excited James wrote to the Pope asking for a subscription towards this new crusade and, warming to his task, authorised the distribution in England of a manifesto so virulent that the English Jacobites were in despair. This threat of vengeance on those who had once betrayed him was hardly likely to win hearts for James's cause. Diplomacy had never been his strong point. A more modified version was printed; but not, alas, before James's daughter Mary had had the original proclamation copied and circulated.

In April James arrived at La Hogue, near Cherbourg. There he waited for a favourable wind to carry the French invasion fleet to England. He waited in vain. Nor did his firmly-held conviction that the English Admiral would come over to him ever materialise. Instead, the French and English fleets were joined in battle. When the French retired in disorder, the English followed them into the bay of La Hogue. From the cliffs above the churning sea, James watched his former subjects scrambling aboard the French ships and setting them ablaze. His reactions to this dramatic scene were, to say the least, unexpected. In Ireland, a couple of years before, when James had heard that a French fleet had beaten an English, he had remarked sharply, 'It's the first time, then.' Now, as his dreams of winning the crown went up in smoke, he cried out proudly, 'Ah! None but my English seamen could do so brave an action!'

For, in spite of this resounding defeat at the hands of his countrymen, James, who had so often been accused of being nothing more than the cat's-paw of the Catholic King of France, still thought of himself, not only as the King of England, but also as an Englishman.

Chapter Six

1

Exile was bringing out the best in Mary Beatrice. Although, during her years in England, she had been known for her charm and her intelligence, she had always been overshadowed by her husband. Twenty-five years his junior, she had been allowed to play no active political role. Nor, in the blindness of her love, had she been able to appreciate her husband's many shortcomings. What had seemed like faults to others—his authoritarianism, his bluntness, his romanising zeal—had seemed like virtues to her. Only of his marital infidelity had she ever been disapproving.

But by now the tables had been turned. James's two failures—in Ireland and at La Hogue—had finally broken the remains of his once-proud spirit. From now on he was to devote himself, more and more, to God. Mary Beatrice, on the other hand, was gaining in poise and confidence. In the exaggerated fashions of the last years of the century—the even longer bodices, the more heavily embroidered fabrics, the towering Fontange head-dresses—she looked more commanding still. With each passing year she was emerging as a much stronger personality than her husband. The French court had always admired her for her beauty, her grace and her vivacity; now they were coming to appreciate her good judgement. 'I never saw anyone understand affairs better than the Queen,' wrote one admirer. During James's absence in Ireland, it was she who organised the court in exile. From that time on she gradually came to take over the management of Stuart affairs; making appointments as vacancies arose, pawning her jewellery to help pay for campaigns, sifting the true adherents from the charlatans. Honest, practical and unaffected, Mary Beatrice was becoming the linchpin of the exiled court.

Now and then she was known to be quite sharp with her stolid husband. One day the two of them were sharing a coach with Louis XIV's brother, the effeminate Monsieur. As usual, Monsieur was holding forth on the subject of his jewels and his furniture.

'And has not your Majesty, who had such great wealth, not built and furnished some beautiful palaces?' asked Monsieur of King James.

'Money!' interrupted Mary Beatrice. 'He never had any. I never knew him to have a half-penny.'

'I had plenty,' countered James, 'but I spent it all on great ships, cannon, guns ...'

'Yes,' snorted the Queen, 'and a lot of good they did you. Why, they have all been used against you.'

None of this is to say that Mary Beatrice was a virago. Far from it. She remained a good-natured woman, tactful and softly-spoken. She had very little taste for the gaieties of Versailles, for the fêtes and balls and spectacles that were such a feature of Louis XIV's court. Indeed, the Queen was happiest when she was furthest removed from all this dazzling social activity; when she was visiting the Convent of the Visitation at Chaillot. This became one of her delights. Overlooking the Seine just outside Paris, the convent housed an order of Salesian nuns, the same order that Mary Beatrice had hoped to enter before she was married to James. Having visited it once or twice, the Queen hired a suite of rooms (the very ones in which James's mother, the exiled Henrietta Maria had once lived) and here she would come in search of tranquillity. Throughout the rest of her life, Mary Beatrice would spend long periods of retreat at Chaillot.

The Queen's chief source of happiness during these first years of exile was her little son, Prince James Francis Edward. By all accounts, he was a lovely child, with his mother's dark eyes. Inevitably, there was criticism of the way he was being raised. One complained of his being dressed like a puppet; another of his being dressed like a child of seven. He should have been swaddled at all times, not only at night, ran one criticism; and was it really necessary, ran another, for him to be tossed up, gurgling, into the air in order to prevent him from contracting what the English called 'Ricket'? Even at two years old, claimed one admirer, the Prince of Wales was 'a great Lover of Music'; while another described him as 'for his age, a lovely child, from the nose upwards all of the Queen, and the lower part and mouth resembling his uncle'—Charles II.

Indeed, with each passing year James Francis Edward gave the lie to the theory that he was not the son of his parents. He resembled them both, having his father's long Stuart face and his mother's black eyes and wide mouth. Sir Godfrey .Kneller, who had painted James II and Mary Beatrice so often that he felt he could paint them from memory, had no doubt that the Prince was their child. 'I say the child is so like both,' he claimed, 'that there is not a feature of his face but what belongs either to the father or mother; this I am sure of...'

But what finally quashed, or should have quashed, any calumnies about the boy's birth was the news, in 1692, that the Queen was once more pregnant. James was delighted. Regally, he summoned his daughter Mary, the Privy Council, and the peers and peeresses of the realm to witness the birth. Only two peers applied to William for leave to do so; both were refused. Nevertheless a suitably impressive body of witnesses were crowded into the room when Mary Beatrice gave birth, on 28 June 1692, to a daughter.

'See what God has given to be our consolation in our exile,' exclaimed James as he put the new-born baby into his wife's arms. And although the Princess was named Louise Marie at an elaborate christening ceremony in the presence of Louis XIV, she was to be known as 'La Consolatrice'. And this is what she would prove to be.

2

James had another son with him at St Germain. This was James Fitzjames, Duke of Berwick, the eldest of the King's two illegitimate sons by Arabella Churchill. Berwick had been eighteen when his father had lost his crown in 1688. Even at that age the young man had shown signs of exceptional military ability, and since turning sixteen he had taken part in various Continental campaigns. Although, for Mary Beatrice's sake, James had kept Berwick well away from court, the young man had joined him on his final flight. Since then, Berwick had been closely associated with James's fortunes. He had accompanied him to Ireland and to La Hogue and when Berwick was not on campaign with the French army, he lived with the family at St Germain.

By now Mary Beatrice had become reconciled to his presence. As a matter of fact, it would have been difficult not to have become reconciled to Berwick. He was a young man of exceptional qualities. He looked every inch a Stuart—tall, long-faced, blue-eyed, dignified. His great personal charm depended not so much on any vivacity of manner as on his sincerity, his directness and his commonsense. Like his father, he was an uncomplicated, methodical man;

but he was far more intelligent. Where James was obstinate, Berwick was pragmatic; where James was a born second-in-command, Berwick was a leader of men. In the often insular, conspiratorial and priest-ridden atmosphere of the Stuart court in exile, Berwick's straightforward presence was like a breath of fresh air. To the ageing James, he brought considerable comfort. However conciliatory Berwick might be, his devotion to the King, to the Stuart cause, to the Catholic religion and to the theory of the Divine Right of Kings was unquestioning.

In 1693, when he was twenty-three, Berwick was given James's permission to serve in the French army. He was made a *Lieutenant-Général.* At the battle of Neerwinden he was taken prisoner and brought before the commander of the enemy forces. This commander was none other than Berwick's cousin—William of Orange. It was a significant meeting.

There they stood facing each other, the small, hunched, hook-nosed William and the tall, erect, handsome Berwick, each very conscious of the other's position in the world. The one was the *de facto* King of England, the other the son of the *de jure* King of England.

William made some polite remark; Berwick answered it with a low bow only. Annoyed, William put on his hat. Berwick, determined that he should not remain uncovered in the usurper's presence, replaced his own hat. More annoyed still, William ordered Berwick to be taken away. Later, as was customary, Berwick was exchanged for some important English prisoners of war.

Before long, Berwick was involved in yet another of his father's attempts to regain the throne. On 28 December 1694, Mary suddenly died of smallpox at Kensington Palace. She was only thirty-two. Although William was apparently overcome with grief, James appeared quite unmoved. No one, he commanded, was to take any notice of his daughter's death; no one was to go into mourning. His lack of compassion was echoed by at least one Jacobite clergyman, who chose as his text 'Go, see now this cursed woman, and bury her, for she is a King's daughter.'

Mary's death led to an upsurge of hope in the Stuart camp. Surely this was the time for a restoration? A fresh rash of Jacobite plots broke out across the face of England; the air was thick with talk of a great Jacobite uprising. Determined to find out the true extent of his support, James sent Berwick on a secret journey to London. The practical young man was not very enthusiastic about the mission. He became even less so when he discovered that his name was being used to rally support for a plot to assassinate William. The plan was for a party of Jacobites to attack and murder William as he entered a narrow lane beside the Thames on his way home from hunting. This would signal the start of the proposed Jacobite uprising. Berwick, who might have countenanced a kidnapping, was certainly not going to sanction a murder. Discomforted, he hurried back to France.

But by now—February 1696—plans for the restoration attempt were well under way. Assured that his adherents would flock to his banner, James called on 'our loving subjects to rise in arms and make war upon the Prince of Orange, the usurper of our Throne.' For a third time, and with considerably less confidence, Louis XIV placed his ships and his soldiers at James's disposal. But this time he sounded a firm warning. The invasion fleet was not to set sail until James's erstwhile subjects had risen. Fair enough; except for the unhappy fact that James's erstwhile subjects had no intention of rising until the invasion fleet had set sail.

So while James waited at Calais for a sign from London, the conspirators waited in London for a sign from Calais.

While everyone waited, the Assassination Plot was uncovered. One of the conspirators, having lost his nerve, blurted out the whole story to William's friend Bentinck. Bentinck warned William and an announcement was made to the effect that the King would not go out hunting that particular day. At this, more conspirators panicked. Two of them revealed further plans for William's assassination. On this, William acted. Wholesale arrests were followed by wholesale executions. Properties were confiscated, papists were banished from London, and Parliament passed an act affirming William's legal right to the throne and the exclusion of King James and 'the pretended Prince of Wales'.

Quite clearly the rising, and the invasion, were off. No bonfires blazed on the coast of Kent to inform James that the rebellion had started. And to give the whole abortive adventure the *coup de grâce,* a raging wind smashed the French transports. Louis withdrew his troops and, on 5 May 1696, James trailed back to St Germain.

But he was not particularly disappointed. For it had been with the greatest reluctance, affirmed Berwick, that James had agreed to take part in the invasion plan at all. By now the King was more concerned with the winning of a heavenly, rather than an earthly, crown. What King James II was after was sainthood.

3

Just as Mary Beatrice had started spending periods of retreat at the convent at Chaillot, so had King James II started visiting the monastery presided over by the Abbe de la Trappe. Lying in a deep, dank, mist-wreathed valley on the edge of a dark forest, the monastery was an appropriately cheerless setting for the harsh discipline within its walls. In total silence, the band of brothers divided their time between praying, fasting, contemplating and trying to grow vegetables in the poor soil. The only words spoken, as a form of greeting, were hardly designed to dispel the all-pervading gloom: 'We must die, brother,' they intoned, 'we must die.'

Convinced that the loss of his throne, and his failures to regain it, were punishments for the licentiousness of his youth, James submitted himself to the discipline with all the single-mindedness of his temperament. His chief concern now was for the salvation of his soul. By prayer, by fasting, by penances, by pilgrimages, by long religious discussions, he set about earning his own salvation. Already he was being looked upon as a martyr to his faith; might he not become a saint as well?

Each day saw him becoming more pious, more melancholy, more convinced that life could hold nothing of interest for him. 'I give Thee, O my God,' began his daily prayer, 'most humble thanks for taking my three kingdoms from me ...' His own death became his favourite topic; it did nothing to brighten a conversation that had always lacked sparkle. 'Remember always,' he wrote as an instruction for his son, 'that Kings and Princes, and the Great Ones of the Earth, shall give an account of their conduct before the dreadful Tribunal of God, where every one shall be judged according to his works. Consider that you are come into the world to Glorify God, and not to seek your pleasure ...'

But if James was ready for God, God was not yet ready for him. As Mary Beatrice once smilingly remarked, she was quite certain that all this talk of death and salvation would not 'accelerate his death by one single moment'. Besides, there were still things of this world to which, like it or not, he was obliged to give his attention. When, for instance, the Polish throne became vacant, James was told that it was about to be offered to him. Louis XIV urged him to accept, but James would not hear of it. For one thing, he had lost his taste for kingship; for another, he felt bound to his countrymen by his Coronation Oath. The crowns of the three kingdoms belonged, not only to him, but to his son.

Louis's encouragement had not been entirely altruistic. He would not have been very sorry to get James off his hands. The English King was proving expensive to keep and his military and political value had been negligible. But, as well as getting James off his hands, Louis wanted to get him off his conscience. For in 1697 the eight-year-long war between France and the Grand Alliance (of the Holy Roman Empire, England, Spain and Holland) finally came to an end. The Peace of Ryswick was signed that September. Its most important clause, as far as James was concerned, was the one by which France finally recognised William of Orange as King of England. This bitter pill was slightly sugared by Louis's recognition of William as *de facto* and not *de jure* King.

And there could have been yet another coating of sugar. It appears that Louis and William had had a confidential discussion on the question of William's successor. As William had no son, and as he had a very poor opinion of Princess Anne, he had talked to Louis about the possibility of the crown passing to the Prince of Wales after his death. One day, before the signing of the Peace of Ryswick, Louis suggested that James cease pressing his claim to the throne on condition that William agree to naming young James as his heir.

Before James could reply, Mary Beatrice cut in. She would rather see her son dead, flashed her answer, 'than possess the Crown to the prejudice of his father'. Tactfully, Louis changed the subject. Who was he, after all, to argue with the theory of the Divine Right of Kings?

To the young Duke of Berwick, who was present at the conversation, it seemed as though an important opportunity had been lost. It was, he wrote many years later, 'a great imprudence to refuse such an offer'.

4

James Francis Edward turned nine in the year that the treaty of Ryswick was signed. Already, he was developing into a striking-looking youngster: tall and slender, with his black, almond-shaped, Italianate eyes vivid in his pale face. His hands, like the hands of all the Stuarts, were long and finely boned. With his long, curled hair, his lace jabots, his many-buttoned, full-skirted satin coats, knee-breeches and stockinged legs, he already looked more like a little adult than a boy. Sometimes he seemed to be the image of his beautiful Modenese mother; at others he looked more like his melancholy father.

And in the same way that he resembled both parents in looks, so did his personality seem like a combination of theirs. Like Mary Beatrice he was sharp, sensible, straightforward, but he also had something of James's withdrawn quality. Without being the least precocious or conceited, he was very conscious of being a prince. This gave him a somewhat reserved air; the boy seemed old for his age. 'Although he is only nine years old,' noted the Duchess of Orleans, 'I am convinced that even now he would govern better than his father.' It was not, perhaps, saying much (the Duchess had a very poor opinion of James) but it was saying something.

Everything in his upbringing was designed to foster this air of self-control. Life at St Germain might not have been as artificial as at Versailles but it was hardly less formal. No matter how meagre the resources (and they were becoming more meagre by the year) royal standards had to be maintained. From babyhood, almost, young James had realised that he must always behave like a prince. Once, when a group of down at heel Scots veterans fell to their knees as his coach rumbled by, he stopped and called them over. Having made a little speech, he gave them his purse. That it contained a mere twelve *pistoles* was not important: what was important was that the Prince had done the right thing and that the old soldiers were delighted.

From infancy young James had had his own suite. Until the age of seven he had been in the care of governesses; since then he had passed into the hands of men. From waking to sleeping, his life was controlled by a governor. And the governor, in turn, was guided by a set of rules laid down by King James. There were no less than twenty-eight of these awesome 'Rules for the Education of the Prince of Wales'. They covered every aspect of the boy's daily life: prayers, meals, studies, audiences, recreations and physical exercises. They allowed, in fact, for everything but a spontaneous enjoyment of boyhood. Even the extent of his friendships was prescribed. Only with his governor's permission, and always in his governor's presence, was he allowed to associate with two or three carefully chosen companions. James II was determined that his son should not be exposed to the corrupting influences of his own youth; therefore young James and his friends were never allowed to 'whisper or run into corners' and they were certainly never allowed out of sight. It was hardly the atmosphere in which natural relationships develop.

Inevitably, young James found that he was more at ease with his sister, Louise Marie, than with other boys. Although four years younger than her brother, Louise Marie was almost his equal in wit and intelligence. She seems to have been an exceptionally lively girl with none of her brother's reserve. Why, his governor once sighed, did James have to cultivate the affability which to his sister came as second nature? Unlike the self-possessed James, Louise Marie was always singing. Years later, well-meaning matrons would remember that the little Princess had used to sing hymns; no, the truthful Mary Beatrice would say, they had been tunes she had learned at the opera.

It says a great deal for the strength of young James's character that this rigid system of upbringing did not turn him into either a delinquent or.a prig. James II had every reason to be proud of his son. By the summer of 1700, when, on turning twelve, young James made his formal début at the court of Louis XTV, he had developed into an engaging youngster: not brilliant, but spirited, polite and well-adjusted, very aware of his responsibilities as the rightful heir to one of the leading royal dynasties in Europe. His deportment, on the glittering but nerve-racking occasion of his debut, is said to have been faultless. Every Jacobite heart beat faster at the sight of this slender youth as he made his obeisance to the Sun King. He was their pride, their Sacred Flame, their hope for the future. He was the 'White Rose' of their aspirations.

5

While the heir to the claimant of the Stuart throne stood facing the dawn of his adult life, the occupant of that throne was staring into the sunset of his. The death of Mary had turned her husband into what he described as 'the miserablest creature on earth'. Never, by any stretch of the imagination a cheerful man, William became progressively more withdrawn, more impassive, more gloomy. His health deteriorated, his unpopularity increased, his dissatisfaction with his new country deepened. William was 'Stadtholder in England,' quipped his critics, and 'King in Holland'.

Bereft of Mary's civilising and graceful presence, William spent more and more time with his companions of the battlefield and the hunting field. He came to move, almost exclusively, in a world of men.

The autumn hunting parties at William's beautiful palace, Het Loo, in Holland, had long been his chief source of happiness. Even during Mary's lifetime he had spent weeks on end in the company of a group of attractive young men. Usually so censorious, William could forgive these roistering youngsters any indiscretions. He lavished on them the sort of rewards and honours that he had always denied his only close female companion—'Squinting Betty' Villiers. In fact, he treated these high-spirited young men more like mistresses and Betty Villiers more like an intellectual equal. In any case, since Mary's death he had broken with Betty completely. He now spent all his leisure time with his male favourites. The Duchess of Orleans, commenting on the gossip that linked William with the *'chateau de derrière,'* wrote 'that it is true that people think King William as belonging to that brotherhood …'

It was not long, therefore, before the Jacobites were reviving all the old accusations of William's homosexuality. Certainly, their gibes were not without foundation. The year 1697 gave them their juiciest scandal yet.

For some years William's close relationship with Bentinck, whom he had created Earl of Portland, had been showing signs of wear. For one thing, Portland was getting a bit old and staid for the King's taste;

for another, his place in William's affections had been taken by a much younger man, 'the handsome and swashbuckling Arnold Joost van Keppel. The entertaining Keppel had risen, with spectacular rapidity, from page to secretary, to Gentleman of the Bedchamber, to inseparable companion. By now he had been created Earl of Albemarle. Keppel, noted one observer, was 'King William's closest companion in all his diversions and pleasures, entrusted at last with affairs of the greatest consequence, had a great influence on the King; is beautiful in his person, open and free in his conversation, very expensive in his manner of living.'

Not unnaturally, Portland was violently jealous of Keppel's position. 'Portland and Keppel agreed together as well as fire and water,' ran one wry comment, and indeed, on one occasion, William was obliged to separate the two courtiers as they started hitting out at each other. Unable to bear the situation any longer, Portland resigned his offices and left the court. William begged him to return. In a series of anguished letters, Portland gave William the reasons for his decision. He also told him about the 'malicious gossip' concerning William's relationship with Keppel that was going the rounds in the army. William was appalled. But he was not so appalled as to break with Keppel. Portland had to admit defeat.

In no time, the story of this emotional triangle was being gleefully bandied about; with each telling it became more *risqué*. Few doubted that the homosexual allusions in Vanbrugh's new comedy, *The Relapse, or Virtue in Danger,* were aimed at the court. Whether, in fact, William's passionate friendships with Portland and Keppel manifested themselves in sexual terms is uncertain, but the bizarre situation provided the Jacobites with plenty of ammunition. 'The King is said to have been in love with Albemarle as with a woman,' declared the Duchess of Orleans, repeating the gossip of St Germain, 'and they say he used to kiss his hands before all the court.'

The fact that this was highly unlikely in no way diminished the relish with which it was repeated.

It was during this stormy emotional period that William again made an approach towards the exiled Stuarts. The question of the succession was once more in confusion. Princess Anne's only child, the frail, hydrocephalic William, Duke of Gloucester, suddenly died of scarlet fever in July 1700. He was eleven years old. With Anne unlikely to bear another live child, something had to be done about her successor. There were those who thought that William ought to marry again. Once before, soon after Mary's death, there had been talk of his taking another wife but William had been no more interested then than he was now. Candidates, suitable and unsuitable, were thrust on him but he ignored them all.

No, the thing would be to find an acceptable successor from among the scores of descendants of the first Stuart King of England—James I.

There was, of course, no shortage of Catholic candidates. If anyone still believed the unlikely story of James II's son having been smuggled into his mother's bed in a warming pan, there was no doubt that his sister, Louise Marie, was the child of her parents. She was thus a legitimate heir to the throne. After her came the descendants of James II's late sister Henrietta (Charles II's adored sister Minette) and, after her—going back a generation—the descendants of Charles I's sister, Elizabeth of Bohemia. In fact, one had to bypass forty-two living Catholic heirs before one could come across a gratifyingly Protestant one: Sophia, the ageing Electress of Hanover.

But, dedicated Protestant that he was, it was to the Electress Sophia that William made his approach. They met at Het Loo, in Holland. Eminently sensible and personally unambitious, Sophia talked William into repeating his offer to adopt James's son as his heir. 'He has learned and suffered so much for his father's errors,' she said, 'that he may make a good King of England.'

So William made another offer. As before, it was refused.

There were represented at St Germain both factions of the Jacobite cause: the Compounders, who were ready for some sort of compromise in order the effect a restoration, and the Non-Compounders, who would allow no tampering with what they considered to be the God-given rights of James II. On this occasion, it was the Non-Compounding philosophy that carried the day. James II was the rightful King; as such, he refused to deliver his son and heir into the hands of Protestant William.

The result was that in June 1701, the English Parliament approved an Act of Settlement. By the terms of this settlement, the Hanoverian Succession was established: after the death of Anne, the crown of the three kingdoms would pass to Sophia, Electress of Hanover and her descendants. In practice, the next King of England would be Sophia's coarse-grained son, George.

The main door to a peaceful, legitimate Stuart succession to the throne had been closed.

6

One day in March 1701, while the English Parliament was still debating the Act of Settlement, James II fainted at Mass in the Chapel Royal at St Germain. A week later he suffered a slight stroke. Louis XIV's doctor suggested that he take the waters at Bourbon. The King returned from his stay there slightly improved but by August he was as frail as before. On 2 September he suffered another, more serious, stroke. For the following two weeks, until his death on 16 September, he did not leave his bed.

The King's sickroom was to be the setting for much drama during this last fortnight of his life. Unshaven, with his long, thin body scarcely disturbing the bedclothes, the dying King lay surrounded by a host of people—priests, doctors, fellow exiles, French courtiers. The curtains of his great bed were drawn back; the air was heady with the smell of incense. The distraught Mary Beatrice seldom left her husband's side. She wept almost continuously. 'Madam,' whispered James to her on one occasion, 'do not afflict yourself; I am going, I hope, to be happy.'

'Sir,' she answered, 'I doubt it not and therefore it is not your condition that I lament, it is my own.' For although few had loved this odd, self-obsessed man, Mary Beatrice's devotion to him had been absolute.

His son, the Duke of Berwick, arrived post-haste from Flanders. Like everyone else, he was struck by his father's happy acceptance of his imminent death. 'Never,' claimed the admiring Berwick, 'was there seen greater patience, greater tranquillity, or greater joy, than when he thought or spoke of death.'

He asked Mary Beatrice to let his daughter Anne know that he had forgiven her. 'He gave you his last blessing and prayed to God to convert your heart and confirm you in the resolution of repairing to his son the wrongs done to himself,' wrote Mary Beatrice to the no doubt discomforted Anne. A better father, she concluded, 'no man could have'.

James sent for his legitimate son, the thirteen-year-old Prince of Wales. Clutching the boy to his bloodstained nightshirt (the King suffered repeated haemorrhages) the bearded old man blessed him, whispered hoarse words of advice and handed him a manuscript in which he had set out the rules whereby the boy was to conduct his life. Sensible and moderate, the tone of these instructions would have astonished those who had always looked upon James II as a tyrannical bigot.

When young James was led out of the sickroom, the nine-year-old Louise Marie was led in. She, too, was given her father's blessing and advice. She must adhere to the Catholic faith, she must honour and obey her mother, she must show gratitude to the King of France.

This same King of France was, of course, James's most important visitor. Louis called several times (always careful to walk up from the gates lest the noise of his coach disturb the dying King) but on his final visit he made an important announcement. 'I am come Monsieur,' he said to James, 'to tell you that, when it shall please God to take you from this world, I shall take your family under my protection, and shall treat your son, the Prince of Wales, in the same manner as I have treated you, and recognise him as King of England, as he surely will be.'

The effect of these words was extraordinary. Ever since the signing of the Treaty of Ryswick, in which Louis had acknowledged William as King of England, it had been suspected that although Louis had recognized James as *de jure* King, he might not extend this recognition to his son. Now he had promised otherwise. To the Jacobites crowded into the sickroom, the announcement came as an immense relief. Their tears of joy and gratitude were so copious that even the normally impassive Louis had difficulty in mastering his emotion. Above thecries of ' *Vive le Roi,'* the grateful James managed to mumble his thanks.

'Adieu, my brother,' said Louis as he took his final leave, 'the best, the most wronged of men.'

James died three days later.

While the sorrowing Queen retired to the Convent of the Visitation at Chaillot, Berwick took charge of the funeral arrangements. The gruesome custom of the period dictated that the King's remains be divided into five portions. The body went to the chapel of the English Benedictines, in the Rue St Jacques in Paris; the other organs and entrails were buried in four other chapels, including the parish church of St Germain-en-Laye. While the body was being embalmed, people came to dip pieces of linen in the blood so that they could be preserved as the relics of a saint.

Presenting the King's body to the English Benedictines, Mary Beatrice's almoner hoped that it would remain in the chapel only 'until it pleased God to dispose the people of England to repair in some measure the injuries they did him in his life by the honour they shall think fit to show him after death.'

But no such honours were forthcoming. Not only was James II denied burial in Westminster Abbey but he was even denied this more modest resting place. For almost a century the body, encased in three coffins—a wooden, a lead and another wooden one—lay unburied in a side chapel. Then, during the French Revolution, the outer coffin was ripped open so that the lead of the second coffin could be melted and cast into bullets. An Irishman, who was being held prisoner by the revolutionaries in the convent, claimed to have been a witness to this desecration.

'The body lay exposed nearly a whole day,' he wrote. 'It was swaddled like a mummy, bound tight with garters. The sansculottes took out the body, which had been embalmed. There was a strong smell of vinegar or camphor. The corpse was beautiful and perfect; the hands and nails were very fine; I moved and bent every finger; I never saw so fine a set of teeth in my life ...'

The body was then carted away for burial. But where James II now lies buried, no one knows.

Part Three

King James III

Chapter Seven

1

On 16 September 1701, at the gates of the Château of St Germain, the thirteen-year-old James was proclaimed King James III of England and VIII of Scotland. While the trumpets blared outside, the represenatives of the Pope, the King of Spain and of Mary Beatrice's brother, the Duke of Modena, were acknowledging the boy as King. As Louis XIV had already recognised James, French ambassadors to the various courts of Europe were commanded to proclaim him King of England. Mary Beatrice, accompanied by the Duke of Berwick and a party of English noblemen, knelt before her son and kissed his hand.

'Sir, I acknowledge you as my King,' she declared, 'but do not forget that you are my son.'

To some, the mother's pledge had an ominous ring. Mary Beatrice was known to be both strong-willed and pious; was she planning to keep the boy under her thumb or, worse still, turn him into a saint? For the following five years, until James turned eighteen,

Mary Beatrice would be Queen Regent. Would she use this period to gain complete ascendancy over her son's mind? There was talk, at Versailles, that James was mere putty in the hands of his possessive mother; he was 'the fruit of wrong upbringing by his mother, who, despite her saintliness, always wished to dominate, and keep him in a condition of fear and dependence,' claimed one Frenchman.

Nothing could have been further from the truth. Mary Beatrice might have been a spirited woman but she had no taste for power. Far from dominating her son, she allowed him greater freedom. With the death of the old King, the atmosphere around the young King lightened: his upbringing became less rigid, the depressing odour of sancticy was dispelled. Although, from this time on, the Queen always wore mourning and was to spend even longer periods at Chaillot, she did not try to restrict her son's enjoyment of life. He was allowed to make new friends, to fence, to hunt and to dance. Everyone commented on his strong opinions and his independent mind. No one who knew him well could ever think of him as being browbeaten.

But he could not be given his head entirely. Until he came of age, Mary Beatrice remained in control, both of his life and of the destinies of the Stuart cause. Within a few weeks of her husband's death, the Queen was having to make a decision concerning James's future. An excited Lord Belhaven arrived at St Germain to invite the young

King, on behalf of a group of Scottish lords, to come to Scotland. When Mary Beatrice would not hear of her son renouncing the Catholic faith ('She would never be the means of persuading her son to barter his hopes of heaven for a crown,' it was reported) Belhaven assured her that all the young King need do was to promise to leave the Established Church intact. This, in principle, the Queen was ready enough to allow. But nothing could make her agree to the sending of a thirteen-year-old boy to head a rebellion in Scotland.

There were decisions to be made nearer home as well. The Queen's most valuable adviser during these years was Lord Middleton, an amiable, realistic Protestant who favoured a conciliatory or Compounding policy. When his Non-Compounding rivals urged the Queen to remove him on some trumped up charge, Mary Beatrice was thrown into a quandary. It was solved by Middleton himself. Conversion to the Catholic religion, he apparently decided, would be the sure way of retaining the Queen's confidence. So Middleton's sudden recovery from a no less sudden illness was ascribed to 'a vision of King James, in the night, who told him he would recover, but that he owed his health to his prayers and that he must become a Catholic.'

Become a Catholic he did, and a delighted Mary Beatrice took him back into her confidence.

It was with the help of this accommodating Lord Middleton (and the Duke of Berwick) that the

Queen drew up and published an important manifesto on behalf of her son. In it was set out the religious policy of James III. It was eminently reasonable. The Established Church would be left undisturbed and the selecting of its dignitaries would be entrusted to the Archbishop of Canterbury and a council of bishops. Parliament would be left to settle the matter of religious toleration. What could have been more moderate? No one, surely, could object to this?

But William's objections, not only to James's manifesto but to the whole question of his recognition by France, was soon made clear. On 7 March 1702 (it was 17 March in France) William signed an Act of Attainder against James. By this Act James was liable to execution without trial if he set foot in England. In addition, anyone supporting him, or corresponding with him, or financing him would lose their property, their titles and, most probably, their lives. In short, the Act of Attainder was a threat of death for all active Jacobites.

2

Who, at this period, were the adherents of the young James III?

The Jacobite movement was made up of all sorts of men: romantics, sentimentalists, adventurers, opportunists, legitimists, nationalists, idealists, reactionaries. They supported the Stuart cause for a variety of reasons, some of them having precious little to do with loyalty to the slender, dark-eyed boy at St Germain.

In England, to a considerable extent, the Jacobites were the spiritual, and physical, descendants of the Cavaliers of the previous generation—those dashing, debonaire, stylishly dressed gentlemen who had rallied to the banner of Charles I. There were Jacobites in every strata of English society; among the great families, among the leading statesmen and politicians, among the doctors and lawyers and tradesmen, and among the masses, who had never forgotten Charles's concern for the poor.

Most Catholics, of course, supported the Catholic King. But so did many Anglicans. For, in refusing to break their oaths to James by swearing allegiance to William and Mary, a great number of Anglican clergymen—including- the Archbishop of Canterbury—had lent tacit support to the Stuart claim of legitimacy. Their stand caused a schism in the Established Church, with many of these so-called Non-Jurors sacrificing their careers rather than break their oaths to the Stuart King.

Then there were the Tories. Although all Tories were by no means Jacobites, their opposition to the Whigs (the descendants of the Parliamentary Party of the Civil War days) tended to make them look more kindly on the exiled Stuarts. The Act of Settlement, by which the crown would pass, after Queen Anne, to the House of Hanover, had been a Whig measure; the Tories would have been only too happy to find some way of scrapping it. If only James III had been prepared to change his religion, he would have had the whole-hearted support of the Tories. And, as the majority of the English people were Tory-minded, James would have regained the throne with very little trouble.

Even as late as the 1770s, Dr Johnson assured the ubiquitous Boswell that 'If England were fairly polled, the present King [George III] would be sent away tonight, and his adherents hanged tomorrow.'

In England, the Jacobites were particularly strong in the West Country: under the slender spires of Oxford, in the honey-coloured manor houses and cottages of the Cotswolds, among the hills and valleys of Wiltshire, Somerset and Dorset. There were Jacobite families also among the glittering lakes and rugged mountains of the North—Cumberland, Westmorland, Northumberland.

Across the Irish Sea, in green and Catholic Ireland, the Irish were ready enough to cheer a Catholic king. But this was not through any deep devotion to the Scottish House of Stuart. Here, among this charming, impoverished, unpredictable people, Jacobitism was more a matter of national feeling. It was a way of expressing Irish antagonism towards their English oppressors. But whatever their feelings might have been, the Irish were in no position to give vent to them. After the defeat of James II in 1690, the Irish Roman Catholics had been so cruelly punished by the English that all spirit of rebellion had been crushed. The harsh Penal Laws had ensured that the Irish would not lightly take up arms against an English King again.

The great Jacobite stronghold was Scotland. For exiled Jacobites, this was the almost mystical heartland of their cause. Stuarts had reigned in Scotland for almost three and a half centuries. Out of every four Scots, they said, three supported the Stuarts. If the Lowlands were more or less reconciled to the new régime, the Highlands—with their misty glens and towering crags, their swiftly flowing burns and frowning castles, their nobles and chieftains and clansmen—were almost all for James. In addition, the Highlands were strongly Catholic. Even the Episcopal Church of Scotland prayed, until as late as 1788, for the Stuarts.

Like Ireland, Scotland resented the foreign domination of England. The Scots had never forgiven Cromwell for stripping them of their rights as a separate kingdom; it was only natural, therefore, that their resentment of England should come to be symbolised by the Scottish House of Stuart.

On the Continent, too, there were Jacobites; and not only those clustered about the court in exile at St Germain. The Jacobite army, which had supported James II in Ireland and during his two abortive invasion attempts, had been disbanded in 1698 in accordance with the Treaty of Ryswick. The regiments of this colourful force had been absorbed into the armies of France, Spain and Naples. So there were now Jacobites—Englishmen, Scotsmen and Irishmen—fighting throughout Europe. In the years ahead, Jacobite names would add lustre to the annals of the French, German, Russian and Spanish armies.

Such then, was the great body of sympathisers who, it was fondly hoped, could be relied upon to rise up and help restore James III to his rightful throne. At its core were to be found the faithful, those who adopted the white rose as their symbol, who sported the white cockade in their hats and who raised their glasses—each with a drop of water caught in a bubble in the base—to drink the health of their absent sovereign. Within less than half a dozen years James would be of age; then would be the time for the great clarion call that would bring back the true King from over the water"

3

At the very moment of achieving the greatest *coup* of his military career—the organisation of a new Grand Alliance of European Powers against France—William HI was struck down. In February 1702 he was riding his horse Sorrel in Hampton Court Park when it stumblec on a molehill and sent him crashing down. Delighted Jacobites, paying tribute to the mole whose hill had caused Sorrel's fall, drank toasts to 'the little gentleman in black velvet'. Although the fall only broke Wiliam's collarbone, the shock weakened his system. Within a few days he had contracted pleurisy while sitting in front of an open window and on 8 March 1702 he died. He was fifty-one years of age.

'It is very rare,' ran the post-mortem report on this essentially chilling personality, 'to find a body with so little blood as was seen in this.'

If the Jacobites had imagined that William's death would lead to a restoration of the exiled Stuarts they were to be disappointed. Anne succeeded to the thrones of England, Scotland and Ireland with very little fuss. Vindictive as ever. Queen Anne belittled both her predecessor, Dutch William, and her rival, half-Italian James, by using her first Speech from the Throne to remind her listeners that she was 'entirely English'. English—and by implication not Dutch or French—interests, would be her only concern, she announced.

But for all her patriotic bluster, Anne could not still her guilty conscience. The fact that she had betrayed her father hung heavily on her mind. One of the last of her many quarrels with William had concerned the mourning to be worn for James II. William, showing more compassion (or perhaps it was simply mote sense of fitness) than James had done on the death of Mary, had decreed partial mourning for the late King. But Anne had refused to settle for violet mourning only, she had insisted on black. When William ordered her to take down the yards of black crepe with which she had festooned her apartments at St James's Palace, she was furious. 'I am out of all patience when I think I must do so monstrous a thing as not to put my lodgings in mourning lor my father,' she protested.

It would have taken more than full mourning, however, to still Anne's misgivings about her treatment of her father and his son. In her heart of hearts she knew that James was her true half-brother. It had been due to her promptings, moreover, that her sister Mary had been led to believe otherwise. Tears of remorse coursed down Anne's fat cheeks when she was shown a miniature of James III: with his dark eyes and his full mouth, he looked so astonishingly like his mother. Pious in an unthinking, superstitious, self-obsessed fashion, Anne was convinced that her long history of miscarriages, still-births and infant deaths had been the punishment of an angry God. Why else should she have been denied an heir? There was only one way in which Anne could atone for her sins against her own flesh and blood: she must recognise her half-brother as her successor.

And here one came to the core of Anne's personal dilemma. As a devout Protestant she could not bring herself to recognise a Catholic heir. Far better to try and stifle her guilt complex in excessive bouts of prayer, in eating and drinking, and in the friendship of the bossy Sarah Marlborough. Time, perhaps, would find a way out of the impasse.

In any case, this was hardly the moment to be thinking in terms of coming to an agreement with Louis XIV's protégé. For in the spring of 1702 England, as a member of the Grand Alliance, declared war against France. It must be a sign that he was growing old, quipped Louis, 'when ladies declare war against me'. The twelve-year-long War of the Spanish Succession, in which the fortunes of James III were to be closely intertwined, was under way.

4

In some ways, these were the most contented years of Mary Beatrice's life. She was in her forties, a still beautiful woman who had come to terms with herself. The sharp edge of her grief at the death of James II had been blunted; she could now write robustly to a depressed relation that grief was 'the most cowardly and stupid, or to speak less harshly, the weakest and laziest of the passions.' With James still not old enough for any military adventures, she was spared the anguish of waiting at home for news from the battle-front; her reply to all over-zealous Jacobites was that they would have to wait until the young man was of age.

Her two children gave her nothing but pleasure. James was becoming more handsome, more accomplished, more level-headed by the year. She could recognise in him so many of her own characteristics, even to his occasional flashes of temper. He was so very much her son. At Versailles they thought him charming: he had, in exactly the right proportions, the liveliness of a young man, the dignity of a king, and the *tristesse* of an exile.

Louise Marie was equally engaging. She was certainly proving to be 'La Consolatrice' of her widowed mother. At the age of thirteen, in 1705, she made her dêbut at the French court. With her lustrous brown hair piled high on her head and cascading in ringlets about her shoulders, Louise Marie looked charming. She had, it was noticed, 'her brother's features in a softer mould'—the same long face, the same dark eyes, the same generous mouth. Like him, too, she was tall and slender. But she did not have his self-control, or his pensiveness. Louise Marie was altogether more open, more joyous, more vivacious. She loved the brilliant social life of Versailles; the picnics, the water-parties, the hunts, the *fêtes,* the musical evenings, the balls. In amber velvet and flashing jewels, she danced in the *galerie des glaces;* her complexion, enthused one admirer, 'reminds us of the most brilliant yet delicate tints of the fairest spring flowers.' No wonder there was talk of her marrying Louis XIV's grandson, the Duc de Berry.

James II's eldest illegitimate son, the Duke of Berwick, had proved to be hardly less of a comfort to Mary Beatrice. His first wife had died in 1698 and a year later he had married a daughter of one of the Queen's ladies. Mary Beatrice had always found Berwick to be so trustworthy, so straightforward, so unselfish. But unfortunately he had not remained long at St Germain. Considering himself as much a Frenchman as an Englishman, he went off to fight for Louis XIV in Flanders; in 1704, with James's permission, he became a naturalised Frenchman. Berwick promised, however, to place his sword at James's disposal whenever he might need him. As James could not possibly need him until he came of age, Berwick went off to help Louis XIV's grandson, Philip V of Spain.

Berwick's brother, Henry Fitzjames (the second of Arabella Churchill's sons by James II) was a distinctly less impressive figure. Saint-Simon considered him to be 'the stupidest man on earth'. He could not, however, have been entirely stupid because instead of marrying, as was rumoured, the daughter of a tailor or the daughter of a poulterer, Fitzjames married an heiress and settled down amidst the splendours of Versailles. At least that got him off Mary Beatrice's hands.

The Queen's association with the Convent of the Visitation at Chaillot continued to give her pleasure of a more tranquil nature. In the scattering of the various bits and pieces of James II's body, his heart had come to rest at Chaillot and the Queen was deeply involved in the rebuilding of the church in which this sacred relic was housed. She gave money, which she could not afford, and organised parties of devout Irishwomen into stitching embroideries for the altar. Sometimes alone, often with Louise Marie in tow, Mary Beatrice would arrive to inspect the progress of the building. Her periods of retreat at Chaillot were still the most satisfying of her life.

But these years brought their troubles as well. The Queen was short of money. Already she had sold most of her jewellery and there was no sign of the yearly allowance of £15,000 promised to her by the English government and agreed to by both William and Anne. Whenever the payment of Louis XIV's annual pension was delayed, she was desperate. Swallowing her pride, she would have to write to the King's wife, Madame de Maintenon, to remind her about it. The position was made no easier by the ever-swelling crowd of Jacobite exiles. Mary Beatrice was very conscious of the fact that their devotion to the Stuart cause had cost these people their positions and their comfortable way of life in England; no less than her son James did these faithfuls face death if they should ever return home. She had to do what she could to support them.

Nor did this conglomeration of idle, unsettled, impecunious Jacobites make life any more harmonious at St Germain. 'The English cannot stand one another ...' reported the Duchess of Orleans gleefully, 'they live like dogs and cats.' The Queen had to balance Compounders against Non-Compounders; she had to thread her way between intrigues and plots; she had to learn whom to trust and whom to send packing. At times it could be bewildering.

Then, in the summer of 1705, she underwent treatment for a growth in her breast. The doctors suspected cancer. But the treatment seems to have been successful and by the end of that year it was reported that "The Queen is much better than she was, and it is hoped that the lump in her breast is not so dangerous as was once thought.' The Queen put her recovery down to the prayers of the nuns at Chaillot.

In June 1706, Mary Beatrice's regency came to an end. It says a great deal for the relationship between the Queen and her son that one of her ladies could write that 'a young man is generally eager to escape from maternal authority, but he is not so'. James was certainly impatient, both to claim his throne and to learn the art of war, but it was not because he wanted to get away from his mother. They were devoted to each other. On 'White Rose Day,' the day on which James attained his majority, Mary Beatrice had every reason to feel that she had raised a son—and a monarch—to be proud of. It was as much from her example of dignity in adversity as from his father's wise, if ponderously worded, set of instructions that James had learned to conduct himself like a king. By now he felt confident of making his mark in the world.

The young King, writes one observer, had 'a secret impulse of glory that spurred him forwards to appear in something worthy of the character that was given him; and of putting in action those rudiments of honour which he had learned with so much pleasure.' He was ready, in other words, to fulfil his destiny.

Chapter Eight

1

In March 1708, the nineteen-year-old James III set out from St Germain to claim his throne. He was going with the highest possible hopes. Never had the time been more, propitious, he had been assured. It appeared that Scotland could hardly wait for his arrival. The Act of Union of 1707, whereby the crown of Scotland, as well as that of England, would pass to the House of Hanover, had proved highly unpopular. Jacobite agents, slipping in and out of Scotland, brought pulse-quickening reports of clans ready to rise; Scottish lords wrote excited letters to St Germain. And, most important of all, Louis XIV was in favour of the adventure. The Duke of Marlborough's series of spectacular victories over the French had convinced Louis that a diversion was called for; anything that could get England to withdraw her troops from Flanders was to be encouraged.

So, having arranged for some six thousand men and thirty ships to be ready to set sail from Dunkirk, the French King presented James with a diamond-hiked sword and sent him on his way. On Friday 9 March, the exultant young James arrived at Dunkirk.

The plan was a simple one. James, with a body of troops, would land on the Firth of Forth. Having been welcomed by his Scottish adherents, he would make for Edinburgh. 'His intention,' explained Louis XIV, 'is not to enter the kingdom by right of conquest but to oblige them to receive him as the legal possessor of it.' Should there be any reluctance to welcome James as the 'legal possessor' of Edinburgh Castle, it would be overcome. The Castle having been taken, the Royal Regalia would be unearthed and James would be crowned King of Scotland. From Edinburgh, with all Scotland behind him, he would march south. Supported by local Jacobites and opposed only by such English troops as were not fighting in Flanders, James's advance on London would be triumphant. Anne, terrified of civil war and convinced of the rightness of her half-brother's claim, would accept the inevitable. By the summer he would, as Berwick so airily put it, 'have been sure of being re-established on the throne of his ancestors.'

It did not work out quite like that. In fact, it did not work out like that at all. No sooner had James arrived at Dunkirk than he went down with measles. He had caught this embarrassingly childish illness from his sister Louise Marie. What with that and an English blockade of the port, it was eight days before the invasion fleet could get under way. Even so, James had to be carried aboard, wrapped in blankets. But his spirits were good.

'My body is weak but my courage is so high that it will uphold the weakness of my body,' he assured his worried mother. 'I hope that when I write to you again it will be from the palace at Edinburgh where I reckon to arrive on Saturday.'

His reckoning was sadly wide of the mark. Saturday found him still aboard the flagship. The invasion fleet had managed to get as far as the Firth of Forth the night before and the French Admiral, Claud de Forbin, had anchored off the Isle of May. From there, wrote one lyrical recorder, 'through a tearful mist of drizzling rain, James looked upon the promised land; up the wide dim water where, beyond hidden hills and the couchant lion of Arthur's Seat, the grey metropolis of his fathers, his own romantic town, made ready for its king. Over that proud ridge of rock springing from the plain to its castled crown, the ruddy lion of his race had ramped in gold for three centuries of thrilling history. There, by the ancient pinnacled palace where Mary [Queen of Scots] had wept, his people awaited him on tip-toe of joyful expectation...'

They waited, whether on tip-toe or not, in vain. Dawn brought the unwelcome sight of no less than twenty-eight enemy ships. The apprehensive Forbin promptly turned tail. A violent gale did the rest. On 25 March, the Admiral had to tell James that he would have to call off the proposed invasion and head for home. The young King was appalled. The jagged, grey-green coastline of Scotland was clearly visible from the heaving deck of the flagship; surely they could not turn back now? But Forbin was not prepared to risk his ships falling into enemy hands. In any case, the Admiral seems to have had secret instructions from the French King not to attempt a landing. Unsuspected by young James, Louis XIV had changed his mind about the advisability of a landing in Scotland; the expedition was to be nothing more than a feint to get England to withdraw her troops from the Continent.

When James could not get the Admiral to agree to a landing, he begged to be put ashore alone. The whole of Scotland was waiting for his arrival, he argued; even without French support he would be able to launch his rebellion. But Forbin remained firm. His orders were to protect James's life. The King must accompany him back to Dunkirk.

So back to Dunkirk they trailed. A combination of disappointment, tiredness, measles and seasickness had left James looking pale and thin, but he was determined to show a good face. Dressed in a richly embroidered suit and a dashingly feathered hat, and with his head held high, he stepped ashore. To cries of 'Long live the King!' from the 'abundance of ladies' crowding the windows of their coaches, James started out on the long, depressing journey back to St Germain.

Far from being 're-established on the throne of his ancestors,' James was from now on to be referred to, by Queen Anne and her government, as 'the Pretender'.

2

Oddly enough, the failure of the Scottish venture ushered in a period of relative contentment for James. As he could hardly sit about at St Germain doing nothing all day long, he obtained Louis's permission to join the campaign in Flanders. For the following three summers, using the title of 'Chevalier de St George,' he fought as a volunteer with the French army. In his equable, self-possessed, undemonstrative fashion, James enjoyed himself hugely. He was certainly very brave. On more than one occasion his companions had to beg him to get out of harm's way. At the battles of Oudenarde and Malplaquet—both of which were defeats for the French and victories for the Duke of Marlborough—James fought with great gallantry.

He never complained. Whether jogging all day in the saddle, or trudging through pouring rain, or sleeping in his cloak beside his horse, or galloping like the wind to escape the enemies' bullets, or leading a charge towards the enemy lines, James was in his element. With Berwick often beside him to advise him, James was learning a great deal about war, and men, and motivations.

The one disappointment of these years was his health. Since boyhood James had suffered from something called quartan ague. This was a type of malaria which made him feel feverish, weak and depressed. And just as James II had suffered from a bleeding nose in times of stress, so did James III succumb to the ague when faced with a crisis. Time and again during these years of campaigning, James was struck down by his complaint. It meant that he had to spend days, sometimes weeks, in bed, feeling shivery and feeble.

Perhaps it was during these bouts of enforced idleness that James began evolving his personal philosophy. As a youngster, he had been drawn to the doctrine of Jansenism, as expounded by one of his tutors. Jansenism, with its emphasis on simplicity of worship, appealed to the sober James far more than did the elaborate, Jesuit-dominated ritualism practised at Versailles. This appeal was strengthened when, at one time, James's illness obliged him to spend several weeks in the company of the saintly Fénélon, Archbishop of Cambrai, who was a believer in the doctrine of Quietism. God's grace, argued Fénélon, could work most efficiently through a passive soul and not through conscious effort on the part of naturally sinful man. Fénélon's teaching, with its emphasis on such things as tolerance ('Grant civil toleration to all, not approving everything as if it were immaterial but suffering patiently what God suffers') struck a responsive chord in James's mind. The somewhat negative virtues of tolerance, patience, impartiality and acceptance had an attraction for James; combined, they gave him, as he matured, a remarkable stoicism.

It was as well, perhaps, that James's adherents were not aware of his gradually shaping philosophy. Such attitudes might be all very well in an enthroned king; they were hardly positive enough to serve a claimant to a throne. To the majority of Jacobites, James remained what he seemed: a brave, handsome, resolute King who would one day 'enjoy his own again'.

This was certainly the impression he gave when, on one memorable occasion, James suddenly came face to face with some of his countrymen. During the campaign of 1710, the two opposing armies were encamped on either side of a river. It was 20 June, James's twenty-second birthday. Both lots of soldiers were resting and the watching James was highly amused by the way in which the French and English were shouting greetings to each othet across the stretch of water. A party of English officers strolled down to the edge and asked after James. When he was pointed out to them, sitting apart on his horse with the blue Garter ribbon aslant his chest, one of the officers bowed low towards him. Several times after that James rode along the bank and never once did the English open fire on him. At one stage he exchanged words with the men; at another the Scots and English officers swept off their hats and bowed to him as he passed by.

For James, these must have been heartwarming encounters.

Later, he had some medals struck. On one side was his likeness, on the other, in Latin, the words 'Restore to whom it belongs'. An English trumpeter, going to and fro between the camps during some peace negotiations, carried some of the medals back to the English camp. When next he arrived in the

French camp, the trumpeter asked for thirty more medals; they were for English officers sympathetic to the cause of the exiled Stuarts.

There can be no doubt that the glimpse of this tall, slender, striking-looking young monarch had stirred the imaginations of the English troops. It would have been difficult to imagine the lumbering Queen Anne engendering, in a similar sort of situation, a similar sort of excitement.

3

As a matter of fact, her half-brother was very much on Queen Anne's mind at this time. Anne's husband, the thick-headed Prince George of Denmark, had died in 1708. The Queen's Whig ministers, knowing how much Anne hated the idea of the Hanoverian succession and anxious to prevent her from opening negotiations with St Germain, suggested that she marry again. Why they imagined that a second husband would be a more successful progenitor than the first is obscure; whatever else Prince George could have been accused of it was not of neglecting his conjugal obligations. In any case, Anne would not hear of the suggestion.

Would it not be a good idea, asked a waggish Irish priest who had been brought into court for refusing to swear the oath of abjuration against James III, if the Queen married the Pretender? But the Pretender was Queen Anne's brother, explained the scandalised magistrates. 'If so,' came the shrewd rejoiner, 'why am I required to take an oath against him?'

The loss of Anne's devoted husband was followed by the loss of her devoted friend. During the last few years Sarah, Duchess of Marlborough, had become even more overbearing. Her husband's series of brilliant victories had made him all but indispensable to Anne; this, in turn, had encouraged Sarah's off-hand treatment of her royal mistress. She badgered her, she scolded her, she criticised her. Once, in the state coach on the way to St Paul's to celebrate yet another of Marlborough's victories, the two of them bickered continuously; when Anne continued her whining on the steps of the Cathedral, Sarah rounded on her and, in front of all that brilliant assembly, shouted 'Be quiet! Not here!'

Yet Anne remained submissive. If Sarah punished her by staying away from court, the Queen—using the pet names of Mrs Morley for herself and Mrs Freeman for Sarah—would write pathetic letters. 'I am very sorry dear Mrs Freeman will be so unkind as not to come to her poor, unfortunate, faithful Morley, who loves her sincerely and will do so to the last moment,' wrote the unhappy Anne.

But not quite, as it transpired, 'to the last moment'. There were limits to the amount of bullying that even Anne was prepared to take from the Duchess of Marlborough. And, what was more significant, Sarah now had a rival at court. A rival, moreover, who was the Duchess of Marlborough's own cousin—Abigail Hill. Much to her subsequent chagrin, Sarah had taken up this poor relation and had found her a place in Anne's service. Softly-spoken, deferential and affectionate, Abigail was very different from the strident Sarah. And although she might not have been anything like as unambitious and self-effacing as she pretended, Abigail was certainly more tactful in her handling of the love-starved Anne. Her marriage, to a page by the name of Masham, who was much younger and decidedly more attractive than herself, seemed to have made no difference to Abigail's relationship with Anne. Gradually, Mrs Masham began to replace the Duchess of Marlborough in the Queen's affections.

Sarah was furious. She could hardly trust herself to speak of 'the black ingratitude of Mrs Masham, a woman that I took out of a garret and saved from starving.'

In many ways it was the story of William, Bentinck and Keppel all over again. Only this time the sexes were different. Whether Anne's romantic attachments manifested themselves sexually any more than William's had done, is uncertain. The Duchess of Orleans, ever ready to repeat a scandalous story, claimed that she had once been told that whenever Anne was drunk, she made love to women; and Anne, by this stage of her life, was quite frequently drunk. Be that as it may, the Queen's relationships, with both Sarah and Abigail, were strongly lesbian in character.

Marlborough, realising that his wife was losing ground to Abigail, warned her not to be too uppity. By staying away from court with the intention of punishing Anne, Sarah was leaving the field wide open to the astute Abigail. Marlborough was right. By the spring of 1710 Anne felt confident enough to break with Sarah completely. With much hysterical ranting on the part of Sarah, the two of them parted company. The Duchess's threatened revenge—to publish the Queen's letters of 'love and passion' to her—came to nothing, and the two women never saw each other again.

But there was much more to this tempestuous love triangle than met the eye. Just as the Jacobites had hoped to turn the earlier rift between Anne and her sister Mary to their advantage, so did they now hope to profit from the break between Anne and Sarah. For Abigail Masham had another cousin—a Tory politician with Jacobite leanings whose name was Robert Harley. With his taste for backstairs intrigue, Harley had quickly appreciated the fact that the Queen's growing infatuation with Abigail Masham could be put to good use. The Duchess of Marlborough was a Whig; once Anne had exchanged her for Mrs Masham the Tories—and the Jacobites—had a friend at court indeed.

With Anne seeing all politics in terms of personalities, it was not long before the break with Sarah began to affect Sarah's husband. Now that his wife was out of favour, Marlborough found his position becoming shaky. And, as Anne began looking more kindly on the Tories—many of whom were Jacobite sympathisers—it became shakier. The thing to do, Marlborough now decided, was to make an approach to James. If Anne were to name her brother as her heir, then Marlborough would be on the winning side. He began sending goodwill messages to James; he asked searching questions about him; he professed himself delighted to hear that James was such an accomplished young man.

Marlborough's approaches threw St Germain into a quandary. Could they trust the man who had been one of the first to desert James for William? On the other hand, could they afford to ignore the man who commanded England's army?

As things turned out, it did not matter either way. In January 1711 Anne dismissed Marlborough as Supreme Commander. Running true to form, she wrote him so vindictive a letter of dismissal that Marlborough hurled it on the fire in disgust.

By this stage Jacobite prospects were beginning to look brighter than ever. For one thing, Anne was by now presiding over an agreeably Tory ministry. Like Anne, the Tories were heartily sick of the war against France and disliked the idea of the Whig-supported Hanoverian succession. Anne's antipathy towards the Hanoverians was entirely personal. George, Elector of Hanover, who was to be the first Hanoverian King of England, had once refused Anne's hand in marriage because of the humble birth of her mother, Anne Hyde. This, Anne would neither forgive nor forget. 'I don't know if this resentment alone will suffice to make the Queen break the Hanoverian succession,' wrote Nathaniel Hooke, 'but it would appear to be a big help to those whose interest it is to revoke it.' Her two leading Tory ministers, Abigail Masham's cousin Robert Harley and Henry St John (afterwards Lord Bolingbroke), were both prepared to recognise James as Anne's successor.

Secret negotiations were opened with the Duke of Berwick on the question of James's possible restoration. The sensible Berwick advised James to accept Anne as Queen of England for the rest of her life on the understanding that she would name him as her heir. Although Anne was only in her forties, she was so grossly fat and in such poor health that she could barely walk. James would not have long to wait.

But neither James nor Berwick ever appreciated the full extent of British hostility towards the idea of a Roman Catholic king. If only James had been prepared to turn Protestant, the whole business might have been resolved in a flash. The Act of Settlement would have been repealed and Anne's crown would have passed to James. 'The Jacobites,' wrote Sir Charles Petrie in his summing up of the situation, 'were prepared to accept James on any terms, and the Whigs would not have him at any price; between these two extremes was the mass of the nation, Tory at heart, and desirous of getting back to the old ways, but fearful of popery and the rekindling of the legendary fires of Smithfield. The choice, in effect, still seemed to be between George, who had nothing to recom-mend him except his religion, and James, to whom the only objection was his religion.'

In May 1711 James sat down to write his half-sister a conciliatory lester. Professing 'true brotherly affection,' he assured Anne that, in the event of his regaining his throne, he would preserve the rights of the Established Church and leave the question of religious toleration to Parliament. 'I conjure you to meet me in the friendly way of composing our difference,' he wrote.

But Anne was not to be conjured. James's letter remained unanswered and Anne's dilemma remained unresolved. As long as James refused to change his religion, Anne refused to bequeath her crown to a Catholic. What then, did she plan to do? She refused to say. 'That,' she declared, 'will be to myself.'

4

In the summer of 1710 James's sister, Louise Marie, turned eighteen If ever proof were needed, wrote one admiring Frenchman, that beautiful souls were housed in beautiful bodies, Louise Marie provided such proof. Besides being vivacious, Louise Marie was 'very affable, and of a sweet, mild temper, full of pity and compassion, which is the distinguishing character of the royal family of the Stuarts.' Remarkable enough in themselves, these virtues seemed even more remarkable in someone so attractive: Louise Marie's dark-eyed beauty was exceptional.

One would have imagined that so glittering a prize would have been snapped up by an eligible suitor.

But matrimonially, Louise Marie was an awkward proposition. On the one hand, she was the sister of a King who might well be restored to his throne in the near future; or, if he should die childless, she might even become Queen of England. On the other hand, if her family did not regain the throne, Louise Marie had very little to offer other than her royal birth and attractive person. She would remain relatively poor and politically valueless. In short, Louise Marie was both too important and not important enough.

There had been rumours, at one stage, that she might marry Louis XIV's grandson, the Duc de Berry. The two of them certainly seem to have been in love. But in the year that Louise Marie turned eighteen, Louis decreed that Berry should marry the King's great-niece, the outrageously spoilt little Mademoiselle de Chartres. The Sun King had the tact, nevertheless, to excuse Mary Beatrice and her daughter from attending the wedding ceremony. They paid a formal call of congratulation afterwards and were said, by the watching Saint-Simon, to be looking extremely downcast.

Another possible suitor was the brilliant young warrior-King, Charles XII of Sweden. James would certainly have welcomed this alliance; with Charles XII's army behind him, his chances of winning back the throne would have been immeasurably increased. But Charles was a Protestant and not particularly interested in the match.

So Louise Marie remained under her mother's wing. Not that she minded; she was devoted to Mary

Beatrice. 'While my mother is alive, I never want to quit her,' she once told the Queen's confessor. 'I am never happy away from her. I can't bear the thought.' She quite happily accompanied Mary Beatrice to Chaillot, and the sight of mother and daughter, arm-in-arm, strolling along the great terrace at St Germain with their little dogs scampering about their skirts, was always a touching one. Occasionally, Louise Marie would join in the revels at Versailles. In a scarlet habit laced with gold, she could turn all heads at a hunt in the Bois de Boulogne. 'Majesty,' enthused one observer, 'sat enthroned on her forehead; and her curious large black eyes struck all that had the honour to approach her with awe and reverence.'

She was very conscious of their poverty. 'We are reduced to such pitiable straits and live in so humble a way,' she once sighed, 'that even if it were the will of Heaven to restore us to our natural rank, we should not know how to play our parts with becoming dignity.' Even at Chaillot mother and daughter were made aware of the sorry state of their finances. For years Mary Beatrice had been unable to pay the rent for their apartments and at one stage the nuns were obliged to let Louise Marie's room to a more profitable tenant.

At St Germain it was worse. Petty pilfering was rife among the household and the keeper of the royal forests was obliged to complain to the Queen about the poaching by her staff. His complaints were backed up by the old parish priest. 'If I were dressed in a hare-skin,' concurred the old man, 'they would poach me.' Louise Marie was appalled by the horde of supplicants who pestered her mother whenever she set foot outside her apartments. Mary Beatrice realised only too well that not all of them had lost their fortunes through loyalty to the Stuart cause. 'Too many who apply to me for relief are ruined spendthrifts, gamblers and people of dissipated lives,' said the Queen. Every misdemeanour by an exile was blamed on her. With James so often away, it seemed, at times, as though Louise Marie was the Queen's only earthly consolation.

The Easter of 1712 saw James home at St Germain. On Good Friday, suspecting that he was about to have an attack of ague, he went to bed. But by the next day it was confirmed that he had smallpox. Mary Beatrice was appalled. His condition worsened to such an extent that he was given Extreme Unction. Before the week was out Louise Marie discovered that she, too, had smallpox. The demented mother was now obliged to spend her time between her two mortally sick children. Louise Marie's condition deteriorated more rapidly and at five o'clock on the morning of 18 April, Mary Beatrice was told that there was no hope. Louise Marie died a- nine that morning. She was twenty years old.

They buried her body beside James II, in the chapel of the English Benedictines in Paris. James was still too ill to be told of her death. When eventually he heard about it, he was desolate. His own recovery was all the slower for the loss of what he called 'our special ornament and joy'.

Mary Beatrice had lost 'La Consolatrice'. Nothing, not ever the sympathetic presence of her son could make up for the loss of this sweet-natured, attentive and affectionate daughter. Her son, she once admitted to the nuns at Chaillot, had solid qualities but her daughter's qualities had been both solid and brilliant. 'I may say so without vanity,' sighed the Queen, 'for I no longer have her.'

5

The twelve-year-long War of the Spanish Succession finally ended in April 1713 with the signing of the Treaty of Utrecht. In exchange for the recognition of his grandson as Philip V of Spain, Louis XIV was obliged to recognise the Hanoverian Succession in England. This, in turn, m:ant that he could no longer acknowledge James as the rightful King. He would have to withdraw his support for the exiled Stuarts, and 'the Pretender' would have to leave France.

He had already done so. Knowing that this would be one of the terms of the Peace Treaty, James had said goodbye to his mother and left St Germain some six months previously. He had made for Bar-le-Duc in Lorraine, where the liberally-minded Duke of Lorraine had offered him a refuge. Housed in a castle which overlooked the jumble of roofs and spires of this tranquil provincial town, James dedicated himself aney to plans for his restoration. He had no doubt that his hour of destiny was about to arrive. Queen Anne was failing fast. When she was not guzzling chocolate she was 'getting drunk every day as a remedy against the gout in her stomach'. Her officially expressed indignation at the Duke of Lorraine's harbouring James had a distinctly hollow ring. The Queen was clearly far more concerned with keeping George, Elector of Hanover, out of England. The death of his mother, the Electress Sophia, in May 1714—which meant that George was now the heir to Anne's throne—did nothing to soften her attitude. He was not to set foot in her kingdom while she lived.

James's last opportunity of succeeding to Anne's throne by peaceful means came early in 1714. Once more he was assured that if only he would change his religion the throne would be his. Once more he refused. 'I neither want counsel nor advice to remain unalterable in my first resolution of never dissembling any religion, but rather to abandon all than act against my conscience and honour, cost what it will.'

What it would cost him, of course, was the crown.

Yet it seemed to James that there would be no need for him to act against his 'conscience and honour' to gain the throne. Wherever he looked, Jacobite activity seemed to be on the increase. There were Jacobites in the government, there were Jacobites in the West Country, there were Jacobites in the North of England, and there were certainly Jacobites in Scotland. On James's birthday, White Rose Day, it seemed as though the entire Highlands were celebrating with toasts and songs and marches. In parts of England the birthday was celebrated with hardly less fervour. A merry party 'in a riotous and shameful manner, passed through the city of Chester in a cart with Musick, playing "When the King enjoy his owne againe." 'The optimistic Berwick reckoned that as many as five out of every six Englishmen were for James.

At St Germain Mary Beatrice received a visit from a Quaker supporter of the cause.

'Art thou the Queen of England?' he asked. Mary Beatrice assured him that she was. 'Well then, I am come to tell thee that thy son will return to England.'

'How do you know this?' asked Mary Beatrice.

'By the inscription of the Holy Spirit,' replied the Quaker. Had he not been convinced of the truth of this prediction, he very sensibly added, he 'would never have put himself to the trouble and expense of a journey from London.'

So impressed was James by this widespread upsurge of loyalty that he began thinking in terms of acting on his own—and without the customary French help—to regain his throne. The opportunity was not to be missed. As soon as Anne died, he must strike.

The moment came on 1 August 1714. Monstrously fat (her coffin was to be 'almost square'), abandoned by her friends, tortured by her conscience, and muttering 'Oh, my poor brother! Oh, my poor brother!,' the forty-nine-year-old Queen died in her great bed in Kensington Palace.

Chapter Nine

1

On a wind-lashed autumn day—6 September 1715—the Earl of Mar raised James's blue and gold standard at Braemar, in the heart of the Scottish Highlands. In the name of 'Our rightful and natural King James VIII, by the Grace of God, who is now coming to relieve us from our oppressions,' Mar invited his fellow Scots to take up arms. Their response was prompt. Within days, all Scotland north of the River Tay was in Jacobite hands.

'The Fifteen,' the first of the two most famous Jacobite rebellions, was underway.

Although the Earl of Mar's stirring call to arms was the first formal declaration of a rising, it was by no means the first indication of Jacobite revolt. Ever since Queen Anne's death, the country had been seething with rebellion. The Jacobites had hoped, during the last days of Anne's life, that the crown could be won legally, that Anne would salve her conscience by bequeathing the throne to her half-brother. Indeed, it was claimed that she had left a document, naming James as her heir, under her pillow. But by some skilful manoeuvring, the Whigs had managed to gain control of the Privy Council just before the Queen died. They promptly destroyed the document and, fearing a Jacobite *coup*, had taken all the necessary steps to protect their position. They had proclaimed King George without any trouble and, six weeks later, the new King had arrived from Hanover to claim his inheritance.

A less prepossessing man than George I would have been difficult to imagine. Fifty-three at the time of his accession, he was short, stocky, pale-skinned, bulbous-eyed and heavy-jowled. Nor was his manner any more attractive. Shy and awkward, the King gave the impression of being a coarse, aggressive and unimaginative man. Unlike the Stuarts, he could speak only very little English and his heart, quite clearly, had been left behind in Hanover.

George lost no time in forming a predominantly Whig ministry. Having won a general election by a considerable majority, the Whigs used their power to harass the Tories. This, in turn, heightened Jacobite dissatisfaction. Soon all England, except for the counties close to London, was experiencing riots and disorders. It was in the West Country, however, that Jacobite opposition was chiefly concentrated and by the summer of 1715 a plan of campaign had been worked out.

There were to be three simultaneous uprisings: in Scotland, in the North of England and in the

South-West of England. The main thrust was to be in the South-West, with Bath as the centre of activity. James would land on the south coast, the ports of Bristol and Plymouth would be seized and—with these two links with the Continent secured—the march on London could begin.

The plan was a good one. But even at the time that Mar was raising the standard in Scotland, things were going wrong in the south. The government had got wind of the conspiracy. Lord Bolingbroke and the Duke of Ormonde, who were meant to head the proposed rising, both fled to France for fear of being arrested. But if they escaped arrest, others did not. Throughout September and October dozens of prominent Jacobites were rounded up. These wholesale arrests unnerved the conspirators who had already assembled at Bath. They promptly scattered. By October only Oxford remained defiant; 'here we fear nothing,' reported one jaunty undergraduate to a friend in London, 'but drink James's health every day.' His jauntiness was not allowed to remain undisturbed long. By the end of October Oxford had been forced to submit to the government forces.

Before it had even got going, the rebellion in the South-West had collapsed.

With the Earl of Mar, things were going only slightly better. His army of 5,000 men, made up of Scottish nobles, chieftains and fierce, kilted clansmen, marched south. Mar's first objective was Edinburgh Castle. He had hoped to take it by surprise but through various delays and indiscretions (Lord John Drummond's raiding party stopped to 'powder their hair' on the way to the Castle) the garrison was forewarned and the attempt failed. Disheartened—and he was easily disheartened—Mar remained in Perth.

In the meantime the Duke of Argyll, head of the Campbell clan and a supporter of King George, marched to Stirling. Here, from Stirling Castle, he could command the road which Mar would have to take south. And that, for the moment, was how things remained: the unadventurous Mar sat in Perth waiting for better days, and the able Argyll sat in Stirling, waiting for Mar.

The rebellion in the south had failed; the rebellion in Scotland was a stalemate; the focus now shifted to the rebellion in the North of England.

This was an altogether more gentlemanly affair. During the first week of October, several Jacobite noblemen and gentlemen (among them James's boyhood friend, the courtly Lord Derwentwater) rounded up their retainers and rode through the towns of Northumberland, merrily proclaiming James as King as they went. They were joined first by a party of Jacobites from the South-West of Scotland and then by a force of Highlanders sent by the Earl of Mar. By the end of the month, the combined Jacobite force numbered several thousand.

It was at this stage that they heard that the Government forces were moving up towards them. What was to be done? Should they march south to give battle, or should they march north to support Mar against Argyll? With opinion divided between the English, who had no wish to march north into Scotland, and the Scots, who had no wish to march south into England, the worst possible decision was taken. They would do neither. Instead, they rode aimlessly along the Cheviot hills that divided the two countries and then—with many of the disgruntled Highlanders having packed up and gone home—they moved down into the Lake District towards Lancashire.

In town after town the Jacobite force was rapturously welcomed. In Lancaster 'the gentlemen soldiers, dressed and trimmed themselves up in their best clothes, for to drink a dish of tea with the ladies of this town.' The ladies, not to be outdone, 'appeared in their best rigging, and had their tea tables richly furnished for to entertain their new suitors.'

This was all very well in its way but it was bringing James no nearer to his crown. At Preston, where this debonair force was planning to march on Liverpool, the Government troops caught up with them. There was a battle and, on 14 November 1715, the Jacobite force surrendered. This rebellion in the North might have been more dashing than its counterpart in the South-West but it had been no more successful.

Now only Mar remained. Finally bestirring himself, he marched south out of Perth. At Sheriffmuir he came up against Argyll's force. An indecisive battle followed. Out of the confusion of charging clansmen, rearing horses, crackling musketry and flashing claymores, each side claimed the victory. What was important, however, was that Argyll had checked Mar and that Mar, instead of continuing the fight, turned tail and headed back to Perth. Not long after this Inverness fell to the Government forces.

This meant that by the end of November 1715 the entire Jacobite rebellion was confined to a relatively small area of Scotland. It would need a leader of exceptional military skill and experience to breathe fresh life into the dying embers of this uprising.

2

James III, alas, was no such leader. And the man who was—the Duke of Berwick—declined to be associated with the venture. As far-sighted as ever, Berwick had been aware of the almost insuperable difficulties. What was needed, he had maintained, was a quick *coup d'état* as soon after Anne's death as possible. When this did not take place, Berwick realised that considerable additional help would be necessary if the. rebellion were to succeed; the movement lacked money, it lacked arms, it lacked trained men, it lacked foreign aid. And try as he might, Berwick could tie down neither France nor Spain nor Sweden to lend support to the venture. Nor did he have any confidence in the various Jacobite leaders. They were too inexperienced, they bickered too much and, like Mar, they were too unadventurous.

An additional cause of concern for Berwick was the fact that he was a naturalised Frenchman. To whom did he owe allegiance? To his half-brother the King of England, or to the King of France?

Berwick's hesitations worried James. So impatient to be off, he resented what he considered to be his half-brother's luke-warm attitude. For the first time in their life-long association, a coolness developed between the two men. The tone of their letters to each other became increasingly strained. James had all along been relying on Berwick to act as the supreme commander of the campaign but as Berwick remained uncommitted, James finally ordered him to take command of 'all our forces by land and sea in our ancient Kingdom of Scotland'.

Berwick refused. Politely but firmly, he pointed out that as a French subject and a Marshal of France, he dare not leave the country without permission; such permission, he wrote, had been 'expressly forbidden'. This was true. As early as August, Berwick had been told that he was not to take part in any proposed Jacobite uprising.

James's reaction was extreme. Displaying an uncharacteristic rancour, he heaped abuse on poor Berwick's head. 'I ... shall write to him no more,' he swore, 'and must suffer the humiliation of courting a disobedient subject, and a bastard too, rather than risk any thing in the main point.' James must have been very angry indeed to have used his half-brother's illegitimacy as an insult.

So James had to set out to conquer his kingdom without any help from Berwick. He left Bar towards the end of October and for the greater pan of the following two months hung about the French coast, waiting for a favourable moment to cross. During this time the rebellions in the South-West and the North collapsed; the only rebellion he could now hope to lead was the one in Scotland. This period of enforced inactivity was enough to try anyone's patience. The weather was stormy, the news from across the North Sea was contradictory, there was quarrelling and jealousy among the leaders, and James was feeling far from well.

It was during this period too that, unsuspected by James, his cause was being undermined by a professed supporter—the same Lord Bolingbroke who had been obliged to flee England to escape arrest by the Whig ministry. At one time a Secretary of State in Queen Anne's government and a Jacobite sympathiser, the ambitious Bolingbroke had since thrown in his lot with James. But not, apparently, completely. Bolingbroke was keeping his options open. An unashamed libertine ('He himself bragged that in one day he was the happiest man alive, got drunk, harangued the Queen, and at night was put to bed to a beautiful young lady, and was tucked up by two of the prettiest young peers in England ...') Bolingbroke had taken up with an ex-nun named Claudine de Tecin. Another of the lady's lovers was the Abbé Dubois—an avowed enemy of the exiled

Stuarts. Thanks to these complicated sexual connections, James's plans, travelling via Bolingbroke, Claudine de Tecin, the Abbé Dubois and the British Ambassador in Paris, reached the ears of King George's government.

It was due, very largely, to Bolingbroke's treachery or indiscretion that the government had been able to nip the West Country rising in the bud. And it was due, also, to Bolingbroke's dragging of his heels, that additional military supplies were so slow in materialising.

But at Dunkirk James still had no reason to distrust Bolingbroke, In fact, it was Bolingbroke who organised the little ship that was to carry James to Scotland. He set sail towards the end of December. For five days the ship battled across the heaving sea; not even James's sense of anticipation could have compensated for his violent seasickness.

It was two days before Christmas, by the English calendar, that James set foot, for the first time in his life, on Scottish soil. The 'bonny Blackbird' of the Scottish Jacobites had arrived home. It was, or should have been, a memorable occasion. Until the death of Queen Anne, the Stuart dynasty had reigned in Scotland for almost three and a half centuries; the arrival of James VIII to claim his ancient kingdom should have been a moment of high drama. As it turned out, it was a singularly lack-lustre affair. Instead of landing, as planned, at Montrose, James's little ship had been forced further north by a suspicious-looking vessel lying outside Montrose harbour. So they dropped anchor off the forlorn-looking fishing port of Peterhead. Because James was so weak, he had to be carried ashore, through the fringe of icy water, by the captain. There was no one to meet them.

All in all, it was a depressingly inauspicious beginning for what was meant to be a glorious adventure.

3

'To believe,' the Duke of Berwick had written earlier in the year, 'that with the Scots alone he will succeed in his enterprise has always been regarded by me as madness.'

Berwick was right. And it did not take the twenty-seven-year-old James long to realise it. Had he delayed his arrival for a few more days, he admitted in a letter to Bolingbroke, he would have been warned not to come at all. The rebellion was crumbling fast. Since the battle of Sheriffmuir the Jacobite force had melted from 10,000 to some 3,000 men. The Highlanders were not ones for hanging about with nothing to do and Mar seemed incapable, either of holding them together or of putting them to some use. The Duke of Argyll, on the other hand, had been greatly reinforced.

There was also considerable reluctance, on the part of some Scottish noblemen, to associate themselves too closely with the Stuart King. When James summoned them to attend him, they made polite excuses—the weather was too bad, they wanted more time to assemble their clans, their men were needed to defend their own lands. A ship, carrying gold ingots from the King of Spain, was delayed. When it finally reached Scotland, it was battered to pieces by violent winds. The precious ingots sank to the bottom.

And if James was disappointed by what he found in Scotland, the Scots were equally disappointed in him. He had brought them nothing—no men, no money, no arms. Nor, during the first few days, was he much in evidence. Because of the strain of the situation, James succumbed to an attack of quartan ague; for several days he lay, depressed and feverish, in the home of the Earl of Keith. When he finally emerged, to make his progress by way of Glamis (where he was the guest of the young Earl of Strathmore) towards Dundee and Perth, he still looked pale and tired. The Scots could hardly believe that this wan young man was the King for whom they had waited so long. His appearance was so foreign. With his strange black eyes and dark complexion, he looked more like an Italian than a Scot. And his manner was so quiet, so gentle, so withdrawn. The ruddy-cheeked, fiercely-bearded, lion-hearted Highlanders had expected someone altogether more swashbuckling. To them he seemed to lack charm, to lack dash, to lack personal magnetism. Was it for the sake of this colourless young man that hundreds of their fellow Jacobites were suffering imprisonment and even death in England? James gave the impression that he hardly cared.

Yet there were occasions when his presence could evoke a show of enthusiasm. James was at his best in private; one could then come to a better appreciation of his exceptional qualities: his bravery, his kindness, his good sense. There was an undeniable aura of kingship about him which was not so apparent amid the hurly-burly of the streets and the parade grounds.

The Earl of Strathmore had been quite bowled over by his royal guest. The young Earl is said to have described James as 'very cheerful, and a very fine gentleman, and a lover of dancing; also of great and uncommon understanding, punctual to his word, very religious, modest and chaste.' At Glamis, James had touched for the King's Evil. Since the days of Edward the Confessor, English kings had performed this healing rite All the patients at Glamis, claimed the adoring young Earl, had recovered.

The climax of James's first few weeks in Scotland was to be his coronation. It would take place at Scone, the spot where Scottish kings had been crowned for centuries. James spent a night at the modest Royal Palace at Scone and the coronation ceremonial was discussed. The regalia, which had always been kept at Scone, had disappeared some ten years before—at the time when the Act of Union with England had decreed that the Hanoverians would reign in Scotland, as well as England, after the death of Queen Anne. Now, in the absence of any regalia, arcent Jacobite ladies donated their jewels so that a new crown could be made. The date was set for 23 January 1716.

But by then, James had other things on his mind. From Scone he had moved to Perth, into the midst of

Mar's disintegrating army. Thirty-Five miles away at Stirling, the Duke of Argyll had been joined by Lord Cadogan. The Government forces now numbered over ten thousand men. Once this superior force came tramping along the icy roads towards Perth, James realised that the Jacobite army would be no match for it. At a council of war, it was decided that they must retreat northwards. Much against James's convictions, it was agreed that the area through which they retreated would be laid waste by a burning of all hamlets and cottages; this way, they hoped to halt the Government advances.

But nothing could halt it. As the Jacobites fled ever further north through sleet and snow, the enemy followed. And with the situation becoming daily more desperate, even James came to realise that they could not hold out much longer. The Duke of Mar now began pressing him to make his escape. James was the only living Stuart King, the lase of his line, the embodiment of the cause; if he were killed or captured, it would mean the end of the dynasty. For him to remain in Scotland would be to invite a thorough search of the whole country and to expose many of his adherents to the danger of discovery. If, on the other hand, he got away safely, he would be alive to fight another day, and the cause would live on.

Convinced by these arguments, James agreed. On 4 February 1716, together with a small party of faithful followers, James sailed from Montrose.

He left a letter for the Duke of Argyll. In it he told him how much he had hated giving the order for the 'scorched earth' policy. He assured him that he was arranging for a sum of money to be paid as compensation to those whose homes had been burnt.

George I did not show anything like the same humanity. With Argyll's punishment of the rebellious Highlanders not proving nearly severe enough for the King, Lord Cadogan, with Dutch and English troops, was put in charge of the final stamping out of the rising. 'Nothing but an entire desolation from Stirling to Inverness,' wrote one Jacobite. 'The Dutch have not left a chair nor a stool, nor a barrel or a bottle, *enfin* nothing earthly undestroyed, and the English troops very little more merciful.'

4

The Fifteen was over. As the coastline of Scotland receded and James crossed the leaden, wintry seas to France, the iron seemed to enter his soul. Once again he had failed. And he realised that, to many of his adherents, his secret and sudden departure must have looked like cowardly desertion. There was certainly some grumbling on the part of those who had been left behind. 'The King's leaving Scotland ...', wrote Colonel John Hay to the (now) Duke of Mar who had accompanied James, 'was a great surprise upon me ... I must own it gives me a great deal of uneasiness to think that your Grace should leave one in the situation that I was in to the mercy of a merciless enemy.'

James was very conscious, too, of the fact that a great many lives had been lost, and a great many hardships endured, for his sake. Gradually, from the impoverished Jacobites who came pouring over from Scotland, he came to hear of the brutal Government repression. And of how young noblemen, such as Lord Derwentwater, with all their lives ahead of them, went to the block for supporting his cause.

Always inclined to be serious-minded, James became increasingly solemn, detached, introspective. Fénélon's doctrine of Quietism, of Christian stoicism, became the ruling philosophy of his life. Gradually, all traces of his youthful spirit of adventure disappeared. The flame that had burned so brightly during those early days at St Germain died down to a flicker. To his victorious opponents, James III now became 'Old Mr Misfortune'.

Chapter Ten

1

'Old Mr Misfortune' was not James's only nickname; another, more engaging one, was 'Jamie the Rover'. The nickname was never more apposite than during the period that followed the failure of the Fifteen. Seldom had James done more roving.

None of it, however, was from choice. James returned from his failure in Scotland to find that no European sovereign wanted anything to do with him. In France, James's champion Louis XIV had died and his nephew, the Duke of Orleans, was Regent for the Sun King's great-grandson. The Regent's only interest in James was to get him out of France as quickly as possible. Nor did the Duke of Lorraine want him back. The other likely countries of refuge—Spain, the Netherlands, the Empire and Portugal—were all too busy trying to befriend England to risk taking him in. The only European power willing to give him refuge was the Papacy and, for political reasons, the Pope was the last person from whom James wanted hospitality. To put himself under the wing of the Pope would be to alienate his Protestant supporters.

But needs must, and when the Regent of France threatened James with arrest, he was obliged to take advantage of the Pope's offer. He made for the Papal possession of Avignon, in southern France.

He did not stay there long. To the British government, the idea of James, with something like five hundred Jacobite refugees, crowding the walled city of Avignon was distinctly unsettling. They threatened the Pope with the bombardment of the Papal territory of Civitavecchia unless James was evicted. So in February 1717, James was obliged to set out on his rovings once more. He headed for Italy. While the rest of his court travelled by sea, James battled across the snow-bound Alps. Any discomfort, to James, was preferable to a sea journey.

In Turin he was welcomed by his cousin Anne Marie—wife of King Victor Amadeus of Sardinia. Her mother had been James II 's sister Henrietta, Duchess of Orleans. This meant that Anne Marie was, by Stuart reckoning, heir presumptive to the British throne. But heir presumptive or not, the Queen of Sardinia was no more anxious to upset England by receiving James with too much ceremony than any other European sovereign. So, after a few hours in Turin, he moved on.

Mid-March found him in his mother's childhood home—the ducal palace of Modena. The reigning Duke was his mother's uncle, Rinaldo.

James immediately felt at home in this ochre-coloured palace with its elegantly pillared loggias, its beautifully bound books and its priceless works of art. Perhaps it was the atmosphere of the ducal palace, or the joy of being among his family, or the headiness of the Italian springtime, or perhaps, after all, it was the grace of the Duke's eldest daughter Benedicta, that caused James to fall so deeply in love with her.

Until now—and James was almost thirty—his name had never been linked with that of any woman. He had certainly not inherited the voracious sexual appetite of his father, James II, or his uncle, Charles II. There had been some talk, ten years before, of his interest in a young lady at Versailles and there was a rumour of a mistress at Bar. Then there is the story that in Scotland, during the Fifteen, two women had been introduced to James on the assumption that he would want one of them as a casual mistress. To the astonishment of his companions, James had confined himself to asking the women about the possible strategy of the Duke of Argyll.

His love for Benedicta, therefore, had all the ardour of a first love. With her tall, slender figure, her dark beauty and her graceful manner, Benedicta looked very like James's mother. Like Mary Beatrice she was well-educated and well-read. In every way, she would have made James an excellent wife. He certainly thought so for, in a very short time, he had asked her to marry him.

Benedicta's father, Duke Rinaldo, torn between the advantages of his daughter marrying the *de jure* King of England, and the disadvantages of offending the *de facto* King of England, asked James for time to consider the proposal. He also thought it best if James were to leave Modena until such time as the Duke had made up his mind. So, in mid-May, James took to the road once more.

He paid a brief visit to Rome during which time it was decided that he must set himself up in the Papal possession of Urbino. To Urbino then, James went, arriving there early in July 1717. Here, in a superb Renaissance palace crowning a steep-sided hill, James spent one of the most frustrating periods of his life. He felt restless, bored, cut off from the world. He suffered from a lack of exercise, a lack of distraction, a lack of meaningful activity. His little court was plagued by the customary intrigue; there was the usual scheming that came to nothing. There was not even the hope of future marital happiness for, while James was waiting at Urbino, he heard that the Duke of Modena had turned down his request for the hand of Benedicta.

Finally, having spent over a year in his elegant prison, James could bear it no longer. The thought of facing a second, snow-bound winter in this isolated spot was more than he could bear. In the autumn of 1718 he left Urbino and made for Rome James's rovings had led him to the one place guaranteed to do his cause the greatest harm: in the mind of what Sir Charles Petrie has called 'public-house Protestantism', James III had finally delivered himself into the arms of the Scarlet Woman.

2

With her strong Italian sense of family, Mary Beatrice had been delighted at the possibility of her son marrying Uncle Rinaldo's daughter. For some years now she had been pressing him to marry. For one thing, a man needed a wife. For another, he was the last of the male line of the Stuarts. If James were to die childless, the cause would probably die with him. At one stage Mary Beatrice had urged him to marry anyone, 'provided she be an honest woman, and a gentlewoman,' but the less enlightened of her courtiers had been horrified at the suggestion. The blood of most noble English families was far too adulterated by that of 'citizens, merchants, lawyers and worse,' they protested. To Princess Benedicta of Modena, however, they could have no possible objection. She would make a perfect Stuart queen.

So Uncle Rinaldo's 'dry and positive refusal' of James's proposal had bitterly disappointed Mary Beatrice. 'I pray God pardon you the wrong you have done to the King my son, and to your own daughter ...' she wrote sharply to Modena, 'and for the grief you have caused me.'

But James, too, was causing his mother grief. Early in 1718 he wrote from Urbino, ordering her to dismiss her old friend and almoner, Father Lewis Innes; James believed that Innes had altered the moderate tone of his proclamation to the Anglican Church. In effect, James was implying that his mother's court at St Germain was far too intolerant of Protestant Jacobites. 'I am a Catholic but I am a King,' explained the annoyed James to his mother's confessor, 'but, as the Pope himself has told me, I am not an apostle. I am not obliged to convert my subjects except by my example, nor to show an obvious partiality for the Catholics which would only injure them in the long run ...' Although believing that Innes was blameless, Mary Beatrice was obliged to dismiss him.

This coolness between her son and herself upset Mary Beatrice considerably. There was so little joy in her life these days. For thirty years now she had lived in exile at St Germain; the companions of her youth were dying off; she found the moral standards of the younger generation disturbing; she was getting poorer by the year; the demands on her charity were unending. Almost sixty, she was often ill and tired. And although she was still a beautiful woman, she looked thin and pale.

'You cannot imagine what my life is like at St Germain,' she once confided to one of the nuns at Chaillot. 'After supper there is absolutely nothing to do except go to my room to read or write letters. The rest of the time I am constantly being asked to take sides in dispuees and quarrels so that I long for the peace and good company I only find here with you.'

But such grumbling was rare. For the most part Mary Beatrice took her troubles philosophically. She could still laugh at her cumbersome, old-fashioned coach that was falling to pieces, and about the fact that she could not afford horses to replace those that had died. Her clothe.; might have been worn and out of date but she was never anything less than perfectly groomed. Walking had always been one of her great celights and when she was feeling well enough, she could still walk any younger woman off her feet. To see her moving across the wide and sun-steeped terrace at St Germain, with her straight back and her firm steps, was to know that one was in the presence of a great lady.

'She had the most noble bearing in the world,' wrote Saint-Simon, 'most regal and impressive, but gentle and modest nevertheless.' At Versailles, they thought of her as a saint.

Mary Beatrice died, after a week's illness, on 7 May, 1718. She had caught a chill which turned to pneumonia; the doctors gave the cause of her death as 'inflamation of the lungs and the great abscess in her side left by her last illness'. This was a reference to the apparently cancerous growth in her breast. Mary Beatrice was fifty-nine when she died.

Her body, and her heart, were buried in the one place whi:h the Queen had loved above all others—the Convent of the Visitation at Chaillot. Other parts of her remains went to the Chapel of St Andrew in the Scots College in Paris and to the parish church of

St Germain. She hoped that her body would one day be returned, together with the podies of her husband and her daughter, for reburial in Westminster Abpey. It never was. Like the other two bodies, it disappeared during the French Revolution.

Writing to James III, Pope Clement XI assured him that the usual masses were being said for the soul of the dead Queen, but 'rather in fulfilment of our duty than in the belief that she has needed or needs them.'

Almost forty-five years had passed since, as a bewildered girl of fifteen, Mary Beatrice had arrived in England to marry the heir to the throne of the three kingdoms. During her husband's short reign, she had been regarded as little more than a symbol of his allegiance to Rome; during her long exile, she had proved herself to be a woman of admirable dignity, great fortitude, sound common-sense and infinite compassion. Mary Beatrice has been described as 'the best of the Stuart Queens'. The next one was to earn for herself a very different reputation.

3

Once James was unable to marry Princess Benedicta of Modena, he did not much care whom he married. The only stipulation, apparently, was that she should not be 'too horrible'. This was all very well but certain requirements would have to be met; his future Queen would have to be young, fruitful, Catholic, royal and, if at all possible, rich.

Two candidates, a daughter and a niece of the Russian Tsar, Peter the Great, had been mentioned. But the daughter was considered to be too important a prize for a King without a crown and the niece was discovered to have been born before the marriage of her parents. For a Queen of England, *de jure* or not, this would never do. So a young Irish captain by the name of Charles Wogan was packed off on a tour of various German courts in search of a suitable bride.

A Princess of Baden was considered to be too small, a Princess of Saxony was considered to be too old, the nose of a Princess of Fürstenberg was considered to be too red. Nor was there anyone suitable to be found in the courts of Westphalia, Swabia or Bavaria. But at Ohlau in Silesia, the zealous Wogan imagined that he had found the perfect wife for King James. She was Princess Maria Clementina Sobieska, youngest of the three daughters of Prince James Sobieski, and thus grand-daughter of the famous Polish warrior-King, Jan Sobieski. As the Polish crown was not hereditary, Clementina's father was now a pretender.

Princess Clementina was sixteen years old, a petite, piquant-faced, high-spirited creature; fittingly devout, impressively well-connected and gratifyingly rich. Her dowry would be enormous. The Princess had always dreamed, everyone was delighted to hear, that she would one day be Queen of England; it had been her favourite childhood game. And if Clementina was just a shade too ardent in her religious observance and just a shade too excitable in her manner, it was assumed that she would soon outgrow these tiresome traits.

So James proposed and Clementina's parents accepted.

But proposal was one thing, marriage another. James suspected that his rival, George I, would 'move heaven and earth' to prevent the marriage. He was right. George had no wish to see the Pretender united to so illustrious a family as the Sobieskis and, through them, to the ruling houses of Austria, Spain and Bavaria. Nor did he relish the idea of the begetting of yet another generation of Stuarts to continue the rivalry for the British throne. So the English King kept a close watch on the situation. When the Princess Sobieska, with her daughter Clementina, their ladies, their maids, their chambermaids, their escorts their chamberlain, their chef, their *mâitre a 'hôtel* and ten footmen, let it be known that they were setting off on a pilgrimage, George was not tooled. Realising that they were headed for Rome, he asked the Emperor Charles VI to prevent the bridal party from leaving the Holy Roman Empire.

The Emperor, torn between arresting his relations and upsettiag the King of England, delayed doing anything in the hope that the party would get away. But the Princess Sobieska foolishly remained in Augsburg getting her jewellery re-set, thus forcing the reluctant Emperor to arrest the party at Innsbruck. Here they were imprisoned in S:hIoss Ambras. The fact that their prison was a comfortable, convenient and imposing-looking castle, set in superb mountain scenery, made it no less of a prison.

For the following six months, from October 1718 until April 1719, the affair of the Pretender's bride took on the air of a comic opera.

Charles Wogan, the dashing Irish captain who had recommended Clementina in the first place, was now determined to conclude the business by rescuing her and delivering her safely to his King. Together with James he worked out a daring plan of action. Then, improbably disguised as a Flemish merchant, Wogan went scurrying about midwinter Europe in an effort to win approval for his plan. Nothing, not pelting sleet, or snow-bound tracks, or unspeakable inns, could weaken Wogan's resolve. He had a secret meeting with an approving Clementina. He talked her mother into agreeing to the plan, he stilled the fears of the understandably apprehensive Prince Sobieski, he assembled a little rescue party. Letters in code flew between the Pope, the Pretender, the Sobieskis and the indefatiguable Wogan. At times, the obligatory use of code gave the messages a distinctly equivocal tone. 'I find him more handsome and more tall by some degrees than when last I saw him,' wrote an apparently enraptured Wogan to James. ' 'Tis certainly the sweetest boy living, and I have my idea so full of him, being just come from him, that I can't help saying it, as improper as it may seem in me.'

Had this letter fallen into hostile hands, Wogan might well have been suspected of-some improprieties, but not of singing the praises of the imprisoned Clementina.

The time for the rescue was finally set for the early hours of 28 April 1719. By then Wogan and his little party had arrived in Innsbruck and had established themselves in an inn below the castle walls. There wasa last-minute hitch when the eager young Prince of Baden, having just heard that George had offered to increase Clementina's already substantial dowry by a further £10,000 if someone else would marry her, arrived at Schloss Ambras to propose. Clementina turned him down.

Once the Prince of Baden had continued on towards Italy, Wogan put his plan into action. Leaving the rest of the conspirators at the inn, he took a good-natured maid by the name of Jeanneton through the black and stormy night towards Schloss Ambras. With the guards enjoying themselves in a nearby wineshop, Wogan used a stolen key to slip into the castle. Having sent the terrified Jeanneton upstairs, he hurried out again. Jeanneton was met by a sympathetic chamberlain and led into the presence of Princess Sobieska and her daughter. Knowing that she was to stand in for Clementina but quite unaware of her identity, the outspoken Jeanneton hustled her along. 'Madam, you kill your friends abroad,' she grumbled, 'they are impatient to see you, and it is full time to be gone.'

Having said goodbye to her tearful mother, Clementina threw Jeanneton's wet cloak about her shoulders and slipped downstairs. Jeanneton was then put into Clementina's bed. Outside, in the deep snow and bitter cold, Wogan stood about in an agony of apprehension. When Clementina finally appeared, he hurried her to the inn where the others were waiting. 'Welcome to you, my brave rescuers,' cried out the undaunted Clementina, 'and may God, who has brought you to my help, be our guide from now on.'

They certainly needed some help. Their two-hundred-mile journey south from Schloss Ambras to the frontier between the Empire and the Papal States was fraught with danger. Hardly had they set out in their berlin, at two in the morning, than they discovered that Clementina's jewel case had been left behind at the inn. Back they went. Not wanting to attract attention by knocking, one of the conspirators simply lifted the inn door off its hinges and snatched up the parcel of jewels. On again they lurched, along frightful roads, through impenetrable mist and whirling snow, over the Brenner Pass and down into Italy. They were forced to eat the most unappetising food, to shelter in the filthiest inns and to live with the constant fear of discovery.

There were good grounds for such fear. With the discovery of Clementina's absence, all hell broke loose at Schloss Ambras. Princess Sobieska, feigning surprise and waving a farewell note from her daughter to prove it, had to face nothing worse than the obscene language of the commander-in-chief of the Emperor's forces at Innsbruck. In the general confusion, Jeanneton was spirited away to safety. But the chase was on. Word went out that Princess Clementina had to be apprehended and a courier was sent galloping over the Brenner Pass after her. His orders were for the conspirators to be arrested and executed.

Although the berlin had had a good start, progress was slow. Clementina's recently rejected suitor, the Prince of Baden, was travelling a few stages ahead of them into Italy and at each staging post the party could find no better replacements than the Prince's worn-out horses. And then, two stages before Trent, the imperial courier caught up—not with the carriage itself—but with two members of the party who had lagged behind with the express purpose of detaining him. Unaware of their identity, the exhausted courier accepted their offer of a glass of wine at a local inn. But he did not stop at one glass. The rescuers plied him with so much wine, liberally laced with brandy, that the courier passed out. They then poured the rest of the brandy down his throat. Having burnt his dispatches, the men hurried on after the berlin.

It was to be twenty-four hours before the poor courier could even think of lifting his head, and days before he could face mounting a horse.

A complete collapse of the carriage was the last of their major problems and at half past three on the morning of 30 April, travelling in a hired cart,

Clementina was jolted past the massive wall that marked the border between the Empire and the Papal States. With one voice, the group cried out 'Alleluia!' Their ordeal was over. The intrepid Wogan had safely delivered his sovereign's bride.

But his sovereign was not there to greet her. James was in Spain, trying, for the third time, to win the crown that would make Clementina *de facto* Queen of Great Britain.

4

'This kingdom which is divided betwixt him and me,' wrote the apprehensive George about James to the Emperor, 'may light a fire that both your prudence and mine would have great difficulty in extinguishing. England is a bloody theatre where factions often arise, and those peoples love a change of master ...'

George had good reason to feel edgy. The Fifteen might have failed but Jacobitism was far from being a spent force. The Scottish Jacobites had merely disbanded, the Irish Jacobites were not nearly as subservient as was imagined and the English Jacobites were toasting the King over the Water as convivially as ever. And now James was in Spain. 'He ought never,' continued George testily, 'to have passed the eyes of your ministers to go to Spain as he has done, the flight should have been guarded against ... Everything is to be feared; a spark may light a great fire.'

James had been trying to light just such a fire ever since his return from Scotland. If the failure of the Fifteen had taught him one tiling, it was that he could not hope to win the crown without foreign help. With Britain now allied to France, the Holy Roman Empire and the United Provinces, James could not expect any help from them; he was therefore obliged to look to Russia, Sweden or Spain for support. Talks with the first two countries came to nothing but during the course of 1718 Spain began to show an interest in, if not exactly James's cause, James's usefulness. When war was declared between Spain on the one hand and Britain and France on the other, Cardinal Alberoni—the power behind the King of Spain's throne—decided to make use of James.

Once again an apparently admirable invasion plan was worked out. Two expeditions were to set sail from Spain. One, under the command of the Duke of Ormonde, would sail from Corunna and land in the West of England. James would travel with this expedition. The other, under the command of George Keith, the Earl Marischal, would sail from San Sebastian and land in Scotland. To coincide with the two landings, there would be a diversion in Ireland.

Once again, everything went wrong. And it was that old enemy of the Stuarts, the weather, that ruined what was to be called “The Nineteen'.

James left Rome on 8 February 1719. Incredibly, it took him a month to sail from Italy to Spain. The wind was ferocious, the sea was mountainous, time and again the ship was forced to put into port for shelter. He suffered from sea-sickness, he suffered from the ague. When James finally stumbled ashore at Las Rosas in Catalonia, he was exhausted. But he pushed on. Travelling overland, he reached Madrid on 27 March. Here he was greeted with all the ceremony due to a reigning monarch by Philip V and his ambitious Queen, Elizabeth Farnese. But james did not stay long. Within a few days he was hurrying north to join Ormonde at Corunna.

He could have saved himself the trouble. The main invasion fleet, which had set out from Cadiz for Corunna in March, had run into the most violent storm off Cape Finisterre. During the ten days that the storm lasted, the fleet was battered to pieces. By the time James arrived at Corunna, on 17 April, all hope of an invasion of England was gone.

The Scottish invasion was only fractionally less disastrous. The Earl Marischal managed to sail from San Sebastian and land on the Isle of Lewis in the Outer Hebrides. Here he was joined by his brother, James Keith, who had brought over several other Jacobite leaders and their followers from France. With an army of about three hundred Spanish soldiers and a thousand Highlanders, the Jacobites crossed to the mainland and established themselves in the castle of Eilean Donan. Here, beside the grey waters of Loch Alsh, they waited for news of Ormonde's landing in the West of England.

It never came. Instead, a British squadron came sailing up Loch Alsh to attack Eilean Donan.

Abandoning the castle, the Jacobites moved inland with a small force towards Glenshiel. Coming face to face with a superior force of Government troops, they decided to defend themselves. In the ensuing skirmish, the Jacobites were soundly beaten.

The date of this defeat, which effectively ended the Nineteen, was 10 June: it was James's thirty-first birthday—White Rose Day.

5

Throughout her dangerous and uncomfortable journey from Innsbruck, Princess Clementina had astonished her companions by her courage, her forbearance and her vivacity. If they had been expecting to transport some proud and pampered princess, they would soon have realised their mistake. She never complained, she was never less than charming, she was often in the highest of spirits. Clementina had, besides her black-eyed beauty and her natural animation, a strong personal magnetism; she could command almost instant loyalty. Her liberators could not praise her highly enough; young Wogan, her gallant knight-errant, was in raptures about 'the majesty of her countenance, agreeableness of her air, beauty of her features, sweetness of her temper and vivacity of her wit.' There is no doubt that Clementina was a young woman of exceptional qualities.

Such then was the bride that was married by proxy to James III in Bologna on 9 May 1719. Wearing an unadorned white dress, a white *coiffe* and the famous Sobieski pearls, she went through the form of marriage which made her, in the eyes of James's supporters, the Queen of England, Scotland and Ireland.

A week later she arrived in Rome. As the travel-scarred but by now repaired berlin came rumbling over the Tiber bridge, Clementina was given a tremendous welcome. Through a rain of flowers she drove to the Ursuline Convent on the Via Vittoria where a sumptuous apartment had been prepared for her. Until such time as James would arrive back from Spain, this was to be her home. She was certainly made to feel at home. The Pope was all kindness; he treated her with the honour due to a crowned head and—what would have been almost as important from James's point of view—arranged to pay her a pension equal to that of her husband. Following the Pontiffs lead, Roman aristocracy lavished gifts and attention on the enchanting little bride.

Not until the end of the hot Roman August was Clementina summoned by James. He asked her to set out immediately for Montefiascone, some seventy miles north-west of Rome. She arrived there on 2 September and went directly to the Bishop's Palace, where James was already in residence. Their first meeting was private. What they thought of each other is not known, but there can be little doubt that the seventeen-year-old, excitable and starry-eyed Clementina would have been very taken by this tall, *triste*, good-looking man, and that the thirty-one-year-old James would have been pleased enough with this small, elfin-faced girl. The match, after all, had been an arranged one, and many a royal bridegroom had been faced with a far less appetising bride than Clementina.

They were married that very day by the Bishop of Montefiascone. Then, having sat through a wedding banquet, an oratorio and a play in honour of Hymen, James—very understandably—declined an offer by the civic authorities of yet more demonstrations of goodwill and took Clementina off to bed.

Part Four

The Old Pretender

Chapter Eleven

1

The palace of St Germain-en-Laye had been the Jacobite centre for almost a quarter of a century; for the following three-quarters of a century, from the year 1719, the Palazzo Muti in Rome was to become the headquarters of the Stuart dynasty. The two places were very different. Where St Germain was an immense, imposing country palace, overlooking the Seine and dominating a leafy park, the Palazzo Muti was hardly more than a large town house, undistinguished in style, gloomy in atmosphere and set at the end of a sunless side street leading off the crowded Via del Corso. Most of the windows, set in the tawny-coloured walls, faced a small courtyard; those at the side looked out across a narrow, dusty piazza to the massive church of Santi Apostoli. It was urban, cramped, unremarkable.

Yet the Palazzo Muti had its compensations. It was in the heart of things, in a fashionable quarter, not far from the Pope's residence of the

Quirinale. Its piazza, although not spacious, was architecturally impressive. The rooms on the first floor were well-proportioned and elegantly furnished. Besides the Quirinale and the Vatican, it was the only residence in Rome to boast a papal guard. It gave off, in some intangible way, the aura of a royal palace.

However the rest of Europe regarded the newly-married James and Clementina, in Rome they were treated as sovereigns. Here they were always referred to as King James III and Queen Maria Clementina. Wherever they went—to mass, to the opera, to musical soirées, to various fêtes and festivals—the two of them attracted attention. If they went out driving, men raised their hats in salute; if they went walking in some Roman park, people fell back to let them pass. They made an impressive couple. With his tall figure, his distinguished air and his sombre clothes set off by the Star and Garter, James looked every inch a sovereign; he had about him an undefinable aura of kingship. Clementina was the perfect foil for her husband; small, pretty, approachable, talkative. Her charm was exceptional.

Guests were impressed by the apparent harmony of the household, by the ease of the host and hostess, by the gaiety of the Queen and the intelligence of the King. English visitors were always surprised at James's knowledge of their country. To them he would explain that he had spent all his life studying English laws and customs as he had no intention of arriving in England as a stranger when the Almighty saw fit to call him to his throne. It was noticed that James preferred English to French or Italian foods; he dined happily on roast beef, 'Devonshire Pye' and a tankard of beer. Still more impressive to strangers was the fact that James arranged for regular Church of England services to be conducted at the Palazzo Muti for the benefit of the Protestant members of his court. Quite clearly, he was far from being the bigot of Whig propaganda.

If James and Clementina were not quite as well-matched as they appeared, they were still, during this early period of their married life, happy enough in each other's company. James was the kind of man who loves once; his love for Benedicta having been thwarted, he was incapable of a passionate, all-consuming romance. But he was fond of Clementina and quite prepared to treat her with a steady affection. And although the mercurial Clementina might have found him a little too temperate, she still saw him as a fairy-book king—a wise, strong and attractive figure, haloed in mystery, steeped in romance.

Within six months of the marriage, Clementina was pregnant. A gratified James announced the news to all the courts of Europe and Clementina was duly paraded before the interested eyes of the Roman populace. Unlike Mary Beatrice, Clementina was quite ready for all and sundry to see her 'great belly' and several people, boasted James, had 'felt it move'. Yet in her eagerness to present her husband with an heir, Clementina seems to have miscalculated. The baby should have been born in early November but it was not until 27 December 1720 that Clementina showed signs of going into labour. Even this proved to be a false alarm and only on the last day of the year, Tuesday 31 December, did Clementina give birth. In the presence of something like a hundred people, cardinals, royalties, ambassadors and other spectators, she was delivered of a fine, healthy boy.

The birth of a Stuart heir was celebrated by jubilant Jacobites throughout Catholic Europe. In Rome fountains flowed with wine, fireworks seared the night sky and the guns of the Castel Sant' Angelo thundered out a royal salute. Bonfires blazed at St Germain, Te Deums were sung at Versailles and even in Cartegena, reported an ecstatic Charles Wogan, there was drinking and dancing and *feux de joie.* Some Jacobites even went so far as to claim that a new star had appeared in the heavens at the time of the birth of this Stuart messiah.

The baby was baptised within an hour of his birth by the same Bishop of Montefiascone who had married his parents. He was given the first names of Charles Edward and created Prince of Wales. It was fondly hoped, by all those present and by a great many who were not, that the baby would one day be known as King Charles III of England, Scotland and Ireland. In fact, he was to develop into the most exotic figure of the whole Stuart saga—Bonnie Prince Charlie, the Young Pretender.

2

From the Jacobite point of view, the birth of Charles Edward Stuart could hardly have come at a better time. George I had been King of Great Britain for some half a dozen years and during that time he had done precious little to endear himself to his subjects. Not only was the sixty-year-old monarch a grossly unattractive figure but his domestic life was hardly a model of royal respectability. He had no Queen. His treatment of his wife, the pretty and feather-brained Sophia Dorothea of Celle, had been positively inhuman. Having got rid of her lover (by murder, it was generally believed) George had divorced her, forbidden her to see their two children and had shut her up in a Hanoverian castle. She was there still; and there she would remain for thirty years.

The King had made good his lack of a consort by bringing with him to England not only one, but two, German mistresses. Both were hideous. Like James II, George seemed to have had a taste for ugly women. One was as thin as a rake, the other as fat as a pig. The thin one he transformed into the Duchess of Kendal and the fat one into the Countess of Darlington. To his unimpressed subjects, however, these two rapacious ladies remained 'The Maypole' and 'The Elephant and Castle'.

The rest of the King's circle was hardly more acceptable. Like his ageing mistresses, they were chiefly concerned with lining their pockets. ('Bah!'

the King is said to have advised a Hanoverian servant who complained of the thieving at the British court. 'It's only English money—steal like the rest!') This money-grubbing, combined with the King's distaste for the grandeur of his position, ensured that the British court became one of the dullest and least cultivated in Europe. Music was the King's only cultural interest. For those who remembered the glittering courts of the Stuart Kings, George's way of life seemed doubly dreary.

Adding to the generally undistinguished tone of the King's circle was George's stormy relationship with his son and heir, the Prince of Wales. In this, father and son set the pattern for almost all future Hanoverian relationships between monarch and heir. For long periods, the two of them refused to speak to each other. In fact, so violent was George's antipathy towards his son that he gave up attending cabinet meetings in order to avoid having to meet him. Inevitably, the son's household at Leicester House became a centre of opposition to the father's court at St James's. It was hardly an edifying situation.

Another source of public discontent was George's all too obvious preference for his native Hanover. He returned to it as often as possible and although he could speak some English, German remained his first and favourite language.

What a contrast it all was, sighed the Jacobites, to James III's harmonious and decorous life in the

Palazzo Muti. Surely the British would not put up with this sorry state of affairs indefinitely?

Then, in the very year of the birth of the Stuart heir, Jacobite hopes began soaring heavenwards. The bursting of the South Sea Bubble—a financial crash which ruined thousands—plunged the country into an economic crisis. When it became known that the King, his German mistresses and his German courtiers, had been implicated in these questionable transactions, the dynasty seemed about to collapse. Immediately the Jacobites fell to plotting. Letters flew between James and his English adherents, and conspirators were hustled up the back stairs at the Palazzo Muti. Yet another plan was worked out and James issued yet another declaration. In rousing phrases he called upon God to witness that his ambition was not so much to wear the crown of his ancestors as to deserve it. He reminded his readers of his English birth and assured them that his heart remained entirely English. He took care, also, to put in a good word for the English Constitution, which he pledged himself to support.

In this latest plan, London was to be the centre of activity (the Tower was to be seized) with simultaneous risings in Scotland, the West Country, the North of England and Ireland. As usual, James would wait at some Continental seaport until the time was ripe for him to land in England.

But the project misfired. In the first place, the dynasty did not fall. It was saved by the political skill of Robert Walpole. By a masterly handling of the House of Commons, this astute politician steadied George's rocking throne and restored confidence in the House of Hanover. Secondly, the Jacobite plot was uncovered and the conspirators rounded up. From then on, the ever-vigilant Walpole was tireless in his efforts to stamp out Jacobite activity.

Walpole's task was made easier by a general improvement in conditions in the country. For by establishing himself as George's chief, or prime, minister, Walpole became a link between the Crown and the House of Commons, so laying the foundations of Britain's successful system of constitutional monarchy. This establishment of a more stable political system coincided with the ushering in of a long period of peace and prosperity. In turn, these factors lessened the appeal of Jacobitism. The Hanoverians might not be perfect, a great many Englishmen now argued, but would the Stuarts be any better? Why rock the boat just when it seemed to be reaching calmer waters?

And there remained the undeniable fact that George, with all his failings, was a Protestant, whereas James, with all his virtues, was a Roman Catholic. The Catholic bogy, in the reign of George I, was as powerful as it had been in the reign of Charles II. Would it not, after all, be better to stick to George, with his boorish manners, his German accent, his grasping courtiers and his hideous mistresses, than to exchange him for James and his priests?

On the Continent, too, things began to look discouraging for the Jacobites. By now all the most important countries in Europe were allied, in some way or other, to England; not one of them was prepared to support a Stuart invasion. In fact, wherever one looked, the flames of the Jacobite fire seemed to be dying down. Not for two decades would they again flare up; and then they would set all Britain ablaze.

3

A second son was born to James and Clementina on 6 March 1725. He was given the names of Henry Benedict and created Duke of York. Like his brother Charles, Henry was a strong, healthy and attractive boy.

Unfortunately, the arrival of another son did nothing towards healing an ever-widening rift between James and Clementina. Since the birth of Charles, some four years before, things had started to go wrong between the two of them. They were such very different types. Where James was reserved, Clementina was effervescent; where he was long-suffering, she was touchy; where he was self-controlled, she was highly-strung; where he was tolerant, she was uncompromising. Yet both could be stubborn. 'Their tempers are so very different that though in the greatest trifles they are never of the same opinion, the one won't yield an inch to the other,' reported a member of the household.

There can be no doubt that marriage to James had proved disappointing to Clementina. Its prelude—her imprisonment, her escape, her triumphant reception in Rome—had all been so exhilarating that the subsequent routine of day-to-day living was bound to seem dull. Clementina was the kind of woman who always needed to be the centre of attention. Yet overnight, almost, her importance seemed to have been diminished. Although she was supposed to be a Queen, she was living a life that was hardly different from that of any other aristocratic young Roman wife.

And not only did the serious-minded James prove to be a less glamorous figure than she had once imagined but he seemed to pay her so little attention. He was always so busy. Clementina was expected to amuse herself while he spent the greater part of the day writing letters or granting audiences or hatching plots. The children afforded her very little pleasure. She was too impatient, too self-centred to be a good mother; she was jealous of the affection that James lavished on them. He never seemed to show her the same indulgence.

Inevitably, there were scenes between husband and wife. At one stage Clementina flounced out to take the waters at Lucca. Yet, so mercurial was her nature, that once she was there, she began to miss James. She wrote him a letter, untidy, mis-spelt but touchingly contrite, in which she assured him that she was trying to master her bad temper, 'so as to appear to you in the future as the best girl in the world'. Equally contrite, James hurried to her side.

But the reconciliation could not last. Once back in Rome, they quarrelled again. Clementina grumbled about being bored; yet when James suggested that she go out, she refused. Instead she sulked, or flung herself, with all the fervour of her temperament, into her religious duties. Gradually, in the claustrophobic atmosphere of the Palazzo Muti, her personality disintegrated. Her vivacity turned to feverishness, her love to possessiveness, her piety to bigotry.

When James decided to replace the four-year-old Prince Charles's governess, Clementina was furious. Mrs Sheldon was a Catholic, and her confidante; the new governor, James Murray, whom James had created Earl of Dunbar, was a Protestant and inclined to be high-handed towards Clementina. The appointment of another Protestant, Lady Nithsdale, to look after the Duke of York, infuriated her still further. And when James made a third Protestant, John Hay, into the Earl of Inverness and elevated, him to Secretary of State, it was almost more than Clementina could bear. She loathed Hay and the story was put about that she suspected Hay's wife of being James's mistress. This is unlikely. James was the last person to take a mistress and Clementina knew it.

No, what Clementina resented was not James's rumoured infidelity but the fact that there seemed to be some sort of conspiracy against her. Why else should James have appointed Protestants to bring up her Catholic sons or have elevated the detested Hays to a position of such prominence? Clementina was too immature and too eaten up with jealousy of Hay's intimacy with her husband to appreciate the political value of the appointments. Egged on by certain Catholics, both in and out of the Palazzo Muti, the hysterical wife demanded the dismissal of those whom she considered to be her enemies. James refused. And the more consistently he refused, the more she ranted.

Before long, the squabbles at the Palazzo Muti had become the talk of all Europe. Spies, some of whom were actually employed in the household, were quick to repeat the gossip. John Walton, the British agent in Rome, whose real name was Baron Philip von Stosch (colourfully described by Sir Compton Mackenzie as 'an expatriated Prussian sodomite') was equally quick to pass it on to his gratified superiors. What right, James's enemies now demanded, had the Jacobizes to criticise the Hanoverian court when things at the Stuart court in exile were hardly more edifying? People who should have known better were only too ready to believe that James was ill-treating Clementina, that the Stuart princes were being raised as Protestants and that James was sleeping with Hay's wife. All in all, the scandal was doing the Stuart cause untold harm.

And just when it seemed that things could not possibly become worse, Clementina took the one step which ensured that they would. In November

1725 she packed her bags, left her husband and sons behind in the Palazzo Muti and took up residence in a convent.

4

Prince Charles was almost five years old and Prince Henry just over eight months, when their mother left the Palazzo Muti. Her going ushered in a period of disruption in their lives for, not long afterwards, James took the two boys to Bologna; some two years were to pass before they were again settled in Rome. Further disruptions came on the death, in 1727, of George I, when James disappeared for several months on a fruitless mission to drum up support; and by the arrival, during his absence, of Clementina to visit her sons. As she spent the time either sobbing on their shoulders or trailing from one church to another, her presence proved a far from stabilising factor in their young lives.

That Prince Charles, or Carluccio as his father called him, needed some stability in his life there is no doubt. His governors—Lord Dunbar and Sir Thomas Sheridan—had their hands full in trying to manage him. Charles was a most attractive boy, fair-complexioned but dark-eyed, and with a devastating personal charm. In temperament, he was very much his mother's son: high-spirited, animated, alternating between the heights of gaiety and the depths of depression. He was blessed with many natural gifts.

He excelled in almost anything that needed no mental effort. He had an ear for languages and could speak English, French and Italian with ease. He was a born musician; his playing of the viola could bring tears to the steeliest Jacobite eye. He could shoot, he could ride, he could master almost any outdoor sport. Such showy accomplishments turned him into the darling of those who did not have to bring him up. To the doting Italian servants or the sentimental Jacobites, Charles was a golden boy indeed.

But he was the despair of his governors. Neither the humourless and unimaginative Dunbar nor the more relaxed but ageing Sheridan knew how to cope with this impetuous youngster. He simply would not learn. 'It is impossible to get him to apply to any study as he ought to do,' groaned Dunbar. Even after Charles had finally learned to read and write, his spelling was poor and his interest in books limited. What made things all the more maddening from his tutors' point of view was that Charles was far from stupid; it was simply that he refused to give his attention to anything that did not interest him. James, who had been such a good and conscientious student himself, was greatly put out by his son's lack of application. Time and again he badgered the poor tutors into driving Charles harder. They tried, but it was hopeless.

Yet, on the whole, James was an indulgent parent. He was devoted to both his sons and very proud of them. Henry, he was pleased to see, was a steadier, more studious youngster and this did have some effect on Charles; the younger boy's natural cleverness eventually spurred Charles on to greater efforts. Both boys, in turn, adored their father. In their company James seemed to shake off some of his melancholia; he took them to festivals, he took them boating, he took them to musical evenings, he took them to balls. They made an attractive little group—the tall, distinguished, elegantly dressed James and his two lively, black-eyed and satin-suited sons. Everyone remarked on the boys' good looks and graceful manners. Visiting Englishmen were gratified to see that they were being raised in as English a manner as possible: they spoke and wrote to their father in English, they dressed in the English fashion, they ate what passed, in Italy, for English food. And from infancy Charles was very conscious of the fact that his father was the rightful King of England and that he was the heir to his father's throne.

Early in 1728 Clementina returned to James. Her presence made very little difference to her sons' way of life. For by now this once pretty, vivacious and charming young woman had changed into a recluse, interested in nothing other than her religion. Having finally accustomed herself to the fact that her married life was not going to be the brilliant adventure of her girlhood imaginings, Clementina plunged herself, with characteristic intensity, into a life of religious devotion. She spent the greater part of her time locked up in her dark and shuttered rooms at the Palazzo Muti, not bothering to dress and with only her maids as company. When she did emerge, wearing black and with a prayer book in her hands, it would be to go to mass. She was forever fasting. While James, with his sons, his guests and the rest of his household, dined at one table, Clementina would sit alone at another, observing her rigid fasts. Not surprisingly, she suffered from malnutrition. Even in the blazing heat of the Roman summer she refused to leave the Palazzo Muti for the cooler air of Albano, where the Pope had presented the family with a country palazzo.

Far from sulking or nagging or making scenes as she had done in the first years of her marriage, Clementina interfered with the daily life of the Palazzo Muti not at all. James was kind to her and the boys treated her with great reverence. But she showed no interest whatsoever in their education or entertainments. Music, with Charles playing the viola and Henry singing in his clear, sweet voice, occasionally brought mother and sons together, but for most of the time she was a withdrawn, sad-eyed, painfully thin figure, always setting out for, or returning from, a church or a convent or a shrine. Romans became accustomed to the sight of Clementina's coach, with the royal arms of England emblazoned on the doors, tearing from church to church in order that she might assist at as many masses as possible.

What Clementina thought of her sons—the dashing, charming, energetic Charles and the graceful, less boisterous Henry—no one knew; she seemed to be living on quite another plane. During these formative years when the boys were most in need of a mother's love, attention and discipline, Clementina simply ignored them.

5

At the dawn of his adolescence, Prince Charles was plunged into a period of activity that was to have a lasting effect on his character. In the summer of 1734, when Charles was thirteen, the Duke of Liria, who was the son of James's half-brother, the Duke of Berwick, visited the Palazzo Muti. He was on his way south to join the Spanish army in its campaign to win back Naples for Spain. The young Charles was very taken with his dashing kinsman. He was even more taken with the idea of joining him on campaign. Liria's visit was followed by one from Don Carlos, son of the King of Spain, who was on his way to claim the Neapolitan crown. The thought of these two young men seeing active service while he was obliged to stick to his books at the Palazzo Muti was almost more than Charles could bear. He subjected his father to an unremitting barrage of pleas. Eventually James gave way. On 27 July 1734 an excited Charles set off to join the forces besieging Gaeta.

Only on certain conditions, however, was he being allowed to go. He must travel incognito, under his father's old title of the Chevalier de George. He was to be under the personal care of his cousin Liria who, on the sudden death of his father a few weeks before, had succeeded to the title of the Duke of Berwick. Berwick was to see that Charles was kept well out of harm's way. Finally, he was to be accompanied by his two long-suffering governors, Dunbar and Sheridan, as well as two gentlemen and two chaplains.

For all the good they did, these six watchdogs might just as well have remained in Rome. Charles was certainly not going to waste any time studying, and the presence of the priests merely confirmed British suspicions that the Stuarts remained firmly locked in the arms of Rome. Charles's letters home were notable only for their brevity and their illiteracy. 'My Lord Dunbar has excused me for not having writ to you hetherto,' ran one typical example. 'I have been very good and umbly ask your Blessing.'

In fact, he had not been very good and James was in no mind to give him his blessing. The conscientious father was greatly distressed by his son's offhandedness. In page after page he lectured him on his 'too natural aversion to all application' and his unwillingness 'to cultivate the talents which Providence has given you'.

But Charles ignored him. He was enjoying himself far too much to take any notice of parental grumblings. Always an exhibitionist, he could now show off to his heart's content. So pretty, so lively, so engaging, so brave, he was fêted wherever he went. Everyone, from Don Carlos to the humblest soldier in the trenches, fell under his spell. Berwick went so far as to describe his manner and conversation as 'really bewitching'. Not only was Charles heir to one of Europe's most romantic royal roles but he seemed eminently suited to play it. Even in his youth James had been a shade too diffident for his part; of Charles's dash there was no doubt whatsoever. It needed all the wiles of the anxious Berwick to keep the ardent youngster out of the trenches; when he did experience some action, his coolness earned him the most extravagant praise.

After the fall of Gaeta on 9 August 1734, Charles attended a triumphant Te Deum with Don Carlos, King of Naples, and then followed the monarch to Naples for his Coronation. Charles's hat is said to have blown into the sea in the Bay of Naples and when it was suggested that a boat be lowered in order to recover it, the boy's answer was characteristically cocksure. The crew need not bother, he quipped, for 'he should be obliged before long to fetch himself a hat [a crown] in England'.

Wherever Charles went in Naples he attracted attention. The cheers of the Neapolitans were certainly no more fervent for their new King than they were for this boy prince who sat his glitteringly harnessed horse with such self-possession.

All this adulation went to Charles's already swollen head. When he returned, to be met by his father and his brother Henry on the road to Albano, he was certainly not incognito. With a guard of fifty men and a gift of two magnificent Spanish horses from the

King of Spain, Charles rode swaggeringly up to meet his father. Beside the thirteen-year-old youth, James, at forty-six, already looked old and tired and disillusioned. His tall frame was beginning to stoop. To some, as they looked from the disenchanted father to the ebullient son, it must have seemed like the end of one era and the beginning of another. In Charles, says one poetic observer, 'the White Rose had budded again and was breaking into full flower'. Even John Walton, the British agent in Rome, had to admit that 'Everybody says that he will be in time a far more dangerous enemy to the present establishment of the government of England than ever his father was.'

So, at first imperceptibly, and then more openly, the Jacobites began turning their backs on the old day to face the new and radiant dawn.

6

Just occasionally, Clementina could still give a glimpse of those qualities which had won so many hearts in the early days. Strangers, meeting her for the first time, would be struck, not only by her obvious piety but by her charm and her quick comprehension. More than one came away with the impression that she would have made a graceful queen. Indeed, had James been a reigning king, Clementina might well have made an excellent consort. An accomplished linguist, an animated conversationalist, an elegantly dressed beauty, a possessor of great personal magnetism, she would have been very happy in St James's Palace of Hampton Court. She would then have been the undoubted centre of attention; she would have been far too busy to resent James's absorption in affairs of state. She would also have been free of the excessively clerical atmosphere of Rome.

But the qualities that might have made her a successful queen had made her an unsuccessful wife for an exiled king. Disillusion, instead of ennobling her, had broken her spirit. James needed to have married a woman like his mother, Mary Beatrice: practical, level-headed, civilised and emotionally mature. Where Mary Beatrice had been a tower of strength at St Germain, Clementina was merely an embarrassment at the Palazzo Muti.

But not for much longer. At thirty-three Clementina was already fading out of life. Her frequent fastings, her stringent penances, her cloistered life, were taking their toll of her frail body. A few months after Prince Charles's return from Naples, on 12 January 1735, Clementina died. Somewhat to the surprise of the household at the Palazzo Muti, James and his two sons were desolate with grief; 'on all sides,' reported Dunbar, 'there is nothing but lamentation.'

Of all the victims of the remorseless fate pursuing the Stuart dynasty, Clementina was perhaps the most pitiable.

If Clementina had not lived like a queen, she was buried like one. Pope Clement XII decreed that she should be given a full state funeral in St Peter's. They dressed her in gold and velvet and ermine, with a crown on her head and a sceptre in her hand. The body was carried in procession through the streets of Rome, like some canopied barque on a river of flickering wax tapers. Every black-draped window and balcony along the route was crowded with faces. After the Requiem Mass, her royal robes were removed to be replaced by the simple black and white habit of a Dominican nun. The body was encased in three coffins and laid in the crypt of St Peter's.

It was meant to remain there, as the bodies of James II and Mary Beatrice were meant to remain where they had been buried, until such time as the Stuarts were restored to the British throne.

Chapter Twelve

1

It was quite clear to James that something would have to be done about Charles. Ever since his return from Naples the boy had been impossible. His moment of glory had made him more conceited, more restless, more averse to study than ever. Dunbar and Sheridan could do nothing with him. Although he rode, hunted and danced with the skill of an adult, he remained essentially childish. The head-shaking James considered him 'very innocent,' 'extreme backwards' and 'woefully thoughtless for one of his age'. And as life in the Palazzo Muti was doing precious little to improve this state of affairs, James decided to pack the youngster off on a tour. Travel might help to mature him. So, in the spring of 1737, the sixteen-year-old Charles set off on a journey through the cities of northern Italy.

He travelled, this time, as the Count of Albany. No one, of course, was fooled by the alias: Charles saw to that. With him, protesting every step of the way, went Dunbar and Sheridan. Also in the party of twelve were two young members of leading Jacobite families—Francis Strickland and Henry Goring. James had agreed to their inclusion on the somewhat naïve theory that, as Jacobites, they would have a good influence on the Prince. The main cities visited by the party were Genoa, Milan, Venice and Florence.

Everywhere Charles was given a rapturous reception. He moved in a whirl of receptions, state dinners and balls. To the fury of assorted British ambassadors, he was accorded full royal honours wherever he went. Even those, like the Doge of Venice and the Grand Duke of Tuscany, who had promised to play down Charles's visit, received him with the most flattering attention.

And Charles was proving himself eminently worthy of it. In public his behaviour was impeccable. He looked enchanting. With his lavishly curled hair (he begged one Irish officer who caught him in morning curl-papers not to let on; the business might so easily be misconstrued in Dublin), his dark eyes, his fair complexion, his uniforms glittering with jewels and orders, he was the prototype Prince Charming. A consummate actor, Charles played his part to perfection. He sat, apparently riveted, through the most boring speeches. He tramped, without showing the slightest sign of flagging, around countless sights. He listened, with powdered head politely tilted, to a toothless old duchess holding forth in excruciating Italian. With becoming, if artful, modesty, he brushed aside any reference to his bravery at Gaeta.

That was one side of the coin. The other was distinctly less brilliant. Charles's overwhelming charm was never directed at his travelling companions; 'particularly [not] to me,' moaned Dunbar, 'who go in the chair with him'. Hector as he might, his tutor could never get the young man to apply himself to anything requiring the slightest mental effort. There was always some excuse for not writing regularly to his father. Nor could Dunbar get the Prince to bed at a reasonable hour. It was usually three in the morning before Charles, overheated 'monstrously' from his tireless dancing, arrived home; 'the later he comes home, the more he wants to sleep.' His Royal Highness really was the wildest, stubbornest, most inconsiderate young man.

On one score, surprisingly enough, Dunbar had no complaints. One would have imagined a young man like Prince Charles to have been an ardent womaniser but he showed not the slightest interest in the opposite sex. He took very little notice of women except when it came to dancing. The most alluring serving wench was quite safe in his company. If Charles's tutors ever gave a thought to this conduct on the part of their charge, it was probably to count their blessings.

Prince Charles arrived back at the Palazzo Muti at the end of July. To mark what James fondly hoped was his son's new-found maturity, his boyhood—if self-induced—curls were cut off, to be replaced by a wig. On his seventeenth birthday he was shaved for the first time. Within the next year or two he filled out so that by the time Charles was nineteen he was a tall, well-built, striking-looking young man. 'Of the two sons of the Pretender the eldest is now in his twentieth year, the second is fifteen ...' wrote the visiting Charles de Brosses. 'They are amiable and graceful, but both are narrow-minded, and less intelligent than princes of their years should be. The youngest is popular here owing to his agreeable presence and pleasant manners. The English, of whom there are crowds in Rome, are always eager to see these youths ... The eldest son is said to be more liked in the family than the second, and is declared to have a good heart as well as great courage; it is commonly reported that he feels his situation acutely, and if he does not come to the fore it will not be owing to lack of energy.'

Nor would it be for any lack of ambition. Prince Charles had an unshakable belief in his destiny, in the restoration of the Stuarts to their rightful kingdom. He would one day be King Charles III of Great Britain. Even more so than his father at the same age, Charles was yearning for action. But where James had been able to channel some of his energy into study or religion until the time was ripe, Charles was incapable of such mental sublimation. He not only loathed book learning but he had no particular interest in religion. Only through violent physical exercise—hunting, riding, shooting, fencing, dancing—could he get rid of his frustrations. The formal dinners, at which he was always so courteous; the dazzling balls, at which he always looked so decorative; the musical soirées, at which he always performed so meltingly; all these were merely ways of passing the time. 'Had I soldiers,' he once declared, 'I would not be here now ... '

2

The monarch who now occupied the coveted throne—George II—was a hardly more engaging figure than his father had been. In neither looks nor manners could George II, who turned fifty-four in the year 1737, match up to his forty-nine year old rival, James III. Fleshy, pop-eyed, bulbous-nosed, he was entirely without the polish that had characterised the Stuart kings. A man of limited intelligence and narrow outlook, George II was obsessed with the less important aspects of his illustrious position; with punctuality, genealogy, uniforms, decorations and court etiquette. His court was hardly less dull than his father's had been, and although his English was better, he shared George I's love of Hanover and would return to it as often as possible. The devil, he once exclaimed, could take 'the whole island, provided I can get out of it and go to Hanover.'

Yet in more Anglophile moods, George II would boast that 'I have not one drop of blood in my veins dat is not English.' The Jacobites might be highly amused at the extravagant claim but, in truth, there were hardly more drops of English blood in the veins of James III.

If George II was very near to being a fool, his Queen was far from being one. Caroline of Anspach was a voluptuous, vivacious and intelligent woman, keenly interested in affairs of state. While allowing her husband to stray sexually (he had the usual Hanoverian appetites) she kept him on what she considered to be the right political path. This meant retaining the services of the late King's prime minister, Sir Robert Walpole. Although the rumours of a liaison between the sensual Queen and the twenty-stone Walpole were nonsense, the two of them were very thick politically. Both astute, both cynical, they were very useful to each other. 'I have the right sow by the ear,' was Walpole's graphic summing up of his relationship with the Queen.

Together, Caroline and Walpole kept the Jacobites at bay. They realised that the two main factors necessary to combat the Stuart threat were contentment at home and peace abroad. Although George II's suspicion that all Tories were Jacobites was exaggerated, there were undoubtedly Jacobites in Parliament; to draw their teeth, Walpole bribed them with crown appointments. And he employed more devious tactics still. On more than one occasion he went so far as to let it be known that he was interested in furthering the Jacobite cause. But James was not taken in.

The death of Queen Caroline, in 1737, opened the first crack in the anti-Jacobite front. In no small measure, it had been Caroline's influence that had kept Walpole in power. Within two years of her death, the unwilling Walpole had been forced to take the one step guaranteed to weaken his anti-Jacobite position; England went to war. The enemy was Spain. Walpole's position was weakened still further, in 1740, by the outbreak of the War of the Austrian Succession. To the delight of the Jacobites, England now found herself at war, not only with Spain, but, more important, with France. This was what they had been waiting for. In February 1742, Walpole resigned. The field now seemed clear for yet another rebellion. Activity among the Jacobites became positively feverish.

James kept his head. He had been through it all so often before. No matter how enthusiastic the letters from England, nor how persuasive the envoys from Scotland, nor how urgent the promptings of his son Charles, James refused to sanction any rebellion without the support of France. And France, in the person of Louis XV, was proving equally cautious. Negotiations floundered on the same old rock; the Jacobites would not rise without the promise of French support and the French would not give their support without the promise of a Jacobite rising.

Then, in the year 1743, things began falling into place. The death of Louis XV's chief minister placed the control of Jacobite affairs in the hands of the more sympathetic Cardinal de Tencin—brother of the promiscuous ex-nun, Claudine de Tencin, who had betrayed the Jacobite cause in the days of the

Fifteen. The belligerent Tencin was all for supporting a Jacobite rising. A few months later the French army was soundly beaten at Dettingen, where the allied English, Austrian and Hanoverian army was personally led by George II. Determined to avenge the defeat, Louis XV began looking towards the Stuarts. On hearing encouraging reports of the amount of Jacobite sympathy in England, he finally made up his mind. He sent a message to Rome, inviting Prince Charles to come to Paris to discuss the mounting of an expedition against England.

Still James hesitated. For his cautious, doubting, logical mind, the whole business was still far too fraught with uncertainties. On the other hand, he could hardly afford to let slip so good an opportunity. Torn by misgivings, he finally gave the eager Charles permission to go. At the same time he issued a Declaration of Regency. As, ran the rolling phrases, 'It will be absolutely impossible for Us to be in Person at the first setting up of Our Royal Standard,' he was nominating 'Our dearest Son, CHARLES, Prince of Wales, to be sole Regent of Our Kingdoms of England, Scotland and Ireland, and of all Our other Dominions, during Our Absence.'

The declaration was given 'in the 43rd year of Our Reign'.

At dawn on 9 January 1744, Charles slipped away from the Palazzo Muti. As the British government must know nothing of the venture, it was given out that Charles was setting off to Cisterna on a hunting trip. Under cover of darkness, he swung round and turned north towards Tuscany. In the utmost secrecy, and in various disguises, he made his way to Paris. The journey, through mid-winter Europe, was both hazardous and gruelling but Charles hardly seemed to notice. He had just turned twenty-four and he was starting out on the greatest adventure of his life.

3

Charles's progress to Paris was eagerly followed by his twenty-year-old brother Henry, Duke of York. The two of them had set out together from the Palazzo Muti on that dark winter's morning but, at the time, Henry had known nothing of Charles's plans: he had assumed that Charles would be accompanying him to Cisterna for the hunting. Only after his elder brother had slipped safely away was Henry told the truth. He was all approval. It was just as well, he afterwards wrote to Charles, that he had not known about his brother's plans; 'for certainly the great love I have for you could not but have showed itself, maybe imprudently on that occasion.' For the brothers were very close, and Henry hero-worshipped the dashing Charles.

Once at Cisterna, Henry kept up the pretence that his brother was still with him; even to the extent of sending wild geese to Rome as though they came as presents from Charles. His only regret was that he had not been allowed to accompany his elder brother. He would gladly 'fly through fire and water' he assured Charles, to be by his side.

But their father was having none of it. Only with the greatest reluctance had James permitted Charles to go. He was certainly not going to risk sending his second son on so dangerous an undertaking.

Whether, in fact, Henry would have proved to be a useful companion in arms is doubtful. He was certainly brave and although he lacked Charles's dazzling looks and magnetic personality, Henry was an attractive enough young man. Shorter, stockier and swarthier than Charles, he looked more like a Sobieski than a Stuart. And despite the fact that he seemed studious only when set against the extrovert Charles, Henry was of a steadier, more decorous nature.

But already, at twenty, the Duke of York was showing disturbing signs of following in his late mother's footsteps: he was becoming excessively, almost neurotically, pious. A few years before, an alarmed Lord Dunbar had presented James with a long report on the Duke of York's behaviour. In it, Dunbar had detailed his charge's daily devotions. From the time that he rose at a quarter to six in the morning until the time that he went to bed, Henry was hardly ever off his knees. On holy days he assisted at no less than three masses; sometimes even four. The minute a meal or a dancing lesson or a riding lesson was over, he would be back in chapel for an hour or an hour and a half.

Dunbar complained that 'in reciting or reacting his prayers he puts his mind in agitation, pronounces his words aloud and crowds them with great precipitation one upon another and I often remark him when he goes abroad after dinner with a blackness about his eyes, his head quite fatigued and his hands hot.'

One would have imagined that anyone so feverishly, so obsessively religious would have wanted nothing to do with his brother's military ambitions. But Henry was a Stuart and, as such, he saw the Stuart cause as a holy one. The Stuarts were kings by Divine Right, and the restoration of their House was therefore a Divine Duty. This was why Henry was so ready to 'fly through fire and water' to be by Charles's side. In time, Henry's sense of religious vocation was to prove stronger than his dedication to the Stuart cause but, at the moment, and because he was still a young and healthy prince, the Duke of York was quite ready to draw his sword in defence of such a righteous cause.

4

Charles's reception in Paris was hardly rapturous. It was not even warm. Remembering the attention lavished on him at Gaeta and during his tour of northern Italy, Charles must have been distinctly put out by this cool French reception. Far from welcoming the Stuart Prince with open arms, Louis XV seemed determined to keep him at a distance. Although, in one of those fancifully spelt letters to his father, Charles assured him that he had 'mett with all that could be expected' from the French King, and that 'all gose well,' there were others who thought that Charles was being cold-shouldered. For someone of Charles's overweening conceit, it was a sobering experience.

But within a few weeks of his arrival, all his reservations were swept away in a pleasurable bustle of activity. Louis XV's attitude towards the Prince might have been aloof but his interest in the proposed expedition remained keen. Late in February, Charles was summoned to Gravelines. Here he joined Marshal Saxe who, with a force of over seven thousand men and a fleet of transports, was preparing to invade England. The main force, with the excited Prince Charles in its midst, embarked at Dunkirk. Things, at last, were under way.

But once again the weather confounded the hopes of the House of Stuart.

A violent storm blew up, damaging not only the French fleet in the Channel but almost destroying the French transports in Dunkirk harbour. Ships were dashed to pieces and many lives lost. And what was worse, from Charles's point of view, was that all thoughts of an invasion were now abandoned. The French forces were withdrawn from Dunkirk and Marshal Saxe went off to fight in Flanders.

To the disappointed young Prince, it all seemed incomprehensible.

There now followed a period of enforced inactivity which, for someone of Charles's mercurial nature, was highly frustrating. He came :railing back from Gravelines to Paris to find himself the centre of a group of idle, dispirited, wrangling and back-biting fellow exiles. And Charles was the very last person to keep himself clear of the general mêlée. He was quite incapable of setting an example of royal dignity, reserve or impartiality. He took sides, he quarrelled, he conspired, he ran up debts, he kept bad company. Time and again poor James was disturbed by report: of his son's unsuitable companions. The Prince seems to have surrounded himself not only with a group of adventurers as hot-headed and impatient as himself but with several of what he referred to as 'very preety yong men'. There was not, as one of his biographers has wittily pointed out, 'a single mention of any preety yong ladies'.

Yet, through it all, Charles kept his main objective in sight: he was as determined as ever to launch a rebellion. To this end, he schemed tirelessly. There was a constant to-ing and fro-ing between the Jacobites in Paris and the Jacobites in Britain. And although there was a goad deal of talk about Scottish support and English support and French support, few were willing to commit themselves. The English Jacobites, grumbled Charles, were 'affred of their own shaddo'. Gradually, he came to the conclusion that he must act alone: that, at the head of a small band of faithfuls, he must land in Scotland and start a rising.

Knowing exactly what his father's attitude to such an enterprise would be, Charles kept James in the dark about his plans. He wrote him reassuring letters, from which James gathered that Charles was still co-operating with the French. Even when Charles urged his father to sell some of the famous Sobieski jewels, bequeathed to Clementina's sons by her father, James assumed that he wanted the money to pay his debts. And all the while Charles was organising his own expedition: borrowing money, pawning valuables, choosing companions, chartering ships, buying arms and ammunition, setting in supplies. By the spring of 1745 he was simply waiting for an opportune moment to get things started.

The moment arrived in May. At the battle of Fontenoy the French under Marshal Saxe defeated a combined British, Dutch, Hanoverian and Austrian force commanded by George II's third son, the Duke of Cumberland. The Jacobites were overjoyed. This, surely, was the time to strike. With Britain demoralised by the defeat, dissatisfied by what it regarded as a Hanoverian war and denuded of troops (even George II had blithely set out for his beloved Hanover) the country had never been more vulnerable. At the end of May Charles sent a letter to a fellow conspirator, John Murray of Broughton, to say that he hoped to arrive in Scotland in July.

Murray afterwards claimed that he had already written to Charles, warning him not to come unless at the head of a force of at least six thousand men, but it appears that Charles never received the letter.

In any case, it is doubtful whether it would have stopped him. By now Charles was completely committed to the venture. As he admitted to his father, when he finally let James into the secret, 'I have taken a firm resolution to conquer or to dye, and stand my ground as long as I have a man remaining with me.' What Prince Charles was after was action, attention and, most important of all, glory; he was certainly not going to get those by cooling his heels in Paris or by dragging them back to Rome.

On 16 July 1745 (the date in Britain was 5 July) the expedition set sail from Belle-Ile off Brittany in two ships, the *Du Teillay* and the *Elisabeth*. The *Elisabeth* was a sixty-eight gun vessel, carrying over seven hundred men; the *Du Teillay*, in which Charles sailed, was smaller. With the Prince on the *Du Teillay* were seven companions who were to go down in history as the 'Seven Men of Moidart'. They were the Duke of Atholl, Francis Strickland, Sir Thomas Sheridan (Charles's one-time tutor), George Kelly, Aeneas Macdonald, John O'Sullivan and Sir John Macdonnell. All in all they were a mixed and unremarkable bunch, hardly deserving of their subsequently hallowed place in the annals of Jacobitism.

It had been decided to sail to Scotland by a route untried by previous Jacobite expeditions: past the tip of Cornwall at Land's End, around the west coast of Ireland and on to the Hebrides, off the north west coast of Scotland. A few days after setting sail, and off the Lizard, the two ships sighted a British man-of-war,

H.M.S. *Lion*. The *Elisabeth* gave battle and was so badly damaged in the action that she was forced to return to Brest. This meant the loss, not only of one of the two ships, but of seven hundred men. But when it was suggested that the *Du Teillay* return as well, Charles would not hear of it. He was determined to go on.

So, quite alone, the little *Du Teillay* sailed north towards Scotland.

On 23 July 1745, by the British calendar, Charles had his first sight of the Promised Land. As he gazed at the somewhat forbidding islands of the Outer Hebrides, an eagle was seen to be hovering over the ship. 'The King of birds is come to welcome your Royal Highness upon your arrival in Scotland,' declared one of his companions gallantly. It was the only thing that did. A member of the party who went ashore on the island of Barra came back with the disturbing news that his brother-in-law, who was expected to welcome them, was nowhere to be found. And the sudden appearance of a suspicious-looking vessel outside the bay convinced them that they must get away to make a landing elsewhere as soon as possible.

They made for the west side of the small and desolate island of Eriskay. In lashing wind and driving rain, Prince Charles set foot, for the first time in his life, on Scottish soil. The place where he landed is still known, in Gaelic, as the Prince's Shore. As he battled up the inhospitable slope, disguised as an abbé, a packet of convolvulus seeds, gathered while Charles had been waiting to set sail from France, fell out of his pocket and was scattered by the fierce wind. To this day, they say, a rose-pink convolvulus grows along this strip of shore. It grows nowhere else on Eriskay. Nor does it grow on any other Hebridean island.

Having spent the night in a rough, smoke -filled, islander's cottage, Charles returned to the *Du Teillay* the following morning. Here he received Alexander Macdonald of Boisdale, who had crossed the two mile stretch of water from the neighbouring island of South Uist. For Charles, it was an important meeting. The Macdonalds were one of the largest clans and were known to be supporters of the Stuart cause. But, to :he consternation of Charles's companions, Boisdale wanted nothing to do with the Prince's adventure. He told Charles that he could expect no help from Scotland. Bluntly, Boisdale advised him to go home.

'I am come home ...' answered the Young Pretender.

Part Five

The Young Pretender

Chapter Thirteen

1

The royal standard was raised at Glenfinnan, at the head of Loch Shiel, on 19 August 1745. Having proclaimed James as King, the aged Duke of Atholl read out the Declaration in which James had appointed Charles as Regent. With this proclamation, 'the Forty Five,' the most stirring chapter in the annals of Jacobitism, had officially begun.

The setting for this momentous ceremony was impressive. Glenfinnan is a narrow valley through which the River Finnan flows into the silvery waters of Loch Shiel. Fringed with mountains, it is a picturesque and tranquil spot. For Charles on that summer's day, however, Glenfinnan had at first seemed just a little too tranquil. He had arrived there expecting to find a mammoth gathering of the clans, but there were only about a hundred and fifty Macdonalds to greet him as he stepped off his boat. For two agonising hours he waited for more clansmen to arrive.

Then suddenly, in the distance, came the heart-swelling sound of pipes, followed by the no less heart-swelling sight of over seven hundred Highlanders 'all plaided and plumed in their tartan array,' pouring down the steep mountainside. They were the Camerons, led by Donald Cameron of Lochiel. Behind them came three hundred more Macdonalds. With an army of well over a thousand men around him, Charles could feel that the day's ceremonial—the unfurling of the red and white banner, the resounding proclamation, the reading of a manifesto, the full-throated roar of the assembled clansmen, the frantic waving of swords and claymores—was a triumphant opening to a campaign that would carry him all the way to London.

That things had reached even this first stage was entirely due to the personality of Prince Charles. The characteristics which served him so badly in time of inacitivity—his restlessness, his obstinacy, his wilfulness, his showiness, his conceit, his inability to apply himself, his need to be always the centre of attraction—became strengths in a position like this. From the moment that he set foot on Scottish soil nothing would shake his determination to organise a rising. And there were a great many who did try to shake it. Boisdale had not been the only one to pour cold water. During the first two weeks that Charles spent in Scotland (he had sailed from Eriskay to Borrodale on the mainland) he received a stream of visitors. Although some minor figures promised support, many of the more important chieftains refused to have anything to do with him. Yet Charles remained optimistic. His companions might be all for sailing back to France, but he would not hear of it.

And gradually his show of confidence began to win adherents. To the more emotional, just the sight of him—so tall, so attractive, so graceful, so charming—was enough: 'at his first appearance,' wrote one impressionable member of the Macdonald clan, 'I found my heart swell to my very throat ...' But something other than the renowned charm and the handsome face, or even the alleged aura of royalty, was needed to win over the more hard-headed chieftains. They found themselves being impressed by Charles's less superficial traits; by his sense of purpose, by his air of optimism, by his show of enthusiasm and, one assumes, by his promise of French support for the venture.

But whether it was by personal magnetism or by powers of persuasion, it says a great deal for Charles that, having landed with only seven companions to back him up, he could talk the Highland chieftains—who had so much to lose if the rising should fail—into giving him their support.

'If he succeeds,' wrote Lord Lovat, 'the whole merit will be his own; and if his mad Enterprize bring misfortunes upon him, he has only himself to blame.'

Undoubtedly, the greatest feather in Charles's cap was his winning over of Donald Cameron of Lochiel. Once he had managed to get this influential chieftain to support him, the Prince felt that the rising could start in earnest. The *Du Teillay* was sent back to France and, with the standard having been raised at Glenfinnan, the march towards Edinburgh could begin.

By now, of course, the Government in London was aware of the arrival of the Young Pretender. A reward of thirty thousand pounds was offered for his capture, and Sir John Cope, who commanded the Government forces in Scotland, moved northwards to check the Jacobite advance. As Charles moved resolutely north-east, beside the string of lochs mirroring the Great Glen which bisects the Highlands, Cope was marching, no less resolutely, to meet him. Both were determined to give battle. Charles was anxious to defeat Cope before he could be reinforced from England, and Cope was anxious to defeat Charles before his insurrection could win more support in the Highlands. The two forces seemed destined to meet in the Corriyairach Pass.

But they did not. As Charles had the good sense to gain control of the Pass and set a trap for Cope, Cope showed equal good sense in avoiding it. He marched away to Inverness instead. This left the road to Edinburgh open. Avoiding the temptation to turn aside and attack Cope in Inverness, Charles took the road south. Only gradually did it dawn on the Jacobites that they had won a great psychological victory.

From now on, their advance became progressively more triumphant. In brilliant sunshine the raggedly dressed but high-spirited army moved down through the Highlands. And as they passed, they gathered more and more adherents. By the time Prince Charles, resplendent in a tartan suit trimmed with gold lace, made his entry into Perth, he could count on the support of such influential men as the Duke of Perth, Lord Nairn, Lord George Murray, Lord Ogilvy, Lord Strathallan, Macpherson of Cluny, Oliphant of Gask and Robert Mercer of Aldie. So impressively reinforced, Charles spent a week in Perth—gathering money, drilling his troops, organising his army and discussing strategy. There was no complaint now, from the assembled clansmen, that their leader lacked dash. Unlike James, thirty years before, Charles was as colourful and inspiring a warrior as one could hope for. To the admiring Highlanders, he became known as Bonnie Prince Charlie.

From Perth, at the head of almost two and a half thousand men, Charles marched on towards the capital. By 16 September, less than a month after the raising of the standard at Glenfinnan, the Jacobite army was encamped on the outskirts of Edinburgh. Realising that he had neither the strength to storm the city nor the time to besiege it, Charles sent a lordly message to the City Fathers demanding its surrender. A deputation asked for more time to consider the terms. Charles gave them a few hours. When they returned to ask for a further extension, he refused.

In the meantime, Charles had secretly posted a group of Highlanders near one of the city's four main gates. When the coach carrying the deputies returned from its unsuccessful mission and the gate was opened to admit it, the Highlanders stormed the gate and entered the city. They were followed by the main body of Charles's army who, with swords drawn and a 'hideous yell,' came rushing through the gate. The small Government force promptly shut itself up in the Castle. Edinburgh had fallen.

At noon on 17 September Charles made his entry into his capital. Avoiding the guns of the Castle, he approached the palace—Holyroodhouse—from the south side. Sitting astride his horse, he looked every bit as impressive as had been rumoured. He was in Highland dress. On his short, powdered periwig he wore a blue velvet bonnet trimmed with gold lace and a white cockade. The Star of the Order of St Andrew glittered on his tartan jacket; a silver-hiked broadsword thudded against his red velvet breeches and military boots. To the mob that crowded the park surrounding the palace, and especially to the women, he looked like a prince in a fairy tale. And his manner was no less princely. With great dignity Charles moved among the excited press of people, frequently stopping so that they could get a better view of him. Then he turned and mounted the stairs which led into Holyroodhouse.

This great, grey, turreted palace—an extension of an earlier tower—had been the home of the Stuart kings for generations. In front of it lay the walled, close-packed city of Edinburgh; behind stretched a wild, undulating landscape; above it loomed the great mass of Arthur's Seat. In it Mary Queen of Scots had lived some of her turbulent life. From it King James VI of Scotland had gone south to become King James I of England. Over sixty years had passed since Charles's grandparents—James II and Mary Beatrice—had lived here as Duke and Duchess of York. And over thirty-five years had passed since his father—James III—had gazed in vain across the wintry waters of the Firth of Forth towards the 'ancient pinnacled palace' of his forbears. Now, at the Market Cross, a hastily rounded up assembly of magistrates, heralds, pursuivants and trumpeters attended the proclaiming of James III of England and Ireland and James VIII of Scotland.

Prince Charles Edward Stuart had indeed come home.

2

But it was not going to be quite as easy as all that. Charles could hardly hope to make himself master of Scotland without firing a shot. Indeed, on the very day that he was entering Holyroodhouse, Sir John Cope's army—having sailed south from Aberdeen—was disembarking at Dunbar, some twenty-five miles east of Edinburgh. Much to Charles's delight, a Jacobite council of war decided that Cope must be attacked as soon as possible. So, as the Government troops came marching towards Edinburgh, the Jacobite force marched out to meet it.

The two armies were pretty well evenly matched. Each numbered about two and a half thousand men. And if Cope and his officers imagined the Jacobite army to be larger than it was, Charles and his officers imagined the Government troops to be better disciplined than they were. By the night of 20 September 1745, the rival armies were encamped near the village of Prestonpans, ten miles from Edinburgh. Between them lay a stretch of marshy ground. Luckily for the Jacobites, one of their men knew of a path leading through the bog, and at dawn the following day, the Highlanders were able to fling themselves on the hastily formed enemy lines.

Within ten minutes it was all over. The Government troops were incapable of standing up to the shrieking, slashing, savagely determined Highlanders. They simply turned tail and ran, as Charles reported to his father, 'likerabets'.

So the sun rose, that day, on a great Jacobite victory. That it had been achieved more by luck than judgement was forgotten in the general Jacobite euphoria. In less than three hours after the battle, the Camerons were marching back through the narrow streets of Edinburgh, with the colours captured from Cope's dragoons rippling in the breeze and the pipers playing the old cavalier song, 'The King shall enjoy his own again'. When Charles re-entered Edinburgh the following morning, it was as an all-conquering hero. Suddenly, everyone was a Jacobite. Those who had been merely curious before were now vociferous supporters of the handsome young

Prince; Charles was assured that the victorious Battle of Prestonpans was to be celebrated in fitting style—with bonfires and balls and general rejoicing.

But he was having none of it. Just as, after the battle, Charles had ordered that the enemy dead be decently buried, the enemy wounded properly cared for and the captured officers civilly treated, so did he forbid any unseemly public demonstration. There was to be no crowing over the defeat of his fellow, if misguided, countrymen, and no want of respect to those of his father's subjects who had lost their lives because of their 'unhappy way of thinking'. Partly for reasons of policy, partly from a natural humanitarianism, and partly from the sincere conviction that he had come to liberate the British people from the foreign yoke, Charles was determined to act the moderate and all-forgiving leader. James would have been proud of him.

And what now? Charles, boyishly flushed with success, was all for marching into England as soon as possible. Field-Marshal Wade was already heading towards Newcastle with a body of. Government troops; surely, argued Charles, the thing to do would be to attack him as soon as possible? He felt confident that he had only to show himself in England to be hailed as a deliverer, and for disgruntled Englishmen to come flocking to his banner.

But wiser heads prevailed. At a meeting of a newly constituted council, it was agreed that Charles should remain in Edinburgh for the moment. It was explained that the Jacobite army was too small, too ill-equipped, too lacking in cavalry, too prone to disintegrate as the Highlanders took themselves off for weeks at a time in order to store their plunder or harvest their crops or sleep with their wives. And, by remaining in Edinburgh, Charles could win more adherents. He would give those wavering chieftains the opportunity of joining what was now being regarded as the winning side. There was even a suggestion that Charles remain permanently in Edinburgh. By denouncing the Act of Union and declaring Scotland independent, the Stuarts could once again establish themselves in their ancient kingdom. Whether, in fact, Charles could have succeeded in doing this is debatable but it is tempting to speculate on the possibility. There had certainly never been a better opportunity than this for a restoration of the Stuarts as Kings of Scotland.

But Charles would not hear of it. His eyes were firmly fixed on London.

The most commanding personality in Charles's council was Lord George Murray, one of his two Lieutenant-Generals. The other was the Duke of Perth. Lord George, a son of the first Duke of Atholl, was a man of considerable military ability and administrative efficiency, but stern, tactless and high-handed. Already he and Charles had had some differences of opinion. But as Lord George could count on the support of most of the other chieftains, his opinion invariably carried the day. More than once Charles had agreed to Lord George's proposals against his own instincts. To some, this looked like youth yielding to experience; to others, it looked like weakness. The lack of rapport between Charles and his forceful Lieutenant-General was to have fateful consequences.

Having been talked into spending more time in Edinburgh, Charles set about consolidating his position. After all, this twenty-four-year-old Prince was now the ruler of Scotland. He levied taxes, he issued proclamations, he established diplomatic relations with France, he wrote honeyed letters to the still undecided chieftains, he reviewed his army, he tried—unsuccessfully—to subdue Edinburgh Castle, which was still in Government hands.

But it was not all work. At night, Holyrood was ablaze with light as Prince Charles held court. The weeks that he spent in this long-deserted palace were always to be remembered as a time of exceptional gaiety and brilliance. Edinburgh society flocked to pay homage to the handsome young man in his Highland dress. The appeal of this romantic Prince, with his unshakable sense of destiny, was all but irresistible. The women were particularly taken with him. With their hair elaborately dressed, their cheeks rouged, their jewels sparkling and their great satin skirts a-swish, they crowded round him, hoping for a glance from those dark eyes or, better still, a few words from those curved, almost feminine lips. All agreed that his manners were faultless. 'Indeed,' noted a young lady breathlessly, 'in all his appearance he seems to be cut out for enchanting his beholders ...'

'In general,' reported one Frenchman, 'all the young and pretty women are Jacobites, and have only become so since the arrival of the young Prince. It is not because he is gallant with them but rather the opposite which attracts the Scottish women who are by temperament serious and passionate, feeling he is a man of depth and constancy, not frivolous by nature.'

But these flocks of serious and passionate young Scotswomen had misread the signs. Charles was not gallant towards them for the simple reason that he was not interested in them. He was polite to the ladies but that was all. And there were some who did not consider him to be especially polite; his behaviour towards women, reports Lord Elcho, 'was very cool'. The fact was that Charles was never really at ease with women; sexually immature, he much preferred the company of men, particularly brave, boyish, impulsive youngsters like himself. 'I had rather,' he once unblinkingly remarked, 'be with one of my brave Highlanders.' In many ways, Charles was one of life's permanent adolescents.

During his stay at Holyrood, he could have taken almost any woman—lady of fashion or chambermaid—that he fancied, but there was never so much as a whisper of sexual scandal concerning him. The same, of course, had been true of his father, but then Charles did not share James's high moral standards or deep religious convictions. He was simply not aroused by the women who pressed so eagerly about him in the candlelit rooms of Holyroodhouse.

In any case, all his attention was fixed on the regaining of the throne. For Charles the invasion of England could not begin soon enough. Finally, having spent almost six weeks in Edinburgh, he persuaded his council into marching south. But which way to go? Charles was all for heading straight for Newcastle to attack Wade. The more cautious Lord George Murray wanted to avoid a battle altogether by marching, via Carlisle, through the north-west of England. By doing this, they would be able to rally support in an area which was traditionally Jacobite. Had not the gallant gentlemen of Cumberland, during the Fifteen, been rapturously received as they went jogging south through Lancashire?

Once more, Lord George's arguments carried the day. Against his own inclinations, Charles 'in a very obliging manner' agreed that the Jacobite army should make for the north-west of England. On 1 November 1745, with banners fluttering and pipes squealing, the five thousand strong force marched out of Edinburgh. At their head rode Bonnie Prince Charlie. Eight days later, having splashed across the River Esk, he set foot on English soil.

3

'The example of my elder son,' wrote James III from the Palazzo Muti to Louis XV, 'naturally influences the younger, and he cannot bear to remain in Rome while his brother is in Scotland. Though the difficulties of leaving this country are greater than ever, he would rather do impossibilities than fail to hasten to Avignon, there to await your Majesty's orders.'

And so, before dawn on 29 August 1745, Henry slipped away from the Palazzo Muti with as much secrecy, and as much eagerness, as Charles had done the year before. While a British squadron (primed by the indefatigable British minister in Florence) kept a lookout for any small vessel that might be carrying the Young Pretender's brother to France, Henry travelled by road to Genoa. Only from there did he sail to Antibes. From Antibes he made for that long-established place of Jacobite refuge—the papal city of Avignon. While awaiting, as James so hopefully put it, Louis XV's orders, Henry developed a fever. Not until November was he able to travel on to Paris.

He could not have arrived at a better time. Charles's spectacular achievements—his entry into Edinburgh, his victory at Prestonpans, his invasion of England—had considerably altered the French attitude towards the Stuart cause. Admittedly, Louis XV had already given Charles some support. He had sent four small ships with volunteers and arms and had accredited a representative, in the person of the Marquis d'Eguilles, to Prince Charles. But by this stage the French King was beginning to think in terms of more massive support. He began to treat James as a power; in practice as well as in theory, he began to look upon him as a fellow sovereign.

On 24 October 1745 a Treaty of Alliance—between Louis XV and James III—was drawn up at Fontainebleau. Among its clauses was one in which Louis promised to help Charles, as far as was practical, against their 'common foe'. This common foe they were,careful to name, not as England, but as the 'Elector of Hanover'.

The meeting between Louis XV and Henry, Duke of York, was hardly an auspicious social success. The French King was never easy with strangers and the interview was marked by awkward pauses. For the twenty-year-old Henry, raised in the pious, impoverished, unsophisticated atmosphere of the Palazzo Muti, the splendour of the French court was almost overwhelming. The audience was further bedevilled by the fact that Henry was obliged to appear incognito, as the Count of Albany; this meant that from the start he was enmeshed in a bewildering web of protocol. None the less, observers were favourably impressed by the young Prince. He had his full share of Stuart breeding and he answered Louis's questions with ease and good sense. On the main purpose of Henry's visit—to solicit more aid from the French King—Louis remained non-committal.

Yet throughout November and December a great invasion force was assembled on the Channel coast. Henry was given the nominal command of the expedition while the actual command was in the hands of the Duc de Richelieu. Headquartered together at Dunkirk, the two men waited for an opportune moment to set sail.

A less compatible pair than Prince Henry and the Duc de Richelieu would have been difficult to imagine. For all the agreeableness of his manner, Henry was a priggish, provincial, deeply devout, young man, introspective by temperament. Richelieu was quite different; relaxed, worldly, sensual, promiscuous. In more ways than one, it seems, did he enjoy his office of First Gentleman of the Bedchamber. And if Henry was scandalised by Richelieu's behaviour, Richelieu was not a little irritated by Henry's piety. The Prince, grumbled the French Minister for War, 'never passes before a crucifix or an altar without genuflecting like a sacristan,' and the Duc de Richelieu dismissed him as an 'Italian bigot'.

The councils of war at Dunkirk frequently degenerated into squabbles between the Prince, who thought that Richelieu was too half-hearted in his attitude towards the proposed invasion, and Richelieu, who considered Henry to be too priest-ridden for his task. 'You may perhaps gain the kingdom of Heaven by your prayers,' Richelieu once quipped, 'but never the kingdom of Great Britain.'

Nevertheless, by December things were getting under way. Already Lord John Drummond, with a thousand-strong Royal Scots regiment, had sailed from France in a twenty-six gun frigate, and the Comte de Maurepas, French Minister for the Navy, was able to assure Charles that the planned invasion was about to take place.

'Here we are at last on the eve of the mighty event,' he wrote. 'We have completed at Dunkirk and neighbouring ports all the necessary preparations for the embarkation of twelve thousand men commanded by the Duc de Richelieu. I have taken very great care over my part in all this; if it goes well with what others have to do, the disembarkation [in England] could take place before this month is out.'

4

And all the while, Bonnie Prince Charlie and his Highland army was marching triumphantly south. Carlisle presented very little problem. Its defences were neglected, its garrison was elderly, its estimation of the strength of the Jacobite army exaggerated and its terror of the savage Highlanders overwhelming. It was widely believed that these unkempt, wild-eyed and raggedly-dressed clansmen were given to eating children. A letter from Field-Marshal Wade to acquaint Carlisle's defenders with the fact that he had no intention of helping them, finally made up their minds. After a six-day siege, the city surrendered. Charles entered Carlisle on 14 November.

A far more significant battle was being fought within the ranks of the Jacobite army itself. Not only was there very little sympathy between Charles and Lord George Murray but there was no sympathy whatsoever between Lord George and the other Lieutenant-General, the Duke of Perth. At Carlisle these long-simmering feuds boiled over. In an insulting letter to Charles, Lord George resigned his commission. From now on, he wrote, he would serve as a volunteer. Infuriated at the tone of the letter, Charles accepted Lord George's resignation. This meant that the Duke of Perth would now be in sole command of the army, under Charles. But the rest of the Jacobite council would not hear of it. For one thing, Perth was a Catholic; for another, he could not hold a candle to Lord George when it came to conducting a campaign. So Perth very sensibly stepped down and Charles asked Lord George to resume his commission.

For the moment, but for the moment only, the quarrel was patched up.

Leaving a small garrison behind in Carlisle, the Jacobite army continued its march south. Although the roads were slippery with ice and the surrounding fields white with snow, they made good progress. Nowhere did they meet with any opposition. At the approach of this, by now, tatterdemalion force of some four and a half thousand men (there had been the inevitable desertions) the local militias simply melted away. Further and further into the heart of England they pressed, through Penrith, Kendal, Lancaster, Preston, Wigan and on towards Manchester. Charles's behaviour, as far as the rank and file were concerned, was exemplary. Only on entering the towns through which they passed did he ride; otherwise he marched with the men. At night he retired only after he was satisfied that the men were decently lodged: he was accessible to all.

'He was never heard to say a rash word to any man,' noted one admirer, 'praised most graciously those that served well, and treated very mildly those that did not; no Prince can have a greater talent to gain the hearts of mankind ...'

The talent might have been abundant but it was gaining very few hearts. For if the Jacobite army was encountering no opposition, neither was it gathering any support. Those hordes of ardent Jacobites, whom Charles had imagined would come flocking to his banner, never materialised. Here and there they picked up a few recruits but, for the most part, the country people watched them pass by in silence.

At Manchester things looked a bit brighter. The city was said to have been taken by 'a drummer and a whore,' for a sergeant, together with his mistress and a drummer, went on ahead of the army to drum up recruits. They were not unsuccessful. Some two hundred men were induced to join the army and were given the grandiloquent title of the Manchester Regiment. Charles, looking as impressive as ever in his Highland dress, was given a gratifyingly warm welcome and, as usual, James was proclaimed King.

From Manchester they marched on towards Derby. *En route,* at Macclesfield, they heard that a Government force, commanded by George II's son, the Duke of Cumberland, was lying to the south of them, blocking the road to London. What was to be done? It was decided that Lord George would lead a small force south-west thus giving the impression that the army was heading towards Wales, while Charles, with the bulk of the army, would move south-east, towards Derby.

The ruse worked. Cumberland fell back, Lord George rejoined the main army, and on 4 December Charles entered Derby.

He was very well received. Bonfires blazed, bells pealed and the town was bright with illuminations. As he rode through the acclaiming streets of this important town, Charles had every reason to be pleased with himself. At Derby, he was in the very heart of England. In a mere three and a half months, since the raising of the standard at Glenfinnan, he had advanced almost five hundred miles. London, as the crow flies, was only a hundred miles away. Even by road, it was less than a hundred and thirty miles, and his advance guard was at Swarkstone Bridge, six miles beyond Derby. Cumberland, outwitted, would have to move fast if he wanted to come between Charles and the capital and, in any case, the Highlanders were spoiling for a fight.

'Never,' wrote Alexander Macdonald, 'were our Highlanders in higher spirits notwithstanding their long and fatiguing march; they had indeed got good quarters and plenty of provisions in their march and were well paid; so that we judged we were able to fight double our number of any troops that could oppose us.'

If Cumberland were to be outmarched or beaten, the hurriedly organised London militia, stationed at

Finchley, was hardly likely to put up much resistance. Already the capital was in a state of panic. There was a run on the banks and if George II had not actually stowed his luggage aboard a yacht on the Thames, he had good reason for feeling apprehensive. It had been in the same month of December, fifty-seven years before, that James II had fled London in the face of the advancing William of Orange; would George II be forced to flee in the face of Charles Stuart? Possession of the capital would enhance Charles's prestige enormously: with the proclamation of King James III, the Stuart restoration would be as good as accomplished.

Chapter Fourteen

1

But Charles got no further than Derby. At an enlarged council meeting on the morning of 5 December, it was decided to retreat. Lord George Murray, backed up by the vast majority of the councillors and commanders present, argued that it would be madness to press on. Ahead of them lay no less than three superior armies: Cumberland was marching from one direction, Wade from another and a third force was waiting at Finchley. If attacked by even one of these armies, the less than five thousand strong Jacobite force would be cut to pieces. Things might have been different, it was explained, if the expected uprising of English Jacobites had taken place or if the promised French invasion had materialised, but the Prince's army was still hardly more than a large band of Scottish invaders who had advanced dangerously far from home into a largely indifferent countryside. Their achievement had been spectacular but it had been fruitless. The most sensible thing to do would be to retreat to Scotland and, from there, to take a fresh look at the situation. No one, claimed Lord George in his stolid fashion, was more anxious to see a restoration than he, but to advance would be to put an end to all hope of any such restoration.

Charles-was appalled. He could hardly believe his ears. In a flash the resolute façade, so easily maintained during the days when things were going well, cracked into a thousand pieces. He became, once more, the immature, petulant princeling of the Palazzo Muti. Instead of meeting Lord George's points with reasoned arguments, he lost his temper. He swore, he shouted, he abused his officers, he became incoherent. But he did not, of course, win anyone round to his way of thinking. Nor did he have the courage to stick to that way of thinking. After all, he was the supreme commander of the army. He could have overruled the others. Even if his council members had reservations about his qualities of leadership, his Highlanders adored him. They were spoiling for a fight; they would have followed him. As it was, no one dared tell the men that they were about to retreat.

For a retreat was what was decided on at the meeting. And Charles, abiding by the majority decision, felt forced to agree. They would start back, along the route by which they had come, at dawn the following day.

The retreat from Derby provides one of the great 'ifs' of history.

Speculation on the decision is no less fascinating for being fruitless. Today, it is generally agreed that

Charles had been right in wanting to continue the advance. Boldness, optimism and an almost mystical sense of destiny had already served him well; who, at the beginning, would have imagined that in less than five months after landing on Eriskay with a handful of men, he would have been within three or four days' march of London? By moving fast the Jacobites could have avoided Cumberland and it is extremely doubtful that the scratched-together force at Finchley (whose members had to be enticed to join with promises of bonuses) would have withstood a charge of the fearsome Highlanders. The Government troops had been cowardly at Prestonpans and they were to prove themselves cowardly again.

Then there was a considerable Jacobite party in the capital and the average Londoner was not particularly enamoured of the House of Hanover. It appears that parties of English and Welsh Jacobites were on the point of moving; a successful battle, an entry into London or even a further penetration towards the capital might well have spurred them into more resolute action. The same held good for Henry and the French invasion force. The fact was that as long as the Jacobites were advancing, the prospects of additional support were more likely; but once the retreat was under way, they melted like snow in the sun.

For the Forty-Five Rebellion, for the Jacobite cause, and for Charles Stuart as a man, the decision to retreat from Derby was a fateful one.

2

If the retreat from Derby was even swifter than the advance, it was due to no effort on Charles's part. On the contrary, he did everything to delay it. No longer was he up at first light to rally the men; no longer did he march briskly at their head, moving from regiment to regiment to avoid being accused of favouritism. Now he rose late, obliging the rear of the retreating column to wait until he was ready to leave, and then he galloped straight on, to arrive at the next halt with the van. He was sulking, and he wanted Lord George to know it. He was also determined that the retreat should not look like flight. Longing for a battle, Charles insisted on prolonged and unnecessary stops. His stubbornness led, of course, to endless disagreements with Lord George; by the time the army reached Carlisle, the two men could hardly bring themselves to be civil to each other.

The retreat had convinced Charles of something else as well; from now on he was going to hold no more councils of war, he was going to be responsible to no one other than his father. He must be the supreme commander in every sense of the title.

The conducting of the retreat, however, Charles left entirely to Lord George He confined himself to harassing his Lieutenant-Gcneral with demands that nothing be abandoned to the enemy. Not even 'one cannon-ball,' he instructed haughtily, 'should be left'. In driving rain, along appalling roads, across swollen rivers, through a populace that had become alarmingly hostile. Lord George urged the disappointed army. The wonder was that it could all be achieved so speedily and so efficiently.

At Carlisle, which they re-entered on 10 December, Charles put his new resolution—to be his own man—into practice. In spite of Lord George's outraged protests, Charles announced that he was going to leave a garrison at Carlisle. His decision to hang on to this indefensible town was quite clearly prompted by a determination to keep the Stuart flag flying on at least one English fortress. In Charles's romantic imagination, Carlisle had become a symbol. His first success on English soil, it represented his hopes for the future.

The head-shaking Lord George was soon proved right. Ten days after the Jacobite army had marched out of Carlisle, the Duke of Cumberland marched in. Cumberland's hope that his father. King George, would show no mercy to the Jacobite garrison was amply fulfilled. Half the captured officers were sentenced to hanging, drawing and quartering, and the rest of the officers and men were banished to little more than slavery in the American plantations.

On 20 December, having crossed the raging River Esk (the Highlanders danced reels to help dry their sopping clothes) the Jacobite army was once more on Scottish soil. But during the weeks that they had been away in England, the situation in Scotland had changed considerably. Government troops had reoccupied Edinburgh and clans which had previously been neutral were beginning to turn against Charles. As he moved through the Presbyterian south-west towards Glasgow, Charles was coolly received; in Glasgow itself, his reception was even more chilly. The sixty new recruits drummed up in the city were as nothing compared to the five hundred that had deserted the army since the return to Scotland.

It was at this stage that Prince Charles took another decision on his own. He would lay siege to the great fortress dominating the Lowlands—Stirling Castle. Once again Lord George objected. He objected, not only to the waste of time and energy that the siege would entail but to the fact that the Prince had not consulted anyone else about it. In his customary tactless, ponderous, self-righteous fashion, Lord George drew up a memorandum in which he suggested that Prince Charles consult his colleagues more frequently. He reminded the Prince that his was an army of volunteers, not mercenaries, and that they should be treated as such.

Charles was furious. In an equally blunt reply, he said that he was sick and tired of being 'hit in the teeth' by the claim that his was an army of volunteers: 'what one would expect from such an army is more zeal, more resolution, and more good manners than in those that fight merely for pay,' he raged. His authority, he declared, could be taken from him by violence, 'but I shall never resign it like an Ideot.'

And that, for the moment, was that. Although Lord George might consider Charles to be little better than an 'Ideot' on occasions, he was too disciplined a soldier to think of usurping his position. He merely gritted his teeth while Charles, reinforced by fresh troops under the command of Lord John Drummond and Lord Strathallan, laid siege to Stirling Castle.

3

There now took place, in Charles's life, a strangely uncharacteristic interlude.

Not even Charles's robust constitution had been able to withstand the biting winds, the soaking rains and the freezing temperatures of the last few weeks; he caught a feverish cold and was obliged to go to bed. He was accommodated, in considerable comfort, in the home of Sir Hugh Paterson of Bannockburn. For the ten or so days that he spent there, Charles was looked after by his host's niece, Clementina Walkinshaw.

Now in her mid-twenties, Clementina was one of a host of daughters of John Walkinshaw of Barrowfield. Born on the Continent, into an exiled, staunchly Jacobite family, she had been named after Charles's mother, who had been her godmother. There was even a rumour that, as toddlers, Charles and Clementina had played together at the Palazzo Muti. Being a staunch Jacobite herself, Clementina must have been following Charles's fortunes with great interest. When her uncle had asked her to act as his hostess at Bannockburn House during the time that Charles was in the district, Clementina must have been delighted. When fate decreed that the romantic young Prince should extend his short stay at Bannockburn to ten days, Clementina would have been more delighted still.

She was a plain girl, with an almost spinsterish air—softly-spoken, scrubbed-looking, sensible. She was a far cry from the beautiful, vivacious and seductive women who had flung themselves at Charles's feet during his stay at Holyrood. To the feverishly ill Charles, Clementina's calm, honest-to-goodness presence must have brought considerable contentment. For once he had found a woman that he need not be afraid of; he did not feel sexually threatened, nor did he feel compelled to prove his manhood. While Clementina moved dutifully around his sick-bed and sat listening to his stories, Charles—for the first time in his life—was able to enjoy feminine company uncomplicated by any sensual undertones. Clementina gave him sympathy, comfort and, most certainly, adoration, but she did not expect him to go to bed with her. She was grateful for any attention that he gave her, and he was grateful for her understanding company. Those who assumed that Clementina Walkinshaw had become his mistress during his stay at Bannockburn did not understand Charles's curious sexual composition.

Perhaps their relationship is best summed up by Charles's parting request of Clementina; she was to promise to come to him if ever he should have need of her. She promised, but seven years were to pass before the call came. The arrangement hardly smacks of unbridled ardour, on the part of either of them.

4

And in the meantime the Government forces under General Henry Hawley were moving up from Edinburgh towards Stirling. By the beginning of January 1746 it was clear that there would be a battle. Charles, recovered from his influenza, was delighted. He was spoiling for a fight. But, to Lord George's exasperation, Charles was not prepared to abandon the idiotic siege of Stirling Castle. A thousand men must remain at Stirling while the rest of the army tackled Hawley's force. Lord George was obliged to acquiesce.

The two armies met near the village of Falkirk on 17 January 1746. Where the Battle of Prestonpans had taken ten minutes, the Battle of Falkirk took twenty. In lashing rain, in driving wind, in fast fading light, the Government forces moved up a slope to attack the Highlanders. When they were ten yards away, Lord George gave the order to fire. The Government line broke and, with broadswords flashing, the yelling Highlanders flung themselves on the enemy. From the resulting chaos, the Jacobite army snatched a sort of victory. It was not that they had fought more efficiently; it was simply that the Hanoverian army had made even more mistakes. Only when the rampaging Highlanders reached Falkirk, to find it evacuated, was the extent of their victory fully realised.

Unfortunately, they neglected to follow it up. Although Lord George was anxious to pursue Hawley, Charles remained mesmerised by Stirling Castle. Only after the Castle had fallen, he said, could they go on. But the Castle was not going to fall; and in the ten or so days that it took Charles to realise this, the morale of his men sank to rock-bottom. Forced to hang about in the far from salubrious conditions of a Scottish mid: winter, they grumbled, they quarrelled, they deserted in droves. Nor were their spirits lifted by the news that the dreaded Duke of Cumberland was arriving in Edinburgh to take command of the Government forces.

When, finally, Charles announced that he was ready to advance, Lord George dug in his heels. It was too late now to follow up their victory. In one of his wordy memoranda, signed by the other chieftains, he declared that there could be no question of an advance. Instead, the Jacobite army must retreat. They must retire into the Highlands and there prepare for a fresh campaign in the spring.

Appreciative of the effect that this plan was likely to have on the Prince, Lord George suggested that Charles's aide-de-camp present it to him 'in the most prudent method'. They were aware, he wrote, 'that it will be very unpleasant, but in the name of God what can we do?'

He was right to be apprehensive. Charles was incensed. For a few moments, in fact, he lost control completely. Bashing his head against the wall until he staggered, he heaped abuse on Lord George. 'Good God!' he raved. 'Have I lived to see this?' In an equally wordy but distinctly less restrained reply, Charles argued against the retreat. Why should 'the conquerors' of Falkirk flee from the conquered? Why should they be any better off in, say, Perth, than they were now? What would the French think of them if they were to retreat? Or the Spaniards? What would become of their Lowland allies? Were they going to abandon them 'to the fury of our Merciless Enemies'? What encouragement would this give others to support them?

But Lord George refused to be won round; not by this letter, nor by a second, more reasoned one, from Charles. Faced by the combined opposition of all the chiefs, Charles was forced to agree to the retreat. He did so, however, with the worst possible grace. 'If you are all resolved upon it I must yield,' he wrote petulantly, 'but I take God to witness that it is with the greatest reluctance and that I wash my hands of the fatal consequences which I forsee but cannot help.'

Charles had good grounds for apprehension. But then so did Lord George. It was too late now to give battle. They should have pursued Hawley's army to Edinburgh on the day after the victory of Falkirk. By not doing this, by fiddling about at Stirling, Charles had let slip their last opportunity of winning a really significant victory. Now, as they began their retreat on the morning of 1 February 1746, the Jacobites were marching to their doom.

5

The retreat, through the Highlands to Inverness, was a shambles. Largely ignored by the apprehensive locals, overcharged for food, slogging through deep snow, thinned out by desertions, plagued by dissensions among its leaders, the Jacobite army staggered north. It was a distinctly unimpressive band that reached Inverness on 18 February. Yet it was strong enough to take the city without too much trouble. The next few weeks were marked by a few minor local victories and by one major disaster—the loss of a quantity of gold, brought over by a French ship. They were marked also, by Charles's final realisation that no military help was to be forthcoming from France. He was on his own.

And every day the Duke of Cumberland's superbly trained and impressively equipped force was drawing nearer.

Yet Charles remained undaunted. As optimistic, as courageous, as enthusiastic as ever, he was determined to give battle. When he heard that Cumberland had reached Nairn, some fifteen miles from Inverness, he marched his army out to meet him. Charles chose, as a suitable field for the coming fight, a stretch of rough, open upland beside the wind-whipped waters of the Moray Firth. That it was far too exposed a position for the Highlanders' particular style of fighting seems not to have occurred to Charles. The place was known as Culloden Moor.

On the morning of 15 April 1746, the Highland army was drawn up at Culloden. But the expected attack did not come that day. It came the next. By then the Highlanders, weak with hunger and exhausted from an abortive attempt to launch a surprise attack on the enemy, were in no shape to face the onslaught. For onslaught it was. A devastating Government cannonade caused havoc in the Jacobite lines and when the Highlanders launched their notoriously fearsome charge, it proved to be less fearsome than usual. By and large the rigid lines of redcoats stood firm. When they counter-attacked, the effect was horrific. In minutes the moor was turned into a scene of the most frightful carnage. When the redcoats had discharged their musket fire, they plunged their bayonets deep into the yelling Highlanders. When the Highlanders were not clambering over their own dead, they were splashing ankle-deep in blood.

Inevitably the clansmen wavered. And once they began to fall back, panic spread through their ranks. They turned and fled. Showing no mercy, Cumberland's men charged after them, bayoneting or shooting or clubbing the wounded to death; many of those that escaped the' infantry were slashed to pieces by the pursuing dragoons. It was all a far cry from the behaviour of the Jacobite army after Prestonpans, when Charles had insisted that the enemy dead, wounded and captured be treated with the greatest respect. At Culloden, the Duke of Cumberland earned his nickname of 'The Butcher'.

In a state of deep shock, Prince Charles galloped off the field. He could hardly believe that his brave Highlanders had lost a battle. In fact, he seems to have had no plan for meeting this eventuality. As far as he was concerned, the business was now over. He had no intention of rallying his scattered army. His only message to his commanders was 'that every one should look out for the means of saving himself as best he could'. For Lord George, the Prince's insouciant message was the last straw. Seething with indignation, he sent him his most acrimonious letter yet. It can have left Charles in no doubt as to what Lord George thought of him. From that time on, Prince Charles's dislike of Lord George turned to loathing.

While the disbanding Highlanders 'sent forth screams and howlings, groaning and weeping with bitter tears at seeing their country at the mercy of the Duke of Cumberland', Charles was riding hell for leather towards the west coast. He was hoping to be taken off by a French ship. 'All the world,' wrote Andrew Lang afterwards, 'has regretted that the Prince did not fall [at Culloden] leaving an unblemished fame, that he did not ride back, if it were alone ... and die with glory.'

Be that as it may, Prince Charles Stuart was to win for himself, during the following five months, a different sort of glory.

Chapter Fifteen

1

To James III, the news of Culloden came as a severe blow. More than the inexperienced Charles, James appreciated that the rising would never withstand this defeat. Already, at the time of the retreat from Derby, James had begun to lose faith. He realised that the retreat would put paid to all hopes of a French invasion. To the disconsolate Henry, still waiting at Dunkirk, James admitted that the only thing to do now would be to keep in with Louis XV; on no account, James cautioned wisely, should Henry let the French see that he blamed them for the fact that the invasion had not been launched. 'It is to be hoped the King of France will make it a point of honour to be kind to your Brother and you whatever may happen,' he wrote.

After Culloden Henry came trailing back to Paris. Determined to strike some sort of blow for the Stuart cause, he asked Louis's permission to serve with the French army in Flanders. Permission was given and the Prince was appointed to the staff of the Comte de Clermont who was besieging Antwerp. But his main concern seems to have been for the safety of his brother. Unceasingly, Henry badgered the French Government to send ships to get Charles back from Scotland. 'It is a cruel thing,' he wrote to his father, 'these frigates are so long a-going, and I am sure it is not for want of pressing.'

James was no less anxious. From the Palazzo Muti he wrote to his eldest son, hoping against hope that he would somehow receive his letters. 'God knows where or when this will find you, my dearest Carluccio, but still I cannot but write to you in the great anxiety and pain I am in for you ... I am, though, still in hopes you may be able to keep your ground in Scotland till you can have assistance from France; but if you really cannot maintain yourself in Scotland, do not, for God's sake, drive things too far, but think of your own safety, on which so much depends. Though your enterprise should miscarry, the honour you have gained by it will always stick by you; it will make you respected and considered'.

James knew his son. This was exactly what Charles wanted to hear.

2

The months, from April to September, that Prince Charles spent in Scotland as a hunted fugitive are generally regarded as the most praiseworthy of his life. This has become his finest hour. Sometimes alone, sometimes with a handful of companions, he survived a series of extraordinary adventures. He endured hardships, ran incredible risks, affected disguises, achieved hair's-breadth escapes, commanded touching loyalty and revealed a daring and a vigour and an optimism that was to become legendary. Although he had a price of £30,000 on his head, he was never once betrayed. The story of that great adventure is as much a testimony to the loyalty of the Scottish people as to Charles's heroism.

As it is, Bonnie Prince Charlie's exploits after the Forty-Five have been enshrined in Scottish song and Scottish folklore; but if he had died, not at Culloden but on the scaffold at the end of these five adventurous months, his name would have been for ever haloed in glory.

The reality, of course, was rather different from the legend. Prince Charles had not suddenly become a paragon overnight. His behaviour was really no braver and his sufferings no worse than those of any of the Jacobites being hounded by Cumberland's men. By expecting help, protection and shelter from the Highlanders, Charles was putting them in grave danger; if he was given constant proofs of devotion, he appears to have expected nothing less. Throughout these adventures he remained strangely negative—never asserting himself, never originating any plan, always content to let others make up his mind for him. There is not really much indication that he was appalled—as his father had been appalled after the Fifteen—by the havoc being wrought in the Highlands because of his rash attempt to restore his House. Homes—whether mansions, farms or crofts, were being burnt to the ground. Men, women and children were hauled out to be hanged or bayoneted. Cattle were driven away. Noblemen were sent to the scaffold and clansmen were being thrown into prison or transported to the colonies. But all Charles could think about was getting safely away in order to organise another rising. In a way, he felt that he had been let down by the Highland chieftains; the least they could now do was to ensure that he would live to fight another day.

Yet for all that, his exploits during these five months were remarkable. Few of Europe's pampered princelings would have been able to endure what he was forced to endure. Charles might have remained as selfish, as conceited and as naive as he had ever been but there was no doubting his courage or his stamina. If those months in the heather did not turn him into a better man, they certainly turned him into a tougher one.

Charles arrived on the west coast, after the rout of Culloden, to find that no friendly French ship was waiting to take him off. So it was decided that he must make for the Islands: it would be easier to be rescued from there. He made the crossing in typically Stuart weather—a raging storm—and landed on Benbecula in the Outer Hebrides. Another piece of typically Stuart bad luck was that Charles had hardly left the mainland before two French ships arrived in Loch nam Uamh to take him off. Unable to contact him, the ships were at least able to rescue a host of other fugitive Jacobites. In spite of being badly crippled in a fight with the twenty-four gun *Greyhound*, the French ships managed to get away safely.

For the following two months, Charles shuffled back and forth between the various islands. With Government ships patrolling the sea and Government troops scouring the land, he lived in hourly fear of capture. He was continually on the run. He walked for miles in drenching rain, he lay huddled for hours in caves or behind rocks, he sheltered in roughly-built foresters' huts, he waded through raging, ice-cold burns, he cowered in open boats, he was scratched by briars and bitten by flies until he broke out in open sores, he ate such appalling food that even his normally cast-iron digestion revolted. Dressed in little more than rags, he looked like a beggar.

Yet he seldom complained. His companions were amazed by his cheerfulness and his resilience. There were even times when his mood was positively boisterous. He joked, he teased, he danced, he sang old Jacobite songs. Much of his joviality was due, it is true, to drink, for it was during these months of wandering that Charles began the heavy drinking that was to characterise the rest of his life. He was for ever calling for another 'dram'. Every day started with a 'hearty bumper of brandy' to 'warm his stomach'. He drank both brandy and whisky neat, simply lifting the bottle to his mouth whenever he felt like it. A bottle of spirits a day became his usual consumption. And not only could he drink his companions under the table but he seems never to have suffered from a hangover. While others would be nursing their heads after a night's carousal, Charles would be up and ready for another session.

A respite from Charles's continuous running came in the middle of May. For three weeks he camped in a forester's hut in Glen Coradale on the island of South Uist. In sunny weather and in the company of seven or eight others, he fished and hunted and received visits from various local Jacobites. From a cave in the hills above his hiding place, he could watch the British warships patrolling the sea, and in the distance he could see the hills of both Skye and the mainland.

But by 6 June he had to move on; the Government troops were getting nearer. For a further two weeks he was able to hide in the hills but by the third week of June the net was closing in. Unless he could get off the island he would almost certainly be captured. The thing to do would be to escape to the island of Skye.

But how to get there? With the waters between the islands teeming with British ships, the desperate little band could not possibly risk a crossing. Captain Felix O'Neil, who was one of the Prince's most devoted companions, decided that there was only one thing to be done. They must ask for help from a young woman whom he had met some days previously. Her mother lived on Skye but she happened to be staying with her brother at Milton, on South Uist. Her name was Flora Macdonald.

3

Flora Macdonald was twenty-four at the time of her meeting with Charles. She was an attractive young woman, short, slight and well-shaped, with large, dark, lustrous eyes and a glowing complexion. Born and raised on South Uist, Flora Macdonald had something of the quality of that other woman with whom Charles had recently been brought into contact—Clementina Walkinshaw. Flora, too, was a calm, sensible, forthright creature and one with whom Charles could feel at ease. Although she had been brought up in a simple cottage and had been educated at home, Flora was an intelligent girl with great natural dignity.

On the death of her father, Flora's mother had married again—another Macdonald—and had recently gone to live on Skye. Flora thus had two homes: one with her mother on Skye and another with her brother on South Uist. She had good reason to move between the two islands.

Charles's companion in flight, Captain O'Neil, had been very impressed by Flora on first meeting her at the Clanranald home on Ben-becula. So when it was agreed that Charles's only hope of getting to Skye would be to disguise himself as a woman, O'Neil immediately thought of approaching Flora for help. Not only was she a practical-seeming young woman but her step-father, who was commanding a company of militia on South Uist, would be able to provide her with a pass for Skye.

On a bright, moonlit night (it was 20 June 1746) Charles, with his friends O'Neil and MacEachain, stole over the hills towards Milton. Flora was sleeping in a hut above her brother's home. Leaving Charles behind the hut, O'Neil woke Flora and told her the plan: Charles was to dress himself in women's clothes and Flora, pretending that he was her maid, was to take him with her to Skye.

She refused to do any such thing. It was too hazardous; it would endanger the lives of too many others; she would be courting malicious gossip. On this last score, O'Neil assured her that she had nothing to fear. With the Prince, her virtue would be as safe as houses. And then, what was the danger when set against 'the honour and immortality that would redound on her by such a glorious action'?

But Flora was not to be won over. Only on being faced by Charles himself—whom O'Neil had summoned out of the shadows—did Flora's resolution begin to falter. Eventually, she agreed to do it. They arranged to meet again at Rossinish, on the east coast of Benbecula, within the next couple of days. In the meantime Flora would get hold of a pass and some women's clothing big enough for Charles.

As it turned out, Charles was forced to hide on the island for almost a week before they could get away. In the meantime Flora had talked her step-father into giving her the necessary pass as well as a confirming letter to his wife, Flora's mother, in which he told her that Flora was being accompanied by 'Betty Burke, an Irish girl' who, as 'a good spinster' would be able to help her with her spinning. (It was as well, perhaps, that Charles was never called upon to illustrate this particular accomplishment.) The clothes proved more difficult to organise. Neither Flora, nor Lady Clanranald, who had been let into the secret, had anything big enough for the six-foot Charles, and the women of the Clanranald household had to spend several days stitching away.

Eventually, by 28 June, everything was ready. Flora arrived at Rossinish with the clothes and a pass for three—for Charles, for herself and for MacEachain, who would be masquerading as her manservant. As sensible as ever, Flora refused to listen to Charles's pleas that the faithful O'Neil be allowed to accompany them. She had a pass for three, she said firmly, and so only three of them could go.

She was equally firm about Charles's intention of stuffing a couple of pistols up his skirt. If Charles should be searched, she said, the pistols would immediately give away his secret. If he were being that thoroughly searched, Charles very sensibly observed, his secret would be discovered in any case. But Flora remained adamant. The pistols remained behind. That evening, as soon as it was dark, Charles, in his sprigged dress, white apron, frilly cap and hooded cloak, stepped into the open boat behind Flora.

The crossing was frightful. For one thing the sea was teeming with British ships; for another, the night was wet and stormy. The five boatmen who rowed them across (and who knew the true identity of Betty Burke) were unsure of their course and the black wildness of the night blotted out all sight of the land. But Charles, as usual, remained cheerful. Gallantly he shielded Flora when the boatmen were fumbling with the sail and blithely he entertained her with old Jacobite songs, including that optimistically titled one, 'The King shall enjoy his own again'.

But, of course, the most memorable song to be associated with this crossing to Skye is the haunting ballad, the 'Skye Boat Song', in which, like a bird on the wing, the bonnie boat carries the lad that's born to be King, over the sea to Skye.

Arrival on Skye did not end their troubles. Far from it. Their boat was fired on by the militia on the shore and they were forced to land further on. The place where they landed is still known as Prince Charlie's Point. Flora hurried ashore to get help from a Lady Margaret Macdonald. Before leaving Charles behind in the boat, she told the boatmen that in the event of any soldiers discovering them, they should curse the Prince 'for a lazy jade,' for not having followed his mistress to Lady Macdonald's home.

It was as well that the lazy jade had not followed her mistress for at the Macdonald house Flora was confronted by Lieutenant MacLeod of the militia. He was there in search of the Prince. With him were four of his men, and the rest of his command was scouring the neighbourhood. Flora, as unruffled as ever, managed to allay his suspicions. The beautiful Lady

Macdonald was not nearly so calm. Leaving Flora to cope with the Lieutenant in the dining room, she hurried out into the garden to consult with her husband's factor—yet another of those numberless Macdonalds, Macdonald of Kingsburgh. To her anguished wail that she was about to be 'ruined forever,' the less excitable Kingsburgh answered that he would get the Prince away to safety. As there were far too many soldiers on Skye, it was decided that Charles must be passed on to the MacLeods of Raasay, a small island lying between Skye and the mainland. Kingsburgh would take him to his own home first.

Finding the Prince hiding on a hillside among a flock of sheep, Kingsburgh invited him home. Flora, making her own way to Kingsburgh's house on horseback, caught up with the two men: she was amused to see Betty Burke loping along with great strides and lifting his petticoats to an indecent height as he waded through a brook. Quite clearly, and despite his somewhat feminine features, Prince Charles made a very unconvincing woman.

This was certainly the opinion of Kingsburgh's daughter when she first, all unsuspecting, set eyes on him.

'O mother,' she cried, bursting into Mrs Macdonald's bedroom, 'my father has brought in a very odd, muckle, ill-shaken-up wife as ever I saw! I never saw the like of her ...'

Mrs Macdonald, hurrying downstairs, was equally horrified. 'I saw such an odd muckle trallup of a carlin,' she afterwards reported, 'making lang wide steps through the hall that I could not like her appearance at all.' She was more horrified still when Charles, with bristling chin, kissed her hand. But the worst horror came when her husband revealed that the 'odd muckle trallup of a carlin' was none other than Charles Stuart.

'The Prince!' shrieked Mrs Macdonald. 'O Lord, we are a'ruined and undone for ever! We will a' be hang'd now!'

But, good Scots housewife that she was, she recovered sufficiently to serve Charles a supper of eggs and butter and cheese. The food eaten, Charles asked for a drink; 'for,' he explained briskly, 'I have learned in my skulking to take a hearty dram.'

Hearty drams in plenty were taken by both Charles and Kingsburgh that night and before it was over, Kingsburgh had become convivial enough to knock Charles's flounced maid's cap off his head.

Understandably, Charles was late getting up the following morning. When Flora dressed him in his Betty Burke outfit, he was in the highest spirits. 'O Miss,' he cried out mincingly, 'you have forgot my apron. Where is my apron? Pray get me my apron here for that is the principal part of my dress.' His hosts stood amazed at this skittishness in the face of danger.

It had been decided that Charles would set out that evening for Portree. From there he would sail to the little island of Raasay. Before he left, he allowed Mrs Macdonald to cut off a lock of his hair and, after he had left, she carefully folded up and put away the sheets he had slept in. She planned to be buried in them.

While Flora rode to Portree, Charles was guided there by way of various cattle paths through the heather. It rained continuously. In a small wood he changed into Highland dress. At Portree he found Flora and MacEachain waiting for him in a little inn beside the rocky shore. Here the party finished one bottle of whisky and bought another. Only towards dawn on 1 July did Charles take leave of Flora. As always, he could be relied upon to strike a suitably histrionic note.

'For all that has happened, I hope, Madam, we shall meet at St James's yet,' he declared, ' and I will reward you there for what you have done.'

His farewell gift to her struck a rather less heroic note. He gave her the garters from his Betty Burke outfit. French, they were, of blue velvet lined with white silk, and with rhinestone buckles.

It was still dark as the little boat set out across the shimmering sea to Raasay.

Not only was Charles unable to reward Flora for what she had done for him but he was never to set eyes on her again. Shortly after reaching her mother's home at Armadale, Flora was arrested. For a year she was im-prisoned, being released under an Act of Indemnity in 1747.

In song, in painting, in prose and in poetry, Charles's relationship with Flora Macdonald has been immortalised. It has become one of the most touching episodes in Jacobite mythology. Yet their association lasted for just over a week and there was not so much as a hint of any romantic attachment between them. Flora was simply a brave, level-headed girl who felt obliged to help the fugitive Prince, and Charles accepted her help as naturally as he accepted the help of any other selfless Highlander.

4

For over two months more Charles was forced to 'skulk' in the heather. From the island of Raasay he returned to Skye and from Skye he returned to the mainland. His comings and goings between the islands had been as nothing compared with his movements on the mainland. For something like three hundred miles he walked or ran or crawled through the Highlands, striking north-east towards Inverness, venturing south as far as Loch Ericht, frequently doubling back on his tracks. With troops guarding the entrance to every glen and with sentries stationed within calling distance of each other, he usually travelled by night. Every other day brought some knife-edge escape. The hills and glens resounded with gunfire as his pursuers chased after him.

No one gave him away. Not one of those thousands upon thousands of impoverished Highlanders took advantage of the £30,000 reward offered for his capture. Instead, at considerable risk to themselves, they passed him on from hand to hand. Often, they had just managed to get him away before they themselves were arrested. Occasionally, and to Charles's genuine astonishment, a chieftain might refuse to have anything to do with him. But for every one refusal, there were dozens of offers of help.

The country through which he was being pursued was a desolation: houses were charred ruins, crops had been destroyed, cattle dispersed. Those Jacobites who had not been arrested were similarly on the run. Charles was forced to sleep in caves or in the open; only rarely did he get enough to eat. At one stage he was sheltered by a band of men, little better than robbers, who gave him, for the first time in weeks, somewhere dry to sleep and something substantial to eat. By then he was looking as wild as they were; red-bearded, weather-beaten, dressed in a filthy shirt, a ragged kilt, a plaid and an old black coat. His feet were bare. He carried a musket, a pistol and a dirk. One of his companions reported taking no less than 'fourscore' lice off him.

Donald Macpherson, meeting Charles in a hut above Loch Ericht, was surprised that he could be so 'gay, hearty and in better spirits than it was possible to think he could be'. For, of course, Charles was having the time of his life. To his still adolescent mind, it was all like some elaborate game of hide-and-seek. He loved the all-male company, the camaraderie, the drinking, the singing, the boasting, the recounting of adventures and escapes, the whole dare-devil atmosphere of the thing. To sit in some dry cave, with a bottle of whisky at his elbow, a plate of hot food in front of him and a circle of admiring companions about him, was bliss indeed. 'Now gentlemen,' he once declared, after a particularly hearty meal washed down with several heartier drams, 'I live like a Prince.'

For the most part, his talk was on a far from elevated level. 'If you happen to drink any cold tiling when you are warm, only remember, MacLeod,' he once cautioned a companion, 'to piss after drinking, and it will do you no harm at all. This advice I had from a friend abroad.' It could have been a schoolboy talking.

Just occasionally, however, he would give a glimpse of that other Charles, or rather, of another facet of the same Charles, of the Stuart Prince who remained conscious of his great destiny. 'MacLeod,' he once mused, 'do you not think that God Almighty has made this person of mine for doing some good yet? When I was in Italy, and dining at the King's table, very often the sweat would have been coming through my coat with the heat of the climate; and now that I am in a cold country, of a more piercing and trying climate, and exposed to different kinds of fatigues, I really find that I agree equally with both. I have had this philibeg [kilt] on now for some days, and I find I do as well with it as any the best breeches I ever put on. I hope in God, MacLeod, to walk the streets of London with it yet.'

But there was small likelihood of his walking the streets of London, whether in philibeg or breeches, while he remained a fugitive in the Highlands. Charles might be enjoying himself but his chief concern remained to get back to France so that he could start all over again. Not until September, however, did he receive definite news of a rescue ship. During the months that he had been in hiding, his friends in France had organised a series of unsuccessful rescue attempts; only on 6 September 1746 did two French privateers, *L'Heureux* and *Le Prince de Conti,* drop anchor in Loch nam Uamh on the west coast. A message was sent, in the most tortuous fashion, to Charles, who was then hiding in an elaborately camouflaged shelter known as The Cage, on the slopes of Ben Alder. He set out at once. Seven days later his party arrived on the shores of the loch. That night, 19 September, Charles was rowed out to *L'Heureux.*

It was well over a year since the *Du Teillay,* bringing Charles to Scotland, had anchored in this same Loch nam Uamh. Here he had first set foot on the mainland of Scotland, and here he had talked the reluctant chieftains into supporting what Lord Lovat had called his 'mad Enterprize'. Now, as he sailed away before dawn on 20 September 1746, Charles was leaving behind a country, to which he had brought untold suffering and, in spite of everything, a reputation for courage and gaiety and chivalry.

Chapter Sixteen

1

During the time that Charles had been away in Scotland, his brother Henry had matured considerably. Twenty-one at the time of Charles's return to France, Henry was developing into an altogether more resolved personality. His manner had become more relaxed, his attitudes less provincial, his religious convictions less feverishly expressed. Henry had always given the impression of being a well-bred young man; now he seemed more worldly, more circumspect, more detached. His experiences—with the vacillating Louis XV, the cynical Duc de Richelieu and the self-interested members of the French Ministry—had opened his eyes to the fact that France had no real interest in the restoration of the Stuarts. The Forty-Five had served Louis's purposes very well. Now that it was over, the French King certainly had no intention of supporting another restoration attempt. Better even than James III, Henry was coming to realise that the failure of the Forty-Five had dealt a death blow to the Stuart cause.

Charles, on the other hand, was coming to no such realisation. He arrived back in France (on 10 October by the Continental calendar) with every intention of drumming up support for the next round. And it was this difference in attitudes—between the rainbow-chasing Charles and the realistic Henry—that was to lead to an irreparable break between them.

At first, though, everything was sweetness and light. As soon as Charles landed, Henry hurried to meet him. For a moment the elder brother did not recognise the younger; it was almost three years since they had last seen each other and Henry was looking much more grown-up. But once the slight awkwardness was over, the two fell into each other's arms. Henry was able to report to the gratified James that Charles was looking extremely well ('which is incomprehensible after all the fatigues he had endured') and that the two of them were now inseparable. 'The Prince sees and scarce will see anybody but myself ...' claimed Henry. They dined together every day.

It was, alas, too good to last. Charles had come back expecting to find Henry exactly as he had been when last he had seen him; an adoring younger brother, ready to accept Charles's leadership in all things. Henry, on the other hand, had not expected to find Charles so essentially unchanged. To Henry's astonishment, Charles was still the showy, sanguine, politically naive creature he had always been. While

Charles reproached Henry (still in 'a loving way') for being a stick-in-the-mud, Henry deplored Charles's 'ill-understood system of pretended popularity'. Charles seemed incapable of understanding what Henry was coming to understand only too well: that France had turned its back on the Stuarts.

It must have been with considerable embarrassment that Henry accompanied Charles on his first official visit to Louis XV's court. The Young Pretender was dressed as glitteringly, it was reported, as 'the star which they tell you appeared at his nativity'. His coat was of rose-coloured velvet, lavishly embroidered with silver thread and lined with silver tissue. His waistcoat was of rich gold brocade, decorated with scalloped rows of 'spangled fringe'. Diamonds flashed with every movement: there was a diamond cockade in his hat, a diamond order on his breast, diamond buckles on his shoes. His carriage procession was hardly less showy. 'Richly dressed pages lolled on the boot' of his coach; resplen-dently liveried footmen walked beside it.

The brothers were kindly received by the King. The French courtiers were quick to notice the difference between the two young men. Although Charles was by no means imperious, he was very dignified, very conscious of his position, very anxious to be thought well of. Henry seemed altogether more at ease. Shorter, squatter and less attractive than Charles, he was more talkative. Music seemed to be his passion.

The days that Prince Charles and the Duke of York spent as the King's guests at Fontainebleau were packed with entertainment. After all, Charles was still very much the man of the hour; everyone wanted to hear about his heroic exploits in Scotland. There was tea with the Queen, Marie Leszczinska, and her ladies, there was supper with the King's mistress—the astute Madame de Pompadour, there were dinners with ministers and banquets with courtiers, there were musical soirées at which the brothers performed with a remarkable professionalism. And, on Charles's insistence, there were several meetings with the King. Yet however affably the normally reserved Louis might treat his guests, he was very careful to commit himself to nothing. If Charles was too flushed with social success to appreciate this, Henry was not. He came away from Fontainebleau more convinced than ever that there was nothing to be expected from Louis XV.

But Charles refused to believe it. With the brothers having settled themselves in a mansion at Clichy, Charles acted out his role—as the future King of Great Britain—to the full. He courted the applause of the adoring Paris mob, he indignantly refused the offer of a pension from Louis XV, he would not hear of marriage to anyone other than a 'King'? dautcr,' he lived in daily expectation of the eighteen thousand men asked for from the French King. To his appalled father, Charles airily explained that the only way to deal with the French Government, whom he described as vermin, was 'to give as short and smart answers as one can, at the same time paying them in their own Coin by Loding them with sivilities and compliments.'

Charles even, in approved royal style, took a mistress. She was not, of course, some attractive young girl who might have outshone him. Marie-Louise, Princess de Talmont was over forty, elegant, intelligent, cultivated, experienced. In other words, she was just the woman to take the sexually immature Charles in hand. She became part-mistress, part-mother, part-mentor. From her, and from her equally influential and vivacious friend, the Duchess D'Aiguillon, Charles could get all the attention, flattery and encouragement that he craved. To them he was an exotic; it amused them to parade him, to champion him, to introduce him—this unintellectual upholder of the doctrine of the Divine Right of Kings—into the company of free-thinking *philosophes.*

But the fact that Charles had at last shown some sexual interest in a woman did not mean that he was sexually resolved; far from it. Nor was it going to take the Princess de Talmont long to find that out.

Of all this flamboyant behaviour on the part of his brother, Henry was highly disapproving. Charles had not been back long before Henry was writing to complain to James about Charles's irresponsible way of life. At the same time Charles was writing to complain about Henry: about his secretiveness, his insubordination, his dislike of being contradicted.

To this James very sensibly answered that Charles should remember that he was Henry's brother, not his father.

When James—in an effort, perhaps, to separate the bickering brothers—instructed Henry to go to Spain to see if he could talk the Spanish King into helping the cause, Charles was incensed. He wanted to go to Spain. Obligingly, Henry bowed out, and Charles went in his stead. He could have saved himself the journey. Ferdinand VI, like Louis XV, was all affability but he promised nothing. Charles returned to Paris empty-handed and resumed quarrelling with Henry. When James wrote, deploring this continuing fraternal wrangling, Charles pooh-poohed his concern.

'Your Majesty may be absolutely shure what any little coldness or broalie that may ever happen to be betwixt us is nothing, but venting one another's spleen, which, God nose, we have occasion enough to have, seeing every day so many follise of our own people, besides strangers.'

But the 'follise,' reckoned Henry, were all Charles's. His brother stubbornly refused to open his eyes to the reality of the situation. With France having started peace negotiations with Britain and with James already wondering whether it would be best for his eldest son to seek refuge in Avignon, Switzerland or Rome, Charles continued to lead his frenetic life and to make plans for a new invasion.

Well, Henry was not prepared to live for ever in his brother's giddily flickering shadow. He was going to make a life of his own. By the spring of 1747, Henry had made up his mind as to what sort of life it was going to be.

Henry's decision might have been understandable but it was the way in which he let Charles know about it that was extraordinary.

Henry had invited his brother to dinner on the night of 29 April. Only after Charles had sat waiting for Henry for several hours, however, was he told that he would not be appearing. He had left for Rome. Charles was bemused. Not until three days later did he receive a honeyed letter from Henry, begging his pardon for leaving Paris without his permission. He was planning, explained Henry, to spend a fortnight in Rome with their father.

Only a month later was Charles told the reason for Henry's sudden and secret departure. It was James who broke the shattering news. As tactfully as possible, he wrote to tell Charles that Henry was to become a cardinal of the Roman Catholic Church.

Without having become a priest first, Henry had been appointed cardinal by the Pope. The practice, which was rare, had originated in the appointing of honorary priests who had the right to take part in the election of bishops. The new cardinal was thus an honorary priest with the right to help elect the Bishop of Rome—in other words, the Pope. By not taking Holy Orders and by remaining in Minor Orders, Henry would no doubt develop into one of those rich, important, influential cardinals whose activities were mainly of a secular nature.

Charles was stunned. So transparently honest himself, he could not get over Henry's deceitfulness. So demanding of unquestioning allegiance, he could not forgive Henry's desertion. So dedicated to the Stuart cause, he could not understand how Henry could betray it. By becoming a cardinal of the Church, Henry had shown the world that he regarded a Stuart restoration as a lost cause. As a man of God, he could no longer take up arms for its sake; as a celibate, he could not father future Stuart princes; if Charles were to die without issue, the dynasty would simply wither away. Charles was fully aware of the anti-papist feeling in Great Britain. What would Henry's acceptance of a cardinal's hat do to Charles's Protestant supporters?

Those two waspish bachelor friends—Horace Walpole and Horace Mann, British Minister in Florence—were thrilled at the news. 'Cardinal Stuart,' reported Mann to Walpole, 'by putting on the Cowle, has done more to extinguish his party than would have been effected by putting to death many thousand of deluded followers.' In short, Henry could not have delivered the cause a more crippling blow. To some, it seemed worse than Culloden.

When Charles could finally bring himself to write an answer to his father's letter, he kept it short. The news, he declared, had been like a dagger through his heart. Or rather, as Charles wrote it, 'a Dager throw my heart'.

For whatever else his mistress, the Princess de Talmont, may have taught Charles, she had not, apparently, taught him how to spell.

2

By the autumn of 1748 the stage was being set for one of history's repeat performances. In the year 1713, when the Treaty of Utrecht was being negotiated, one of its clauses had stipulated that France should no longer offer refuge to James Stuart, the Old Pretender. Now, thirty-five years later, when the Treaty of Aix-la-Chapelle was being drawn up, one of its clauses likewise insisted on the banishment of the latest Stuart thorn in Britain's side—Charles Stuart, the Young Pretender. But here the similarity ended, for the reactions of the two Pretenders to these provisos were quite different. Whereas James had had the good sense to get out of France even before the ratification of the Treaty of Utrecht, Charles refused to budge, neither before nor after the Treaty of Aix-la-Chapelle had been signed.

His first act of defiance was to issue a high-sounding statement in which he dismissed as 'null, void, and of no effect,' anything in the Treaty which acknowledged any King of Great Britain other than 'the most high and most excellent prince, James the Third, our most honoured lord and father.' And then, far from lying low during the peace talks, Charles did everything to attract attention to himself. Always flashily dressed, he flaunted himself in public; he had a medal struck which carried the defiant inscriptions of *Carolus Walliae Princeps* on one side and *Amor et Spes Britanniae* on the other; he bought new furniture and ordered a magnificent service of plate. Quite clearly, he had no intention of moving. When he was told that this was not really the best time to buy himself a house in Paris, he replied jauntily, 'If I won't make use of it, my ambassador to France might.'

In his stand, Charles was being backed up by the Princess de Talmont. It was almost certainly she, with her fashionably advanced ideas, who encouraged him to turn himself into the darling of the Paris crowds. With them behind him, reckoned Charles, Louis would never dare expel him. Having digested a few half-baked theories from the *philosophes,* Charles began to think of himself as a sort of Noble Savage; as a simple Highlander who, by standing up to the King, would win the applause of the mob. He even imagined that the English would approve of his defiance of the French monarch.

But Louis was neither intimidated nor impressed. He was merely concerned with getting rid of Charles in the kindest possible way. Once the Treaty had actually been signed—in October 1748—the French King tried every means, other than force, to get him out of the country. He offered a generous allowance, he suggested an alternative place of residence, he sent one emissary after another to plead with him. He appealed to James; he appealed to the Princess de Talmont. It was all to no purpose. Charles refused to go. When, finally, the Comte de Maurepas warned Charles that unless he left voluntarily he would be forcibly expelled, Charles replied 'with the greatest disdain,' that Maurepas was to tell the King that Charles had been born 'to smash his ministers' plans'.

There was only one thing left for Louis to do. On 8 December 1748 he signed the order for Charles's arrest. But even now he was showing consideration; by making sure that all Paris knew about the impending arrest (Charles was to be seized on his way to the Opera) Louis was giving him the opportunity of getting away to safety. Charles ignored the gesture. Always the actor, he was looking forward to this particular drama. He felt sure that a public arrest would lead to a public outcry.

Perhaps the authorities felt the same way. They certainly deployed an extraordinarily large force—no less than twelve hundred men—around the Opera House at the Palais Royal that night. They had even brought locksmiths, hatchets and scaling ladders in case Charles should shut himself up in some nearby house. As the Prince's carriage came trundling along the Rue St Honoré, a warning voice, positively Shakespearian in tone, cried out: 'Prince, return, they are going to arrest you. The Palais Royal is beset.'

But Charles paid no attention. As he stepped down from his carriage, he was seized by six soldiers. After he had been formally arrested in the name of the King, he was tied up with 'ten ells of crimson silk cord' and bundled into a waiting coach. He was imprisoned at Vincennes.

Four days later, having given his word that he would leave the country on his release, Charles was escorted to the border between France and Savoy. He made for the old Jacobite refuge of Avignon. In no time Charles had fallen out with the Archbishop of the city (it appears that His Grace had objected .to Charles's introduction of prize-fighting) and for this, and other reasons, Charles thought it best to move on. On the last day of February 1749, with only his friend Henry Goring as equerry and three servants, Charles rode out through the gates of Avignon. Nobody, least of all Charles, knew where he was going.

One of the strangest periods of his strange life was about to begin.

3

With malicious glee, Horace Walpole noted down the latest rhyme to be going the rounds. 'In royal veins how blood resembling runs! Like any George, James quarrels with his sons.' For, by the 1750s, the Stuart family rows were equalling anything the Hanoverians could manage. Firstly, Charles had fallen out, not only with Henry, but with James. Once Henry had accepted a cardinal's hat, Charles vowed never to return to Rome. And although James and Charles continued to write to each other, their relationship steadily deteriorated. Secondly, between James and Henry things were going far from smoothly. By the year 1751 there was an open break between them.

At the time that Henry returned to Rome from Paris, everything between father and son seemed rosy. James quite happily accepted the fact that Henry wished to enter the Church. Perhaps he imagined that his son would not actually take Holy Orders: that by remaining in Minor Orders—and by not becoming a priest—he could be released should he ever be called upon to serve the Stuart cause in an active capacity.

But Henry had no such intention. In just over a year after becoming a cardinal, he was ordained priest.

The first few weeks of Henry's ecclesiastical life were given over to those splendidly theatrical ceremonies by which the Duke of York was formally admitted to the Sacred College of Cardinals. On 30 June 1747, in the presence of James III and his court and the Cardinal-Protectors of England, Scotland and Ireland, Henry received the Tonsure at the hands of Pope Benedict XIV. A few days later, wearing his sumptuous scarlet robes, he went in state to the Vatican to receive, under the magnificent ceiling of the Sistine Chapel, his Red Hat. The following week he was at the Quirinale Palace, enacting for the Pontiff the bizarre rite of opening and closing his mouth to symbolise the discretion required of his office, and to receive the customary sapphire ring.

These ceremonies completed, Henry was appointed Cardinal Deacon of the Church of Santa Maria in Campitelli.

From the start, almost, it became apparent that, in gaining a cardinal, Rome was not losing a prince. Far from it. Henry remained very conscious of his royal status. He insisted on being addressed as 'Royal Highness and Eminence' and saw to it that his scarlet cape was trimmed with royal ermine. Only after considerable debate did he allow his cardinal's hat to be placed above his princely crown on his coat of arms. Other cardinals, coming to pay their formal call of congratulation, were obliged to wear full scarlet robes and not merely the usual black cassock and, when speaking to his canons, Henry insisted that they remain standing as a mark of respect for his royal person. It is hardly surprising that his colleagues were soon grumbling about his royal pretensions and his imperious manner. Even the tolerant Pope Benedict XIV was heard to exclaim, after granting an audience to the opinionated young man, that if all the Stuarts had been as boring as Cardinal York, he was not at all surprised that the English had driven them out.

To be in occasional contact with this precocious twenty-two-year-old was irritating enough but to live with him under the same roof—as James was doing, for they still shared the Palazzo Muti—was infinitely more difficult. Not that James himself was the easiest man to live with. Now in his sixties, James was as melancholy as ever and his health was beginning to fail; in addition to a hernia and the quatran ague, he suffered from chronic indigestion. Inevitably, father and son quarrelled. Henry resented being treated as a child and James disapproved of his son's way of life. So inured to relative poverty, James could never appreciate that Henry was on his way to becoming a very rich cardinal indeed; he grumbled continually about his son's extravagance.

James disapproved, too, of the company Henry was keeping. With his strong literary and musical interests, Henry moved in Rome's artistic circles; to the dyspeptic James, the writers, painters and, above all, musicians that crowded the hitherto empty salons of the Palazzo Muti, were simply 'low company'. His son was altogether too social, too worldly, too full of himself for the serious-minded James.

What annoyed James most of all, however, was Henry's dismissal of his English chamberlain, Monsignor Leigh, replacing him with a Genoese priest named Lercari. James saw it as a deliberate slap in the face for England. Besides, he considered Lercari to be far too 'pushing'. James insisted that Henry dismiss his new chamberlain. Henry refused. James appealed to the Pope. His Holiness, taking James's side, compelled Henry to dismiss his chamberlain. Forced to comply, the Cardinal took himself off, in a huff worthy of his late mother Clementina, to Bologna. Here he remained, and here he seems to have made up his mind to stay, until a sharp letter from the Pope brought him to heel. The Pontiff reminded Henry that cardinals were expected to live in Rome and that he should show more respect to his father who was, after all, a king. Chastened, Henry wrote his father a contrite letter. James was all forgiveness.

'Return, therefore, my dear child, without delay and with all confidence, into the arms of a tender father and true friend, who will forget what is past, and who will be as he always has been, wholly taken up with whatever may contribute to' your real good and satisfaction. I beseech God to bless you and give you a good journey, and tenderly embrace you, my dear child.'

So back to his father and the oppressive atmosphere of the Palazzo Muti came Cardinal York. Out of his defeat he had been able to snatch at least one small triumph: James allowed him a separate dining room in which he was free to entertain as much 'low company' as he pleased.

Chapter Seventeen

1

In the autumn of the year 1750, Prince Charles took two extraordinary steps. He visited London, and he was converted to the Anglican faith.

Ever since riding out of Avignon on that winter's morning the year before, Charles had been leading a mysterious life. The wanderings of Jamie the Rover during the early years of the century had been as nothing when set against the wanderings of his son. For seventeen years, from 1749 until 1765, Charles was to cross and re-cross the face of Europe—sometimes in disguise, invariably in secret, seldom with any fixed purpose, occasionally pursued and increasingly showing signs of some deep psychological disturbance.

At one moment he is in Venice, at another in Paris, at another in Liège. Sometimes he is living in Lunéville, sometimes in Ghent, sometimes in Basle, sometimes in Bouillon. Now he signs himself as Mr Douglas, now as Mr Williams, now as Mr White, now as Wild Man; and, in wilder moments still, as Cousin

Peggie. It was almost as though, by moving in this atmosphere of romantic secrecy, Charles was trying to recapture the boyish excitement of his days in the heather.

The only place in which Charles refused to set foot was Rome. No matter how desperately poor James might beg his son to return home, Charles would not hear of it. To arrive back at the Palazzo Muti with his tail between his legs would be to admit defeat. While he remained on the move, Charles could create—if only to himself—an illusion of activity and purpose. Who was to know that he was not busily contacting fellow Jacobites? That he was not negotiating with various foreign powers? That he was not on the point of launching a new campaign?

His sudden arrival in London, on 16 September 1750, certainly seemed to lend weight to these possibilities. For some time there had been signs of a revival of Jacobitism in England. The traditional Hanoverian rift between monarch and heir (in this case between George II and his son Frederick, Prince of Wales) had given the Jacobites fresh hope. By ganging up with the Prince of Wales against his father they planned to reap some benefit for their cause. There was even some heady talk of Frederick giving up the succession to the throne in favour of Charles. Frederick, they said solemnly, would keep the colonies.

An important and patently pro-Jacobite speech by Dr William King at Oxford (he repeated the word *redeat*—may he return—no less than six times) was wildly applauded, and a few months later Dr King was able to list the names of no less than 275 gentlemen who were willing to give Charles their support. A new Jacobite medal, showing a vigorous young shoot springing from a withered tree, sported yet another of those cheering Latin words: this time *Revirescet*—it will flourish again.

Charles followed this little Jacobite flurry with the keenest interest. In fact, it seems to have gone to his head. He distributed his own medal with his own bit of Latin: *Laetamini Cives*—Citizens Rejoice—ran the somewhat hectoring inscription. He asked his father to renew his commission as Regent. *He* instructed his agent in Antwerp to get hold of 26,000 muskets. And on 12 September, heavily disguised, he sailed to London from Antwerp.

Charles spent a week in London. As the visit was made in the strictest secrecy, not much is known of his movements. He is said to have stayed with Lady Primrose, widow of the third Viscount Primrose, in her home off the Strand. Accompanied by a Colonel Brett, and showing breathtaking audacity, he walked the streets of the city that might have been his own capital. He even inspected the very building into which George II would have been only too happy to fling him—the Tower. One of its gates, he decided, could quite easily be blown in. At a house in Pall Mall he attended a meeting of several leading Jacobites at which the question of a possible restoration attempt was discussed. But his offer to lead a rising if four thousand men could be mustered was coolly received. As usual, the English Jacobites were prepared to do little more than talk.

The ubiquitous Dr King, whom Charles received a day or two later, was even less encouraging. 'If I was surprised to find him there,' noted King, 'I was still more astounded when he acquainted me with the motives which had induced him to hazard a journey to England at this juncture.' Dr King told him, quite bluntly, that his schemes for a restoration were 'utterly impracticable'. Quite obviously, the good Doctor preferred his Stuarts over the water.

But at some stage during that week-long visit Charles took one step which he imagined would improve his chances: he was formally received into the Church of England. This took place 'in a new church in the Strand,' which could have been one of several churches. Practical considerations alone induced Charles to change his religion. Unlike his father James and his brother Henry, he had no strong religious feelings; he had always worn his Catholicism lightly. But if his conversion did not mean much personally, it meant even less politically. Instead of winning him more Protestant supporters, it merely alienated his Catholic ones. It was too late now for this sort of gesture. Even before the Forty-Five a conversion would not have made much difference. It was James, forty years before, who should have changed his religion, not Charles. In any case, Charles's conversion was not to prove a lasting one. Rome did not take it seriously and nor, before many years had passed, did Charles.

Finally realising that there was nothing to be gained by remaining in London, Charles returned to France.

2

From having at one time shown very little taste for feminine company, Charles, by now, was seldom out of it. Women tended to give him the uncritical adulation his nature so ardently craved. Lectured by his father, disapproved of by his brother, ignored by the authorities, cold-shouldered by a great many Jacobites, Charles was still looked upon as a hero, as a figure of high romance, by certain of his women friends. Chief among these remained the Princess de Talmont. It was mainly for the reassuring pleasure of her company that Charles risked returning to Paris; for something like two years, both in Paris and on the Princess's estates at Lunéville, Charles and Marie-Louise de Talmont kept up their association.

But the course of their love, whether true or not, was running anything but smooth. No sooner had they been reunited than they were quarrelling. The Princess found that she was having to contend, not only with Charles's selfishness and petulance, but with his drunkenness. He was seldom sober these days. But, drunk or sober, he treated her in the most cavalier fashion: he was forever insulting her or ignoring her or picking quarrels with her.

The truth was that Charles was incapable, not only of wholehearted love but of conducting a relaxed and affectionate relationship with anyone, male or female. He compensated for his emotional and sexual insecurity by mental and physical brutality. He had to be the master. With Charles there was no give and take; he had to have his own way and when he did not get it, he resorted to violence. Charles was to be sexually involved with only three women throughout his life and all three of them were beaten by him; not in some excess of sexual excitement but as a release for his sexual immaturity. He attacked them as a frustrated child might attack its nurse—shouting at them, insulting them, pummelling them. He left them bruised, shaken, and in tears, but never ravished. Afterwards he sulked.

It was no wonder that Marie-Louise de Talmont was bewildered. She was not to know that Charles could simply not love anyone. In letter after hysterical letter she complained that he did not return her love, that his indifference was breaking her heart, that his coolness was killing her. 'I am dying,' ran one of her impassioned outpourings. 'I love you too much and you love me too little.'

A welcome relief from the Princess's rantings was to be found among the well-born ladies of the Convent of St Joseph in the Rue Dominique. Charles was in hiding there for several months, and in the company of such women as the Marquise de Deffand, Madame de Vassé and Mademoiselle Ferrand, he was infinitely more relaxed than he was with the frenetic Princess de Talmont. His relationship with these cultured, intelligent and serious-minded women was free of any hint of sexuality. With them he felt safe. As he basked in their admiring company, Charles became his old, charming, courteous self. He seems even to have been able to take part in their dauntingly intellectual conversations and to have exercised his mind to the extent of penning some unoriginal philosophic ideas.

But neither in the eager arms of the Princess de Talmont nor in the erudite atmosphere of the Convent of St Joseph could Charles hope to find a permanent home. 'What can a bird do that has not found the right nest?' he asked plaintively at about this time. 'He must flit from bough to bough.'

The bough to which he flitted in the year 1752 was the city of Ghent. And the mate with whom he now decided to share a nest was none other than the plain, sensible Scottish spinster who had nursed Charles at Bannockburn during the Forty-Five: Clementina Walkinshaw. Whether Charles actually sent for Clementina or whether she suggested that she join him, is uncertain, but by the spring of that year they had set up house together in Ghent.

The picture presented by Charles and Clementina was hardly that of love's young dream. At thirty-two Charles was no longer the brave, attractive, idealistic young warrior-prince of the Forty-Five: drink and disillusion were turning him into a fat, slack and cantankerous neurotic, given to black and violent moods. Clementina, also in her thirties, had none of the beauty or sparkle or wit that one would have expected in a royal mistress: she was just a plain, loyal, undemanding jane. As such she suited, or should have suited, Charles admirably.

If Charles seemed happy enough with Clementina, many Jacobites were not. They suspected that she was a Government spy. Lending weight to their suspicions was the fact that one of her many sisters (in fact, her sister Catherine) was in the service of the Princess of Wales, at Leicester House. They became more suspicious still during the secret negotiations concerning the Elibank Plot. This was another of those elaborate schemes whereby, with the help of a foreign power—in this case Charles had hopes of Frederick the Great of Prussia—the Jacobites in Britain would topple the régime. Both St James's Palace and the Tower would be seized (not without reason, apparently, had Charles inspected the Tower during his visit to London) and there would be the inevitable rising in Scotland. But through a spy in the jacobite camp, referred to as 'Pickle the Spy,' the Government came to know all about the plot. They nipped it in the bud.

As Pickle the Spy had started sending the British Government his reports at the very time that Charles took up with Clementina, many Jacobites believed that she supplied the information. This was highly unlikely. At that stage Clementina adored Charles. She would have had neither the desire nor the reason to betray him. Loyalty was probably her most outstanding virtue.

During the first eighteen months or so of their association, Charles and Clementina were fairly happy. Pickle (he was believed to be Alastair Ruadh Macdonell) reported that 'the Pretender keeps her well, and seems to be very fond of her.' In October 1753 Clementina gave birth to a daughter. Baptised in the Church of Our Lady of the Fountains at Liège (if Charles had forsaken Rome, Clementina had not), she was given the name of Charlotte. The father was entered in the parish register as the noble Seigneur William Johnston and the mother as the noble Dame Charlotte Pitt.

The baby's life would prove to be as star-crossed as that of any Stuart exile.

3

While Charles drifted steadily downhill, his brother Henry was moving resolutely upwards. Almost every other year brought an enhancement in the status of His Royal Highness and Eminence, Cardinal York. From the Church of Santa Maria in Campitelli he was moved to the important Church of Santi Apostoli, the church opposite the Palazzo Muti and in which his mother's heart was buried. A few years later he was appointed to the post of Camerlengo: it is the duty of the Cardinal Camerlengo to organise the Conclave which elects a new Pope. When Pope Benedict XIV died in 1758, it was Henry who presided over the election of the new Pope, Clement XIII. Then, in the same year, in a ceremony of almost overwhelming magnificence, Cardinal York was consecrated Archbishop of Corinth.

And not only was Henry becoming increasingly important, he was becoming increasingly rich. To the monetary rewards of his cardinalate were added the benefices bestowed on him by the Kings of France and Spain. In time, he was to become the richest member of the Sacred College of Cardinals. Even by his early thirties, the Cardinal Duke was looking every inch a Prince of the Church. Everything—his penetrating eyes, his aristocratic nose, his imperious manner, his dignified carriage, his sumptuous, ermine-trimmed robes and massive diamond cross—combined to give him an air of authority. No one could doubt, when they met him, that they were in the presence of one of the brightest stars in the Roman galaxy.

In the year 1761 the vacant See of Frascati was presented to the Cardinal Duke. As Cardinal Bishop of Frascati, Henry became one of the six senior members of the Sacred College of Cardinals. Lying some fifteen miles south of Rome in the wooded Alban hills, Frascati was one of the suburban sees of Rome; from the Piazza outside the Cathedral one could look out across the close-packed houses and narrow streets of the little town to the distant dome of St Peter's. And not only was Frascati one of the most picturesque of the six suburban sees, it was one of the most fashionable. In the summer one could hardly move for the nobility escaping the heat of the capital. Every hillside sported the splendid, shuttered, cyprus-shaded villas of the great Roman families. The Pope's summer residence of Castelgandolfo dominated one little village; James III's Palazzo Savelli dominated another. The Cardinal Duke was housed in the medieval castle of La Rocca. Here Henry lived as lavishly as any of his aristocratic neighbours; he maintained, it is said, 'grooms, lacqueys and serving men without number, all of pleasing appearance and of commanding stature, as a great Prince should.'

Henry's enthronement as Cardinal Bishop of Frascati on 13 July 1761 was a superbly staged ceremony. His coach, with his coat of arms emblazoned on the doors and his footmen in royal livery, headed a cortège of carriages through the decorated streets of the town. Having received a deputation of various municipal dignitaries in the Piazza, the Cardinal Duke moved on to the Cathedral. With his splendid vestments billowing about him, he knelt on the Cathedral steps on a gold-embroidered cushion to kiss the crucifix held by a priest. Then, in stately procession, he passed through the great open doors and up the aisle. The scene within the Cathedral was one of kaleidoscopic brilliance—red damask hangings, glittering candles, gleaming plate, embroidered vestments, snowy surplices. Solemnly, the Cardinal Duke was escorted to the sanctuary and seated on his episcopal chair.

'One Stuart at least,' writes one of Henry's biographers, 'had gained a throne.'

4

Nothing in Clementina Walkinshaw's past had prepared her for the sort of life that she was living with Prince Charles. Until her first meeting with him, at Bannockburn in 1746, Clementina seems to have led an eminently respectable life; she claims to have lived 'in great plenty'. What she did in the years after the Forty-Five is uncertain. She once hinted at having been 'bred to business about Whitehall' and, as her sister Catherine was in the service of the Princess of Wales, there might well have been some truth in Clementina's boast. There were darker hints of having been 'undone' during this period, but what is certain is that at the time of her reunion with Charles, she was on the point of becoming a canoness in one of the Noble Chapters in the Low Countries—an educational institution for well-connected but impoverished young ladies. It was, perhaps, to avoid this somewhat cheerless-sounding future that Clementina decided to kick over the traces and take up with Charles. For a plain, thirty-two-year-old spinster, the prospect of living with one of Europe's most romantic figures must have appeared glamorous indeed.

Poor Clementina was soon disillusioned. Living with Charles proved to be anything but glamorous. Once their daughter had been born, things started to go wrong. They were for ever on the move. Driven by goodness knows what compulsion, Charles shifted from one place to another. They lived in Paris, they lived in Basle, they lived in Bouillon. At one moment he was complaining that France was an 'abominable Country', the next he was hankering to get back there. And wherever they lived Charles felt that he was being hounded, spied upon, betrayed. Their debts were enormous. For the well-brought-up Clementina, the struggle to make ends meet, to raise a child and to keep up appearances was almost overwhelming. No wonder that she could cry out at one stage that she was in 'a poor, strange place, starving indeed'.

She could expect no help from Charles. Everything was left to her. With every passing day the figure of her once-shining Dream Prince was becoming progressively more tarnished. He was restless, feckless, extravagant; at times his moods could be terrifying. They quarrelled almost continuously. All Europe was being diverted by the stories of their private and public rows. At one time Charles declared that 'my mistress has behaved so unworthily that she has put me out of patience and as she is a Papist too, I discard her ...' Yet when his Jacobite friends encouraged him to do exactly that, he refused to consider it. He might assure Clementina that he wanted nothing more to do with her but she claims that his jealousy was such that he surrounded her bed 'with chairs placed on tables, and on the chairs little bells, so that if anyone approached during the night, the bells would be set a-ringing.'

Although Charles was fond enough of his little daughter Charlotte, he was prepared to make no effort with her whatsoever. If he were in a good mood or convivially drunk, he might play with her or fondle her, but he never concerned himself about such things as her education, her daily needs or her future. Clementina had to see to all that.

From Rome, James begged Charles to get rid of his mistress. For Charles to regain the British throne with an unblemished reputation had proved difficult enough; how could he hope to do it with so blackened a one? James wanted Charles to settle down, to marry, to ally himself to some royal house, to father Stuart heirs, to present himself as an honourable candidate for the throne. In 1760 Charles would turn forty. What chance would a dissolute, middle-aged bachelor have against the *de facto* heir to the British throne, the English-born, highly respectable and deeply religious young prince who would one day become King George III?

But Charles ignored his father's pleas. He was not intetested in marriage, and that was that.

When James could get no further with Charles, he turned to Clementina. If she would consent to leave Charles, James would support her. In the early days, Clementina would not have considered it, but as year after miserable year dragged by, with Charles becoming both more off-hand and more violent towards her, she began to think of leaving him. She let James know that her conscience was troubling her (she no doubt imagined that this was what he wanted to hear), that she was anxious to silence those Jacobites who accused her of being a Hanoverian spy, that she wanted to give her daughter a good convent education. Only too ready to approve of these 'reasonable and pious desires,' James encouraged Clementina to make the break. If she and Charlotte would go and live in a convent, he would provide for them.

In July 1760, eight years after she had started living with Charles, Clementina left him. Secretly, for she knew his temper, she took the seven-year-old Charlotte and made for Paris. She entered the Convent of the Visitation in the Rue St Jacques.

Charles's reactions were typical. At first he was furious. He was determined that Clementina and Charlotte should return to him. Clementina's answer to this was unequivocal. 'She would sooner make away with herself than go back, and as for the child, she would be cut to pieces sooner than give her up.' Faced with Clementina's resolute stand, Charles turned maudlin; he was now to be found either drunk, or in tears, or both. He refused to see anyone.

This, as far as the good-hearted Clementina was concerned, proved more effective. She wrote him a long and touching letter: apologising for her desertion of him, reproaching him for his ill-treatment of her, and wishing him 'all manner of happiness and that everything that is good and great may for ever attend my Dearest Prince.'

But she refused to return to him. 'You pushed me to the greatest extremity, and even despair,' she explained, 'as I was always in perpetual dread of my life from your violent passions.'

So Clementina and Charlotte remained in their convent in the Rue St Jacques and Charles gradually lost interest in them. And there, for the following twelve years, the matter rested.

5

Like his uncle, Charles II, some eighty years before, James III took an unconscionable time a-dying. For years that indefatigable British Minister in Florence, Sir Horace Mann, had been sending back reports of James's imminent death. 'He is so emaciated and weak,' he wrote cheerfully in 1760, 'that it is not natural to suppose that he can hold out long.' At one stage Mann is reporting 'some organick disorder in his stomack,' at another 'two apoplecktic fits'. Yet each time James rallied. Sir Horace Mann must sometimes have wondered if the Old Pretender might not outlast him.

In the year 1765 James turned seventy-seven. Although more stooped and thin and frail than ever, he still gave off his indefinable air of kingship. Like any reigning monarch, James lived a highly regulated life. For years his routine remained unaltered. On New Year's Eve there would be a reception at the Palazzo Muti at which the old man, with the pale blue Garter ribbon aslant his black clothes (George I had introduced the darker blue ribbon to distinguish the Hanoverian from the Stuart knights) would receive congratulations on the anniversary of his son Charles's birthday. The fact that he had not set eyes on the prodigal Charles for about twenty years merely added poignancy to the occasion.

On 17 January James would attend mass in St Peter's for another of those wayward figures in his life, his long-dead wife Clementina. In May, escorted by a troop of brightly uniformed Papal Guards, he would drive out to his country place at Albano. His first visit would be to the Pope at Castelgondolfo and the two old men might be seen, on a fine spring morning, slowly pacing the gravelled terraces. James would return to Rome for St Peter's Day and remain there until September, when he would go back to Albano for six weeks. The beginning of winter would see him back at the Palazzo Muti.

James lived an increasingly lonely life. One by one his companions were retiring or dying off and the servants were being replaced. After all, he had lived in the Palazzo Muti for almost half a century. He did not even have Henry to quarrel with as the Cardinal Duke now lived, in considerably more state, at Frascati. Henry had a home in Rome as well. In 1763 he had been appointed Vice-Chancellor of the Holy Roman

Church and with this important post went the splendid Renaissance Palace of the Cancelleria. Although James was proud of his Cardinal son, the two of them were not really very close. But Henry managed his father's affairs and was always on hand to administer the last rites whenever it seemed as though the old man could not possibly survive another relapse.

Charles, of course, was constantly on James's mind. His most ardent wish was to see his 'dearest Carluccio' again before he died. In letter after letter he begged his son to come home. 'Is it possible,' wrote James on one occasion, 'you would rather be a vagabond on the face of the earth than return to a father who is all love and tenderness for you?' It was possible. No matter how much the distressed father urged his son to pull himself together, to remember the dangers and hardships he had so bravely endured, to think of the 'applause and glory' he had once won, to prove himself worthy of those who had died for the Stuart cause, Charles refused to listen. He remained where he was, living the kind of life that he had chosen.

Henry, who knew Charles better, tried another way to bring his brother to heel. If Charles would return to Rome, not only would Henry have his papal pension made over to him but he would renounce, in Charles's favour, any money that he might inherit from their father. But even this was not enough enticement for Charles. He would return to see his dying father only if the Pope promised to recognise him as the true heir to the British throne, and as the true King on the death of James. Henry, who was just as anxious for this papal recognition, promised to do what he could. But the important thing, he wrote, would be for Charles to get back to Rome as soon as possible. James could not last much longer.

Finally bestirring himself, Charles set out for Rome. But before he could reach it, James died. The date of his death was 1 January 1766; he was in his seventy-eighth year.

James was given a magnificent funeral. If he had lived the life of a king in exile, he was buried with all the pomp due to a reigning monarch. In royal robes of crimson'velvet, with a golden crown on his head, a sceptre in one hand and an orb in the other, he was laid on a bier of purple silk and carried to the Church of Santi Apostoli, in which he had worshipped for forty-five years. Twenty cardinals followed his remains. They placed the body under a canopy hung with purple velvet and gold lace and topped by a great golden crown. Below it swirled the triumphant legend, JACOBUS TERTIUS MAGNAE BR1TANNIAE REX.

When the Requiem Mass had been sung, the body was carried in procession through the streets for its final burial in St Peter's. It was Stuart weather, dark, windy and bitterly cold. But the funeral route was crowded, and the procession—with its flaring torches, its colourfully-dressed Papal Guard and its hundreds of slowly pacing Church dignitaries—was brilliant. After a second Requiem Mass, James's body was laid to rest beside that of Clementina, who had died over thirty years before.

For more than sixty-four years James had been *de jure* King of Great Britain. His was the longest reign in British history. George III was to reign for sixty years; Queen Victoria for sixty-three. Had James III been *de facto* monarch, six other monarchs would not have reigned: William III, Mary II, Anne, George I, George II and George III. If he had succeeded to the crown in the normal way, James III would probably have developed into one of Britain's most memorable kings, for he was a remarkable man; intelligent, tolerant, humane, high-principled. But it was not to be, and his life was a melancholy one; as tragic, in a different way, as that of his son Charles.

To his enemies James seemed to have led a worthless existence, to have been weak, wavering, bigoted and unlucky. To them he remained Old Mr Misfortune. But to generations of Jacobites he was a paragon: a man who had faced the many disappointments of his life with great fortitude, who had always behaved with exemplary dignity, who had never looked for solace in self-indulgent living, who had unfailingly shown wisdom, tact and courage. His life, to them, had been one long martyrdom. If James had been prepared to change his religion at some stage during the last few years of Queen Anne's life, he may well have regained his father's throne. But by refusing to trade his faith for an earthly crown, James III had won, claimed his many admirers, an infinitely more glorious one.

Part Six

King Charles III

Chapter Eighteen

1

The man who now regarded himself as King Charles III of Great Britain had turned forty-five on the day before his accession. He looked a good ten years older. Of the dazzlingly good looks that had set so many hearts a-flutter in Edinburgh a couple of decades before, hardly a vestige remained. His face was bloated and blotchy, his complexion spotty, his expression hang-dog. He was stooped, paunchy, lethargic. 'Upon the whole,' wrote a woman who met him at this time, 'he has a melancholy, mortified appearance.' No one now would have dreamed of calling him Bonnie Prince Charlie.

But not quite everything had been lost. Occasionally, when he took the trouble, Charles could still impress strangers with the nobility of his bearing and the charm of his conversation. With the pale blue Garter ribbon across his scarlet, gold-laced coat, he looked regal enough and his manner still showed traces of the dignity and authority of a king.

But, alas, there were very few who regarded Charles as a king. His ringing announcement that he would return to Rome only if he were welcomed as the rightful sovereign of Great Britain had carried no weight whatsoever. Pope Clement XIII had refused to recognise him. When Henry, resplendent in floating purple and a diamond cross, drove out to meet his brother on the outskirts of Rome, it was to break this unhappy news. The Cardinal Duke had done his best to talk the Pontiff into acknowledging Charles as King, but it had been hopeless: the French Government had let the Pope know that they were prepared to recognise only George III as the rightful King of Great Britain. This unequivocal French attitude had swept away the last of Clement XIII's own doubts on the matter. Encouraged by the French directive, by the advice of his assembled cardinals, and by the fact that Charles had at one stage renounced the Catholic faith, the Pope refused to grant recognition.

So it was a deeply disappointed Charles who drove, unheralded, through the streets of Rome to take up residence in the Palazzo Muti. Only within its echoing rooms, he now realised, would he be accorded the title of 'Majesty'.

Charles could not really have expected anything else. To imagine that George III would not be generally regarded as the true King was to be living in a dream world. And besides, George was an altogether more admirable person. The passing of time had reversed the Stuart and Hanoverian images. The Hanoverian was now the young, virtuous and cultivated Englishman while the Stuart was the coarse, ageing and dissolute foreigner. Even to George himself, Charles was no longer a threat; the King hardly gave him a thought.

While Charles sulked, Henry did what he could to cheer him up. Whenever they went out driving together, the Cardinal always allowed his brother to be seated on his right, like a reigning sovereign; when he entertained him at Frascati, it was in full regal style; he saw to it that Charles had enough money to keep up his royal pretensions.

But the more Henry treated Charles as a king, the more Pope Clement XIII insisted that he should not be treated as one. The Pontiff issued a declaration to the effect that he expected all his subjects to follow the example of the Holy See in not acknowledging Charles; he banished the heads of the English, Scots and Irish colleges in Rome for having offered up prayers for King Charles III; he ordered that the British royal coat of arms be stripped from above the entrance to the Palazzo Muti. It was now as treasonable, reported a delighted Horace Mann to his friend Horace Walpole, to acknowledge Charles as King in Rome as it was in London.

This state of enmity—between Charles and the only power ready to give him shelter—could not last indefinitely. Once again it was the urbane Henry who patched things up. He arranged for Charles to be received by the Pope. Only as 'the brother of the Cardinal of York,' however, and not as a sovereign, would Clement XIII grant an audience to Charles. But the meeting went well enough. Despite the fact that Charles had to remain kneeling until the Pope told him to rise and that Henry was allowed to sit while Charles stood, Charles 'seemed well enough content'. He liked to be on show and he enjoyed exercising his still considerable charm.

He was in a position to do both now that he had been officially received at the Quirinale. Using the title of the Count of Albany, Charles was able to move about in Roman society. And for a while this social activity diverted him. But not for long. Attending musical soirées and chatting to overdressed old ladies could hardly compensate for the pointlessness'of his life, and Charles was soon drowning his disillusion in what Henry called the 'nasty bottle'. There were innumerable stories about his drunken behaviour: how he once chased after his attendants with a drawn sword, how he had lurched about in his box at the opera, how he had dismissed three of his most faithful servants for having refused to accompany him in his coach because of his disgusting state.

For over four years, from 1766 until 1770, Charles lived an increasingly degenerate life. He was being forgotten, it seems, by almost everyone other than his brother Henry and the often exasperated household at the Palazzo Muti. Then, in his fiftieth year, things suddenly began looking up.

France started paying him attention once more, for although the French Government had no interest in Charles as a king, they did have some interest in him as a pretender. For over three-quarters of a century France had always had an exiled Stuart up its sleeve for use in its game against Britain; faced with the realisation that the Stuart line would die out unless Charles produced an heir, the French decided that he must marry. They got his cousin, the Duke of Fitzjames, to write to him, offering him a pension of forty thousand crowns a year if he agreed to marry a suitable bride.

Charles jumped at the offer. He did not, of course, favour it for any romantic or sensual reasons (since his break with Clementina Walkinshaw, ten years before, Charles seems not to have looked at another woman) but because it would place Kim in the spotlight once more. At one stroke he would become a centre of attention, secure a handsome financial settlement, and gain someone to comfort him in his approaching old age. The choice of bride he was prepared to leave to France.

The choice, in fact, was not proving easy. Charles could hardly hope for a King's daughter but then nor could he be fobbed off with just anyone. After some scrabbling around, the French uncovered a suitable candidate: she was Princess Louise Maximilienne Caroline Emmanuele of Stolberg. Her late father had been a prince of the Holy Roman Empire, her mother could claim descent from the Bruces of

Scotland. Such blood was surely blue enough for a king without a throne.

And then, in addition to her impressive ancestry, Louise had other advantages. She was nineteen, which meant that she was neither too young nor too old; she was pretty in a piquant, dark-eyed, animated fashion; she was poised, self-possessed and intelligent; and, perhaps most important of all, she knew exactly what she was doing. Despite her airy complaint that she had 'learned nothing' at her convent at Mons, Louise does seem to have learned one thing: as a princess with no dowry, she could do worse than marry a pretender to a throne. After all, she would not be the first penniless princess to be married off to a portly, middle-aged and drunken husband and at least she would be marrying into one of the great royal dynasties of Europe. She would be, if only in the Palazzo Muti, a Stuart queen.

So, with her eyes wide open, Louise accompanied her gratified mother to Paris. Here, on 28 March 1772, she was married to Charles by proxy. Like the last Stuart Queen, Charles's mother Clementina, Louise was then escorted to Rome by one of those obliging Irish Jacobite officers—this time a Colonel Ryan. Charles, who had travelled from Rome to meet his bride, first set eyes on her at Macerata on Good Friday, 17 April. They were married on the same day. The bridegroom signed the register with a flourishing Charles III and saw to it that his bride signed her name in the same regal fashion. To the dwindling band of loyal Jacobites, Charles's young bride became Queen Louise, but she was to be more generally known, and with good reason, as the Queen of Hearts.

2

Hardly had Charles and Louise settled down to married life in the Palazzo Muti than that ghost from Charles's wayward past, Clementina Walkinshaw, returned to haunt him. Ever since leaving Charles, Clementina and her daughter Charlotte had been living as *dames pensionnaires* in convents: first in the Convent of the Visitation in the fashionable Rue St Jacques and then—as James III's death had meant the end of her annual allowance—in the humbler Convent de la Miséricorde at Meaux-en-Brie. For Clementina, who now styled herself Countess of Albestroff, it was a miserable life; dull, impoverished and lonely. She must often have cursed those ten so-seemingly glorious days at Ban-nockburn during the Forty-Five when she had first been thrown into the company of Bonnie Prince Charlie. Her association with him had brought her nothing but unhappiness.

Yet, her allowance from James having dried up, Clementina was obliged to turn to Charles. As soon as he reached Rome after his father's death, she wrote to him. Would he be so kind as to continue, or even increase, her allowance? Clementina should have known Charles better than that. He ignored her request and it was left to his long-suffering brother to come to her rescue. Fighting down his distaste for the whole matter of Charles and his mistress, Henry undertook to continue her allowance. But his terms were the same as his father's had been; Clementina and her daughter must remain, out of sight and out of mind, in their convent at Meaux-en-Brie.

Having settled that particular problem, Henry was promptly faced by another. By 1767 (five years before Charles's marriage to Louise of Stolberg) Rome was seething with the rumour that, at some stage during their association, Charles had married Clementina. This, in Henry's anguished eyes, would not only make Clementina Walkinshaw the Queen of Great Britain but her daughter Charlotte would be Princess Royal. The horrified Cardinal dashed off a letter to his bankers in Paris, instructing them to arrange for Clementina to sign a statement to the effect that she had never married Charles: 'such a report of marriage or anything relative to the least tendency of that kind, is void of all foundation ...' ran the outraged phrases of the document. Obligingly, Clementina put her name to it.

With her own letters bringing no answer from Charles, Clementina urged their daughter, Charlotte, to write. But neither the series of somewhat cloying notes to 'Mon Auguste Papa' from 'Pouponne,' nor the covering letters from Clementina giving glowing details of Charlotte's scholastic skills, were able to soften Charles's heart.

He went on behaving as though his mistress and daughter did not exist.

A more direct appeal, Clementina then decided, was what was needed. She encouraged Charlotte to beg her father to re-establish communication; without her father's help, wailed Charlotte, she would be condemned to a life of poverty, futility and misery. Charles's answer to this filial *cri de coeur* was to offer to receive Charlotte into his household on condition that she broke with her mother completely. Charlotte refused.

As long as Charles had remained single, Clementina had apparently been content to remain fairly docile. But his marriage to Louise of Stolberg obviously decided her that the time had come for some sort of show-down. She wanted a settlement from Charles. And so, with the nineteen-year-old Charlotte in tow, Clementina came sailing once more into Stuart waters. She arrived in Rome in the spring of 1773.

For all the good that it did the two of them, Clementina and Charlotte might just as well have remained in Meaux. Charles would not see them, Henry would certainly not see them, and when they did manage to see the Cardinal Secretary of State, his only advice was that they leave Rome immediately. Charlotte's final appeal was to her uncle, the Cardinal Duke: would he at least allow her to exchange her dreary convent at Meaux for something more lively in Paris? Henry's answer was very much to the point.

She could live wherever she chose, he replied haughtily, as long as she expected no more money and as long as she remained in a convent. In short, where Henry wanted Clementina and Charlotte was under the carpet. Disheartened, mother and daughter trailed back to France.

3

For the first year or two of her marriage, Louise was happy enough in the Palazzo Muti. The newly-married couple had had a flatteringly triumphant entry into Rome, Louise had been thrilled to be addressed as 'Your Majesty' by the faithful Jacobite household, and the Cardinal Duke had presented her with a gold, diamond-encrusted box decorated with his portrait and containing a banker's draft for forty thousand crowns. Louise had not even had cause to complain about Charles. Her ageing husband seemed to have made some effort to pull himself together. He was looking slimmer, fitter and more neatly dressed, and the 'nasty bottle' was not nearly so much in evidence.

In a very short time the musty atmosphere of the Palazzo Muti had been dispelled by light and bustle as Louise played her role of royal hostess for all—and rather more—than it was worth. She organised receptions, she received visitors (considering herself royal she was careful not to return these visits), she held *salons.* With her ardently professed interest in the arts and the intellect, she gathered about her a circle of artists and poets and philosophers. And when Louise was not entertaining, she would be accompanying Charles to the opera, to formal parties, to masked balls or on drives through the city. This, she very soon decided, was a good deal better than life in the convent at Mons.

'Prince Charles Edward's house,' wrote one of the guests, 'was a charming miniature court; you were there with the King and Queen of England, surrounded by three or four chamberlains or ladies in waiting, everything enhanced by the charms and gaiety of the Queen.' Charles, when he regaled the company, *ad nauseum,* with stories of the Forty-Five, could be boring, but then one could always rest one's eyes on the Queen's considerable charms.

To find herself so greatly admired was a source of considerable gratification for Louise. With her toweringly-dressed blonde hair, her retroussé nose, her rose-petal complexion and her dark, intensely blue eyes, she was certainly a beauty. The rise and fall of that milk-white, lace-framed expanse of bosom was enough to set any male heart pounding. And it did. Not only for the sparkle of her conversation, it seems, did all those ardent young poets and painters come flocking to her *salon.* Nor would Louise have wanted it to be. She might have been a cultured young woman but she was also a flirt. She basked in the warmth of masculine attention; she had an almost schoolgirlish conception of love.

Charles, needless to say, was hardly the man to fill that conception.

Although he was doing his best to make himself more attractive to his vivacious young wife, he was far from being the knight errant of her romantic imagination. In any case, Charles's reformation had not lasted long. He was soon back on the bottle. Sir Horace Mann, who was reporting home on the activities of the Young Pretender as assiduously as he had done on the Old, claimed that 'having abstained from any great excess in wine [he] has given in to it again as much as ever, so that he is seldom quite sober.'

And the more Charles drank, the more he resented the fact that the Pope still refused to accord him royal honours. He had hoped, for some obscure reason, that his marriage would lead to a papal recognition of his claims. 'One of the first conditions of the marriage,' he protested with more heat than accuracy, 'was that the Queen should be treated like the late Queen.' But Charles's lordly announcements to the effect that the 'King and Queen of England' were doing this or that, fell on deaf ears at the Vatican. No matter how often, or in what manner Charles badgered the Pope for recognition, His Holiness remained adamant. Finally, having worked himself up to a pitch of fury about the matter (Charles was to be invited to the Pope's jubilee as Count of Albany and not as King of England) he decided to leave Rome. He would not return, he swore, until the Pope had granted him official recognition. His Holiness, needless to say, was delighted to hear it.

So in August 1774, Charles and Louise (she was just as obsessed with this matter of royal status as he was) left Rome. They took a villa between Pisa and Parma. And it was here, according to a widely believed Jacobite rumour, that Louise gave birth to a son.

The improbable story goes that a young Scottish physician by the name of Beaton was visiting a church one evening when he was approached by a stranger. He was asked to come and help at an urgent *accouchement.* On agreeing to do so, the doctor was blindfolded and bundled into a carriage. When he arrived at his destination, Dr Beaton was led into a large *salon* and his eyes unmasked. He found himself in a sumptuously furnished room, on one of whose crimson damask walls hung a portrait of James III. It appeared, however, that he had arrived too late. Nevertheless Dr Beaton was taken in to see her. He found, lying in bed, a young woman whom he described as being of great refinement and, in the arms of a nurse, a baby generously wrapped in silks and laces. A portrait on a writing table of Prince Charles—or Charles III by the doctor's reckoning —made him realise the identity of the newly confined mother.

His suspicions were confirmed when, a few days later, in the *Florentine Journal,* Beaton saw a notice to the effect that the Countess of Albany was recovering from a recent illness.

Not long after this, the ubiquitous Dr Beaton was at Leghorn. And who should he see there but the very gentleman who had asked him to help at the *accouchement.* Accompanying him was a woman—presumably the nurse—with a bundle in her arms. Woman and bundle were helped into a little boat and rowed out to a British frigate lying at anchor in the bay. As soon as they had boarded it, the ship 'bore off,' as one version of the legend so mellifluously puts it, 'slow and still and stately towards the west.'

Why the birth of a longed-for Stuart heir should have been kept secret or why the baby should have been shipped off to England, was never explained. But there was many a romantically minded Jacobite only too ready to believe the preposterous tale, and, in years to come, to believe that Bonnie Prince Charlie's son, and grandsons, were still alive.

From their villa near Pisa, Charles and Louise moved on to Florence. Here they lived, first in a palazzo which had been lent to them and then in the Palazzo Guadagni, in the Via Sebastiano, which Charles bought. It was the first home of his own; on its roof he erected a weather vane carrying the proud royal inscription 'CR 1777'.

The change of scene brought no accompanying change of lifestyle. Charles continued to drink, to sulk, to fall asleep in his box at the opera and to resent the fact that the Grand Duke of Tuscany had no more intention of recognising him as the King of England than the Pope had had. His health began to fail; the delighted Mann, who now had his subject under his very nose (he had to report on 'King Here' to 'King There' was his way of describing his task to Walpole) was able to catalogue vomitings, coughings, bleedings, piles, swollen legs, 'sickness of the stomach' arid an 'insupportability of both stench and temper'.

Louise, too, continued to lead much the same sort of life. She read, she walked, she entertained, she went to the theatre, she flirted, she wrote gushing letters to her poetic young men. 'There remains still at the bottom of my heart a fire not fully extinguished which needs only you to re-light it,' ran one romantic effusion. 'For me to be madly in love,' ran another, 'would be something unique. Ah, how delightful that would be. Only a being like you could perform this miracle, and each of us would lead the other on to see who would do more mad things.'

Whether, at this stage, things went any further than the exchange of such titillatingly amorous little notes between Louise and her admirers is doubtful. Charles was careful not to let her out of his sight. He insisted that she accompany him on his walks and drives and visits to the theatre; even in the burning heat of the Florentine summer, he would drag her with him for fear that she might get up to some mischief if left at home. 'All the avenues to her room, excepting through his own,' tattled Sir Horace Mann, 'are barricaded.' The legitimacy of the Stuart succession, explained Charles, must not be in any doubt.

If Charles was determined to keep others out of his wife's bed, it was not because he was so anxious to be in it. And it was not long before the heartless Louise was taunting him with his lack of virility. Surely, she wrote in one of her malicious letters to him, he was not in his dotage? 'It would certainly do you no honour in the world to have people imagining that you, who have always had the reputation of a gallant, had degenerated to the point when you did not want to spend more than a few hours in bed with a young woman who is pretty and who loves you,' she wrote.

All in all, it was not an edifying situation. Neither character—not the drunken, jealous and cantankerous elderly husband, nor the pretentious, coquettish and scheming young wife—was deserving of much sympathy. One ingredient only was needed to turn the situation into a conventional *opeéa bouffe* of the period—the young lover. And in the year 1778 this character made his appearance in the person of a handsome, ardent, arrogant, twenty-seven-year-old poet and dramatist named Vittorio Alfieri.

4

Louise and Alfieri suited each other perfectly. From the time of their first meeting in Louise's salon (Alfieri had already admired her from afar) they felt that they were destined for each other. Both were passionate, romantic, histrionic; both had what they claimed was a burning interest in literature; both were yearning to embark on a grand, all-consuming love affair.

Alfieri had already had some practice. But after three major romances with married women, he was ready, he declared fervently, for a deeper, more intellectual relationship. This is not to say that he was not attracted by Louise's more obvious assets (he was in raptures about the striking contrast between her dark eyes and fair hair) but he saw her as his inspiration, his Egeria, the Beatrice to his Dante. And this is exactly how Louise saw herself. Although she, too, was very taken by Alfieri's part-soulful, part-virile good looks, she was equally thrilled by the prospect of encouraging his talent.

But Alfieri saw Louise in another light as well, as a frail, fresh, flower-like creature at the mercy of a cruel and loutish husband. Louise was not, of course, exactly that, but it did not take her long to begin looking upon Alfieri as her deliverer from tyranny.

How this delivery was going to be effected without Louise losing everything—or almost everything—that she had married for, was a difficult question. Love was one thing, love in a garret another. Louise might profess a fashionable republicanism in her little scented notes to her lover but she enjoyed the advantages of being a queen of sorts. No, the thing would be to escape from Charles without having to forfeit her position. He must be seen to be in the wrong.

In the meantime, and in mounting frustration, Louise and Alfieri carried on their liaison. Charles, suspecting nothing, did not object to Alfieri's frequent visits. The *cavaliere servente*—the male escort or companion to a wife—was a perfectly acceptable role in Italian society. What could be more fitting than that Charles's clever little wife should inspire this poet and playwright; particularly when he was working on projects such as *Maria Stuarda*—the tragedy about Charles's famous ancestress? Not that Charles ever left them alone to get on with either the play or their love-making, but one imagines that just occasionally, when a surfeit of Cyprus wine had caused him to nod off, the lovers would take what advantage they could.

For two years Louise and Alfieri were forced to bide their time. The first step towards deliverance came on St Andrew's Day, 30 November 1780. As usual, Charles had been drinking to the patron saint of Scotland with such single-mindedness that he could barely stand. But stand he did and, once on his feet, he lurched into Louise's bedroom. There, according to the feverishly excited Mann, Charles accused her of adultery, beat her up, ravished her and tried to strangle her. Mann may have been exaggerating but whatever Charles did to Louise was enough to bring the servants rushing into her room in answer to her screams.

Louise might indeed have been shocked by Charles's attack but nothing could have suited her better. There had been several witnesses to his brutal behaviour. Who could now deny that Louise had every right to escape from what Alfieri was quick to call 'the tyranny of an unreasonable and perpetually drunken master' ?

The lovers organised the 'deliverance' with great skill. A few days later Louise, all honey-sweet, announced that she wanted to inspect the lace-making in a nearby convent. As always, Charles insisted on going with her. On arriving at the convent Louise and a woman companion hurried up the stairs. By the time Charles had toiled up behind them, the door had been shut in his face. His outraged hammerings finally brought the Mother Superior to the grille. Crisply, the Reverend Mother informed him that the Countess of Albany had sought refuge in the convent and that she would remain there under the protection of the Grand Duchess of Tuscany.

Having made one astute move, Louise made another. She threw herself on the mercy of her brother-in-law, the Cardinal Duke. The guileless Henry, suspecting nothing of Louise's relationship with Alfieri and knowing everything about Charles's boorishness, was all sympathy. He promised to do what he could to help. Assuming that Louise wished to retire permanently to a convent in order to lead, as he naively put it, a 'higher life,' the Cardinal suggested that she come to Rome. He would place her in the Ursuline Convent. Henry's letter was backed up by one from the Pope. His Holiness promised the poor, ill-used Louise all the help, protection and peace that she so richly deserved.

Gritting her teeth, Louise resigned herself to the idea of spending some time in the Ursuline Convent. With touching gratitude and becoming modesty, she thanked Henry for his solicitude. Dutifully she travelled to Rome in the coach so thoughtfully provided for her by the Pope (His Holiness was not to know that Alfieri, disguised as a coachman, travelled on the box for part of the way) and took up residence in the convent.

She stood it for three months. Then, in her melt-in-the-mouth manner, Louise asked her brother-in-law to allow her to leave the convent and take up residence in his town palace, the Cancellaria. This way she would be under his protection. Henry agreed. He also arranged for half of Charles's papal allowance to be paid over to her. Thankfully, Louise settled herself in a second floor apartment, and Alfieri, who had already moved from Florence to Naples, now moved to Rome. He took up residence in the Villa Strozzi which was set in an almost countrified position on the Esquiline Hill. Under the unsuspecting noses of the Pope and the Cardinal, the lovers resumed their liaison. From now on, however, there would be no need to wait until Charles had dozed off over his glass of Cyprus wine before stealing a kiss.

Chapter Nineteen

1

Yet another of the women in the Stuart story who had been obliged to learn to look after her own interests was Charles's illegitimate daughter, Charlotte. Having turned twenty-one in 1774, Charlotte was a big girl-tall, blonde, blue-eyed, pink-cheeked. In short, she was a feminine version of her father at the same age. Unlike her mother, the subservient Clementina, Charlotte was a bossy young woman, very conscious of her Stuart parentage. She never forgot that at least half the blood coursing through her veins was royal: nor that she was entitled to one of the more tangible advantages of her birth, a financial settlement appropriate to her status.

With her father resolutely refusing to contribute one sou towards the support of her mother and herself, and with her Uncle Henry's grudging allowance just covering the cost of their dismal lodgings in the convent at Meaux, Charlotte decided to appeal to Louis XV. In a 3,000-word effusion she outlined her plight; of how she was forced to live 'without relations, without friends, without a name, unacknowledged and without a home' as a *dame pensionnaire* in a provincial convent. Reminding the King of their common descent from Henry IV of France (no Stuart begging letter ever failed to draw attention to this fact) she asked for his help in achieving a way of life worthy of her royal birth.

Her letter remained unanswered.

The death of Louis XV and the accession of Louis XVI gave mother and daughter a fresh excuse for a begging letter. This time it was Clementina who wrote. Had her daughter been brought up as a Protestant, ran her somewhat curious argument, the English court would have lavished on Charlotte the same benefits that it had lavished on the bastards of Charles II and James II; but as Charlotte had been raised as a Catholic, it was up to the French court to show the same generosity. Clementina's tortured reasoning cut no ice with Louis XVI.

Nor was Clementina the only Stuart connection to be bothering the French King; Louise had already badgered him for money. 'Do not speak to me of the Stuarts,' he said. 'They are an unlucky family.'

But then Louis XVI was not going to be so lucky himself.

With one avenue closed, the practical Charlotte tried another. She applied to be admitted as an honorary canoness of the Noble Chapter of Migette, a convent near Besançon. Her application was successful.

And it led, before long, to a success of a quite different sort, for it was at a dinner party at Besançon, in 1776, that Charlotte met the Archbishop of Bordeaux, Prince Ferdinand de Rohan. The Archbishop, like most of the men of his illustrious, influential and colourful family, was a great womaniser. Never for a moment did he allow his ecclesiastical status to interfere with his sexual activities. One look at the blonde, big-breasted, twenty-three-year-old Lady Charlotte Stuart (as the new Canoness now styled herself) was enough for His Grace. Within weeks Charlotte had forsaken the Noble Chapter of Migette for a distinctly ignoble town house in the Rue St Jacques in Paris.

The Archbishop's love nest could hardly have been better placed for a Stuart mistress. In one direction lay the Convent of the Visitation in which Charlotte's mother, the unprotesting Clementina, had been freshly installed; in another was the English Benedictine monastery in which the bodies of James II and his daughter, Louise Marie, lay buried. So whether dead, alive, legitimate or illegitimate, Stuart descendants came pretty thick in the Rue St Jacques.

And Charlotte lost no time in adding more. She might not have been the worldly Archbishop's only mistress but she bore him three children. A daughter Aglaë was born in 1778; another daughter, Marie, in 1780; and a son, Charles Edward, in 1784. Clementina, who was in no position to throw stones, took charge during her daughter's pregnancies and arranged for the babies to be packed off to wet-nurses in the country. With understandable vagueness, for neither her father nor the Cardinal must ever suspect her liaison, Charlotte always referred to her ecclesiastical lover as *ami* and to their three love-children as *mes fleurs*.

2

For two years Louise and Alfieri were blissfully happy. Although they had not been quite so bold as to live openly together in the Cardinal's Roman palace, they spent as much time as possible in each other's company. 'In the evening I descended [from the Villa Strozzi] into the city,' wrote the starry-eyed Alfieri, 'and restored from my fatigues of study by the lovely sight of Her for whom alone I existed and laboured, I returned from it more contented to my hermitage, whither I retired never later than eleven at night. An existence more gay, more free ... one could never find, nor one more agreeable to my nature, character and occupations.'

To the amusement of Roman society, Louise even went so far as to use Alfieri as a go-between in her dealings with her unsuspecting brother-in-law, the Cardinal. 'Since I noticed, my dear brother,' she wrote with saccharine sweetness to Henry on one occasion, 'that your' fine library lacked a good copy of Virgil, and since I knew of a most beautiful edition, I am sending you the very book; and I take the liberty of sending it to you by the hand of Count Alfieri, who has dined today at my house, and has told me he was going tomorrow to pay you his respects. I hope, my dear brother, you will do me the honour of accepting my gift as a mark of my tender and sincere attachment to you But for neither Louise nor Alfieri was it all play. He had never worked harder and she had never involved herself more closely with his writing. During this period, when Alfieri was busy on some of his greatest plays, Louise was proving to be the perfect Egeria. If she had not made much of a success as a king's consort, she was undoubtedly succeeding as a playwright's mistress. Both Louise and Alfieri took themselves very seriously indeed but never more seriously than in their roles as Muse and Poet. One of the highspots of their literary and romantic partnership was the performance, at the Spanish Embassy, of Alfieri's tragedy, *Antigone.* Bedecked in the Stuart and Sobieski jewels, Louise was the centre of attention; she had every reason to feel proud, both of herself and of her talented lover. Let Charles grumble as much as he liked; secure in the love of Alfieri and in the protection of the Pope, Louise was certainly having her cake and eating it.

It was all too good to last. In the spring of 1783 Charles became dangerously ill. Henry, whatever he might think of his brother, could hardly leave him to die like a dog, so he hurried north to Florence to see him. Charles did not die but, lying back on his pillows, told Henry the full story of Louise's affair with Alfieri. Henry was shocked. And not only shocked, but enraged. Strongly puritanical and very conscious of his dignity, he resented having been made to look silly in the eyes of the more worldly Romans. On getting back to Rome he arranged for a papal order expelling Alfieri from the Pope's domains. Louise, miserable but not quite miserable enough to risk becoming an impoverished outcast by following her lover, retired to the Alban hills. From here she wrote anguished letters, not only to Alfieri, but to anyone who cared to listen.

'I love him more than myself,' she wailed. 'It is a close union of souland mind that we ourselves alone can understand. In him I findeverything I can require, and he is all in all to me.'.

It was an impossible situation. What with Louise wretched in the Alban hills, Alfieri wretched in Sienna and Charles wretched in Florence, there seemed to be no way in which this particular triangle would ever be anything but eternal.

Like a fresh breeze into this turgid atmosphere blew King Gustavus III of Sweden. Meeting Charles in Pisa in the winter of 1783, the Swedish King was appalled by the state of the man who had once been the most colourful figure on the European stage. With characteristic tact, efficiency and generosity, Gustavus set about putting Charles's affairs in order. He first unravelled the complicated financial arrangements between Charles and Louise and reorganised them to the satisfaction of both. He then arranged for a legal separation. Charles, having been convinced that he was taking a wise step, wrote a pompous deed of separation. Louise, only too delighted to be at liberty (and allowing herself just a fleeting flirtation with the Swedish officer who helped arrange the separation) shook the dust of Rome from her feet and made for Colmar in Alsace. Here she was reunited with the faithful Alfieri.

She did, however, have one thought for Charles. 'May Heaven grant him some measure of repose and content in his old age!' she declared. Surprisingly enough, her wish was to come true.

3

No sooner had Charles's wife gone out of his life man his long-neglected daughter Charlotte re-entered it. For suddenly, in the spring of 1783, the unpredictable Charles decided to legitimise the thirty-year-old Charlotte and to invite her to make her home with him in Florence. With Louise gone, Charles wanted a less demanding companion to look after him in his declining years. So overnight, the hitherto forgotten young woman became Her Royal Highness, the Duchess of Albany. The legitimisation was ratified by the King of France and the delighted Charlotte enjoyed the heady experience, not only of being received by Marie Antoinette, but of being granted the coveted right—the etiquette of which had at one time driven Mary Beatrice almost to distraction—to sit on a stool in the French Queen's presence.

One thing only prevented the ecstatic Charlotte from answering her father's.summons immediately—she was pregnant with her third child by the Prince de Rohan. Not until her son—Charles Edward—had been born early in 1784, was she free to set out for Florence. As usual the obliging Clementina arranged for the baby to be put out to a wet-nurse in the country. The Archbishop, who had shown no interest in *les fleurs* at any stage, certainly showed none now and Clementina undertook to look after all three during Charlotte's absence.

Charlotte arrived in Florence at the beginning of October 1784. Her arrival caused an immediate stir. Although it was generally agreed that she was too tall, too robust, too like her father to be a beauty, Charlotte struck observers as being a lively and good-natured young woman. The essential shallowness of her nature was masked by a certain briskness of manner. Inquisitive Florentine society ladies flocked to her door to leave their cards; they were gratified to find that the Duchess of Albany, unlike her step-mother the Countess of Albany, was quite ready to return their calls. The Palazzo Guadagni, which had rapidly been becoming as dismal as the Palazzo Muti, suddenly sprang into life. Charlotte, who was never happier than when organising, gave little dinner parties and little balls and little musical evenings. Through them all Charles happily nodded off to sleep.

And when Charlotte was not receiving; she could be seen all ablaze in the family jewels, which Louise had been obliged to give up, sitting beside her father in his newly decorated box at the opera. No one could deny that Charlotte had taken her sudden, Cinderella-like transformation in her stride.

An extremely capable woman, Charlotte knew exactly how to handle Charles. After all, she had no reason to love him, so she was able to treat him with a breezy detachment. He had sent for her (again, not because he loved her) because he needed company and attention, and this is exactly what Charlotte was prepared to provide. While seeming to defer to him, she managed him. She nursed him when he was ill, she jollied him along when he was depressed, she kept him out of sight when he was drunk. When, before very long, she discovered the chaotic state of his finances, she applied her businesslike mind to improving things.

How much she missed her mother and children is difficult to say. Charlotte's letters to Clementina were crammed with more instructions than with expressions of affection. She commissioned her mother to buy her the newest in dresses and hats (including one of those cumbersome turbans that were the *dernier cri* in pre-Revolutionary Paris) and begged for the latest news of the Diamond Necklace scandal. It was, of course, Charlotte's lover's brother, Cardinal Louis de Rohan, who was linked with Marie Antoinette in this mystifying affair.

Charlotte's concern for her three children seemed mainly confined to hastily scrawled postscripts to her letters, although she did, from time to time, instruct her mother to watch over their health and see that they wanted 'for nothing'. She seems to have had word, at last, from her negligent *ami:* the Archbishop, she solemnly assured her mother, 'seems fonder of me now that I am further away from him'.

All in all, though life with the ill and unpredictable Charles could be extremely trying, Charlotte was enjoying herself. Any inconvenience was worth being able to refer airily, in letters and conversation, to 'the King, my father' or 'my grandfather, King James'. Now that she was Charles's legitimate heir, she saw herself as *La Prétendente.* Charles encouraged these pretensions by proposing to have a medal struck for her showing a storm-tossed ship sailing towards England and carrying *the* inscription 'Deliverance depends on a small, last hope.' Whether or not this small, last hope ever saw herself as the future Stuart Queen of England is uncertain.

On St Andrew's Day. 1784, which Charles celebrated more soberly than in days gone by, he invested his daughter with the Order of the Thistle. Sitting in a Chair of State, he gave her a ceremonial tap on the shoulder with his sword; the gratified Charlotte afterwards moved among the assembled Jacobites to smile her ready smile and to crack her little joke: *Je suis Chevalier.*

4

Watching all these junketings with an extremely jaundiced eye was *La Prétendente*'s uncle, the Cardinal Duke. Henry disapproved most strongly of Charles's legitimisation of Charlotte. He saw the Act of Legitimisation as a blow to his own rights as the Stuart heir and he resented the fact that the title of Albany, which traditionally belonged to the second son of the King of the Scots (before becoming a cardinal Henry had sometimes used the title of Duke of Albany), should now go to this daughter of Clementina Walkinshaw. Several self-confident letters from Charlotte did nothing towards softening Henry's attitude. On the contrary, he reacted to her advances by first cutting off her allowance and then issuing a strongly-worded protest against her recognition.

The Cardinal's rebuff opened Charlotte's eyes to the precariousness of her situation. She had long ago realised that he was the key figure in the family triumvirate; without her uncle's approval and protection she could never hope to secure her future. So she changed her tactics. From this point on she directed her talents towards winning Henry round. She wrote him an extremely contrite letter in which she apologised for annoying him and took care to sign it simply 'Charlotte Stuart'. This letter opened the way to an improvement in their relationship. Then, taking advantage of the warmer atmosphere, Charlotte set about working towards a reconciliation between Charles and Henry. In a stream of astute letters she stripped away any illusions which the unworldly Henry might still have harboured concerning Louise of Stolberg. The Cardinal was appalled to discover, from his niece's copious correspondence, that Louise's infidelity was not confined to Alfieri: a German count had followed Louise to Paris, a *valet de chambre* had had to be sacked by the jealous Alfieri.

Having successfully turned Henry against Louise, Charlotte decided that the time had come to meet her uncle face to face. In October 1785 the Cardinal paid official visits to several towns in the Papal States. When he reached Perugia, Charlotte was waiting for him. The meeting went off extremely well. Charlotte could hardly help being impressed by this erect, dignified and imperious Prince of the Church and Henry was very taken with his forthright niece. Together they agreed on a full family reconciliation. Charles, they decided, must return to Rome. For Charlotte, it had been a considerable triumph.

On 1 December 1785, Charles and Charlotte left Florence for Rome. The journey took them eight days. At Viterbo, to greet their cavalcade, was the Cardinal Duke. To Charlotte's great satisfaction, the two brothers embraced each other warmly, and it was as a united little family that the three Stuarts entered the Palazzo Muti. Within the four walls of this unpretentious, ochre-coloured Roman palace, Charles III was once more in his make-believe kingdom.

5

Charles turned sixty-five in the month that he returned to Rome. By now he was very ill. His legs were monstrously swollen, his breathing was laboured, his blood pressure was high. He was often, as he put it, 'bothered in the head'. Yet he refused to lead the life of an invalid. On the contrary, the Palazzo Muti was said to be 'one of the gayest' houses in Rome. With her father's full approval, Charlotte entertained lavishly; night after night the high-ceilinged rooms of the palazzo blazed with light and resounded with chatter as the Duchess of Albany held court.

Charles, more neatly dressed than in earlier days and always wearing the Order of the Garter would sit smiling benignly on the animated crowd. He could still impress, if not by his looks, by the charm and courtesy of his talk. Charles was not an unintelligent man and even when he was not being particularly interesting or amusing, he remained one of the sights of Rome. People came to see him as they came to see the old buildings or the famous monuments. To the Europe of the late eighteenth century, a Europe on the very brink of revolution, Charles was like a relic from another age. Two generations had grown up since the Forty-Five. It was hard to believe that this lumbering wreck of a man had once inspired that highly romantic adventure.

But Charles never forgot it. Even after forty years the memory of that stirring campaign could move him to a state bordering on hysteria. One day an

English visitor asked him some questions about those far-off days.

'His eyes brightened,' runs Ewald's famous description of the scene, 'he half rose from his chair, his face became lit up with unwonted animation, and he began the narrative of his campaign. He spoke with fiery energy of his marches, his victories, the loyalty of his Highland followers, his retreat from Derby, his defeat at Culloden, his escape, and then passionately upon the awful penalties so many had been called upon to pay for their devotion to his cause. But the recollection of so much bitter suffering—the butchery around Inverness, the executions at Carlisle and London, the scenes on Kennington Common and Tower Hill—was stronger than his strength could bear. His voice died in his throat, his eyes became fixed, and he sank upon the floor in convulsions.'

Alarmed by the noise, Charlotte came rushing into the room.

'Oh! Sir,' she cried out to Charles's guest, 'what is this? You must have been speaking to my father about Scotland and the Highlanders! No one dares to mention these subjects in his presence.'

Charlotte herself, by now, was in need of cosseting. Although still in her early thirties, she was not well. For some time she had been suffering from severe pains in her abdomen. Not wanting to upset her father, she told him nothing about them; and not, perhaps, having much faith in doctors, she dosed herself and hoped for the best. But when she was not playing the hostess, she became increasingly depressed. Queening it. at the Palazzo Muti had its compensations but she was beginning to miss her mother and her children. Two, three years had already gone by since last she had seen them and she sometimes wondered if she would ever set eyes on them again. She did not dare suggest, to either Charles or Henry, that Clementina—and still less her three illegitimate children—be allowed to join her in Rome.

Charlotte was ill in bed when, on 11 January 1788, she was told that her father had suffered the first of a series of strokes five days before. She sent at once for Henry and for the following weeks uncle and niece did what they could to comfort the sinking Charles. He died on 30 January 1788. The date of Charles's death was singularly ill-omened for it coincided with the anniversary of one of the blackest days in the Stuart calendar, the execution of his great-grandfather, Charles I. So 31 January was given out as the official date. The date had further significance in that exactly a century had passed since Charles's grandfather, James II, had been forced to flee from England. Not for a hundred years had a Stuart King sat on the British throne.

The Cardinal Duke asked Pope Pius VI to grant Charles the same burial rights that had been granted to their father; he wanted Charles to be buried as a king in St Peter's. But the Pope could not agree to it. As the Holy See had never recognised Charles as king in his life, they could hardly do so at his death. Henry's Cathedral of Frascati, then, it would have to be, and it was here that Charles was buried on 3 February 1788.

Nothing in the way of royal trappings was missing. Charles's body was dressed in royal robes, the crown was on his head, the sceptre was in his hands, his breast glittered with orders and decorations. His cyprus-wood coffin, bearing the unequivocal inscription CAROLUS III MAGNAE BRITANNIAE REX, was covered by a magnificent velvet pall emblazoned with the royal coat of arms. Henry celebrated the mass. When it was over, the coffin was placed in what was optimistically hoped to be a temporary resting place. Above the vault Henry erected a memorial tablet, surmounted by the British royal coat of arms in bronze and triumphantly inscribed with the names and titles of his dead brother. It might not have been St Peter's but it was something. St Peter's would come later.

Sixty-seven years old when he died, Charles had spent not much more than a year of his life in the public spotlight. And it is for this year that he is remembered. The forty-three-year-long anticlimax of his life has been largely forgotten. Charles's personality was one which depended on success; when that was denied him, he had nothing to fall back on. Without inner resources, he could not adjust to those long years of exile. Both his grandfather, James II, and his father, James HI, had been sustained by their deep religious convictions; James II by his obsession with saving his soul, James III by the doctrine of Quietism. In a way, exile had brought out the best in both men. But in Charles, exile—and failure—had brought out the worst. Only success could have ennobled Charles. His forty-three twilight years were unrelieved by a single wise or generous or noble act.

Yet with all his faults, Charles remains the most fascinating figure in the saga of the exiled Stuarts. Like that other tragic Stuart—Mary Queen of Scots—he has caught the imagination of the world. It is as Bonnie Prince Charlie—standing beside the wind-whipped standard at Glenfinnan, riding through the acclaiming streets of Edinburgh after the victory of Prestonpans, taking leave of Flora Macdonald in the inn at Portree, scrambling through the mist-shrouded heather to escape the redcoats—that he is remembered. To admit all his failings is not to deny his attraction; nor to deny the extraordinary effect that he had on his contemporaries.

As Lord Balmerino stood facing execution for his part in the Forty-Five, he had this to say about the man whose escapade had brought him to the scaffold.

'I am at a loss when I come to speak of the Prince; I am not a fit hand to draw his character. I shall leave that to others. But I must beg leave to tell you the incomparable sweetness of his nature, his affability, his compassion, his justice, his temperance, his patience, and his courage are virtues, seldom to be found in one person. In short, he wants no qualifications requisite to make a great man.'

Prince Charles Edward Stuart was soon to lose all these shining virtues and he was never, of course, a great man, but for all that, he was, and remains, an extraordinarily interesting one.

Part Seven

King Henry IX

Chapter Twenty

1

Never did the Stuart claim that they reigned 'not by the desires of men but by the will of God' seem more ironically appropriate than on the Cardinal Duke's assumption of the title of Henry IX, King of Great Britain. Very few men indeed now desired to acclaim Henry IX as their rightful sovereign. So little thought, in fact, did the average Englishman give to the man who claimed to be their true King that a few years after his self-styled accession a party of Oxford dons laid a bet on whether or not the Cardinal Duke of York was still alive. And when one remembered the career of the last English King to bear the name of Henry—the rumbustious, much-married, anti-papal Henry VIII—the Cardinal Duke's assumption of the title of Henry IX seemed doubly bizarre.

But to Henry it all made perfect sense. He was not merely asserting his rights for the sake of appearances; nor was it a case of doing what was expected of him because he happened to be the last member of the dynasty. Henry firmly believed that the crown was his by Divine Right and legitimate succession. In fleeing his kingdom a century before, James II had not abdicated his God-given right to the throne, and that right now belonged to Henry. It was his Divine Duty to claim it. That he had never set foot in England and that he spoke English with a strong Italian accent, was neither here nor there.

To indicate his elevation to the state of Majesty, Henry took various steps. He had the coronet on his coat of arms replaced by a crown, he arranged for the striking of an accession medal, and he issued a resounding manifesto. 'We have no intention of ever renouncing those rights of succession and fealty which we hold and ever intend to hold over those kingdoms and over all else appertaining to Us, as true, last and legitimate Heir to Our Royal House ...' read the triumphant phrases.

But even Henry could hardly be expected to be treated as a King and a Cardinal-Bishop at the same time. So he announced that he would retain the title of Duke of York, except that from now on he was to be addressed, not as Cardinal Duke of York but as Cardinal *called* Duke of York. This, he explained earnestly, would point the fact that Duke of York was merely an incognito title. In his own mind, though, Henry was now the Cardinal King.

Once this little accession flutter was over, Henry settled back to his own life. There was nothing else that he could do; or that he wanted to do. He was perfectly content with the ordered, privileged, luxurious and highly civilised existence that he had been leading for the past twenty-seven years. It had not needed the death of his brother Charles to reveal Henry's kingly qualities: his demeanour had never been anything less than majestic. He certainly looked like a king. Now in his early sixties, he had a strong, high-coloured, hardly lined face; the glance from his dark eyes was as imperious as ever. Although not as tall as Charles had been, Henry carried himself better: all his movements were dignified, unhurried, sure. In common with all Roman clergy of the time, he did not always wear the robes of his office. Out of the public eye, he dressed like any late eighteenth century aristocrat; most often in a black coat lined with scarlet, a scarlet waistcoat, black velvet breeches, scarlet stockings and black, scarlet-heeled shoes. On his breast would gleam a plain gold cross.

His day was highly organised. He would rise early and after Mass in the chapel of his palace of La Rocca, he might go to pray in his Cathedral in Frascati. Often he would spend the morning in the Seminary, studying in the library or talking to the students. This Seminary was Henry's special pride. He had spent a great deal of money in restoring and enlarging and re-organising it. The nine-year-long course of study had been revised, with leading scholars and professors being engaged as instructors. A printing press had been installed, a stage erected and a superb library assembled. In this library was housed the Cardinal's own valuable collection of books', manuscripts and engravings; indeed, the library at Frascati was said to be one of the most splendid in the Papal States.

Henry's beloved Seminary had provided him with a more intimate interest as well. One of its most brilliant pupils had been a young man by the name of Ercole Consalvi. The Cardinal had been especially attracted to the young Consalvi and after he had left the Seminary to join the Ecclesiastical Academy in Rome, Henry often invited him to stay at La Rocca. Like the Cardinal, Consalvi was a cultured man, deeply interested in the arts; he shared Henry's passion for music. The young man's subsequent rise to eminence (as Cardinal Secretary of State he was to prove himself an accomplished diplomat) was in no small measure due to Henry's patronage. The Cardinal treated his protégé, noted guests, 'like a dearly loved son'.

After the midday meal, the Cardinal's coach, emblazoned with his coat of arms and drawn by six superb horses, would be brought round. A crowd of beggars would always be waiting at the palace gates in the hope that the Cardinal would distribute alms. He never disappointed them. But Henry's concern for the poor was not confined to the flinging of a handful of coins from his carriage window. His interest in his flock took a more lasting form. He built schools and orphanages, he distributed food and money, he improved medical services. Far more than the majority of his colleagues, Henry showed a real interest in his pastoral and episcopal duties. He was known as often as the Protector of the Poor as he was as a Patron of the Arts or a Prince of the Church.

Henry concerned himself with those who suffered in a more mystical fashion as well. He used sometimes to touch for the King's Evil. As the Hanoverians had never claimed to possess this royal healing touch, Henry IX was the last royal descendant to practise it.

Most afternoons, in a cloud of dust and preceded by running footmen, the Cardinal's coach would go tearing off to Rome. Here Henry would attend to his duties as Vice-Chancellor of the Holy Roman Church and, if he were kept late, he might spend the night in his palace of the Can-celleria. But he always preferred to get back to the 'splendid tranquillity' of Frascati. At night, in the sumptuously furnished rooms of his palace, he would entertain on a scale unsurpassed by most of Europe's princes. Everything—the blazing chandeliers, the gleaming plate, the ruby-red wine, the liveried servants, the scarlet and purple cassocks, the powdered wigs, the gilt furniture, the damask and velvet and brocade—epitomised the elegant, luxurious, self-confident world of the *ancien régime;* a world into which Henry always fitted so comfortably. One could almost believe that one was at the court of a reigning Stuart King.

And it was appropriate, if ironic, that it should be in the year 1788 that this autocratic upholder of absolute monarchy should, if only in his own eyes, inherit the Stuart crown. For the following year was to see the outbreak of the French Revolution: a convulsion that was to turn the world of the Cardinal King upside down.

2

With the death of Charles, his daughter Charlotte, Duchess of Albany, had good reason to imagine that most of her problems would be solved. As his heir, she should inherit enough money to make life comfortable, not only for herself, but for her mother and her three children. Although Charlotte's first letter to Clementina was full of conventional sentiments about her heart being 'torn with indescribable pain' at the death of 'the best and tenderest of fathers,' she very soon got down to more practical concerns. 'Be at rest, my dear mother, about your future,'she promised, 'depend on my heart which only longs to make you as happy as you deserve.'

There could be no question, however, of an early return to Paris. Charlotte had far too much to do. She busied herself with such matters as the correct mourning to be worn and bombarded her long-suffering mother with requests for mourning buttons, ribbons and earrings. Obsessed with her royal status, Charlotte put her late father's twenty-six retainers into mourning on the grounds that this had been done 'pour le roi Jacques'. She even seems, in a mad moment, to have toyed with the idea of declaring herself heir to the throne; but this, she admitted somewhat wistfully to her mother, 'cannot happen without an Act of Parliament'.

Charles's will brought her back to earth. He had not left nearly as much as she expected. But good businesswoman that she was, Charlotte lost no time in improving her financial position. She arranged for Charles's French pension to be paid to her; she persuaded the Cardinal to make over to her any money which might, at some future date, come to him from the British Government; she sold Charles's Florentine palazzo for a very handsome profit. Any ideas that her *ami,* the Archbishop, might have had about selling their love nest in the Rue St Jacques, were firmly scotched by the practical Charlotte: he must continue to pay the rent.

She even seems, now that she was something of an heiress, to have turned her mind to marriage. She was visited, that summer, by the young Duke of Berwick. Like Charlotte herself, Berwick was an illegitimate descendant of James II. Charlotte took the young man out to Frascati to meet the Cardinal. Henry was charmed. What a pity, he said, that Berwick was so young; he would have made an excellent match for Charlotte. Charlotte, at thirty-five, was equally regretful. 'As a grandee of Spain,' she sighed, 'he will have a rent roll of three hundred thousand.'

Before many months had passed, however, Charlotte was in no position to contemplate marriage. Her abdominal pains had worsened considerably.

As her doctors could suggest nothing better than a change of air, Charlotte travelled to the baths at Nocera for a cure. But they could not help. From here she went to Bologna to stay with her friend the Marchesa Lambertini-Bovis. In November 1789 a cancerous tumour was diagnosed. She was operated on but it was no use. The Marchesa, in reporting to the Cardinal of his niece's illness, assured him that although there was small hope of recovery, he need have no fear about the 'poor Signora Duchess's Christian sentiments'; they were excellent.

Charlotte died on 17 November 1789. All in all, her life had been an unfortunate one. Bossy, mercenary and superficial she might have been but she surely deserved more out of life than to be the mistress of one selfish man and the nursemaid of another. The three years that she had spent with Charles had been rewarding only when contrasted with the make-shift quality of her previous life. And at the very moment when happiness of a sort seemed to be within her grasp—when she was in a financial position to rejoin and help her mother and children—she was struck down.

'What has your family done, Sir,' an exasperated Jacobite once asked of Charles, 'thus to draw down the vengeance of Heaven on every branch of it through so many ages?' Whatever it was, it seemed a pity that not even Charlotte should escape it.

And fate had one more blow in store for her. The church in Bologna in which she was buried was destroyed by the French in the Revolutionary wars. No trace remains of the grave of this 'small, last' Stuart hope.

3

On 20 January 1793, in the newly named Place de la Revolution in Paris, Louis XVI was guillotined. It seems to have been this significant event that finally opened the Cardinal's eyes to the dangers that were facing his particular world. Until now the old man had been relatively immune from the revolutionary tide that was sweeping through Europe. The doctrines of the Rights of Man and the Sovereignty of the People, the cries of Liberty, Equality and Fraternity, even the spread of unrest to the Papal States themselves had hardly ruffled the tranquil surface of life at Frascati. Henry had been far more upset by the fact that Pope Pius VI had finally recognised George III as King of Great Britain (the harsh revolutionary winds were huddling the sovereigns of Europe closer together) than he had been by the eruptions in Paris. The Pontiff's act of reconciliation had brought forth a wordy protest from the Cardinal: 'henceforth,' he ended his complaint,' 'I intend to pass my last few years of life in deep retirement amongst my flock at Frascati.'

He was allowed to do no such thing. In the spring of 1796 the French Revolutionary army, under the command of the brilliant young General Bonaparte, invaded Italy. As it swept triumphantly south towards

Rome, with Bonaparte issuing spine-chilling promises to 'free the Roman people from their long slavery,' the Holy See took fright. A delegation was sent to Tolentino to negotiate with the victorious young General. Bonaparte's terms were harsh. Harshest of all was the size of the indemnity to be paid to the conquerors. But if the French were to be kept out of Rome, the money would somehow have to be raised.

Papal treasures were hurriedly rounded up and of all the donations given by various noblemen and cardinals, none equalled that given by the Cardinal King. Despite the fact that he had already lost his French allowance (and was soon to lose his Spanish), Henry handed over almost all of his personal fortune. All those magnificent Stuart and Sobieski jewels (among them the pigeon-egg sized Great Ruby of Poland, worth over fifty thousand pounds) were yielded up to save the city.

But Rome was not saved. The Holy See had merely been given a respite. Within a year rioting in the streets gave the French the excuse they needed to march in. On 15 February 1798 the Roman Republic was proclaimed. Pope Pius VI, ill and over eighty, was placed under 'protective custody' and carried off to France; six cardinals were put under house arrest; Henry's friend and protégé, Ercole Consalvi, was imprisoned in the Castel Sant' Angelo; and Henry himself, now seventy-two years old, was forced to flee. Accompanied by his secretary and a valet, and taking only such silver plate as he could carry, the Cardinal escaped to Naples.

He was not allowed to remain there long. Within ten months the huddle of aristocratic and ecclesiastical refugees, headed by the Neapolitan royal family and protected by the British fleet, was obliged to seek refuge in Sicily. In their wake yet another republic—this time of Naples—was proclaimed.

At Messina Henry, who was by now limping from having hurt his leg during the flight from Naples, had to share a house with three other fugitive cardinals. Only by selling off, piece by piece, the silver plate with which he had escaped, could he cover his expenses. Already he had heard that the French troops had sacked and plundered both his Roman and Frascati palaces. He was now almost penniless.

Yet Henry's main worry at Messina seems to have been about a conclave to elect a new Pope in the all too probable event of the death of the old, ailing and imprisoned Pope Pius VI. The question had already been discussed before the flight from Rome and it had been decided that, failing Rome, Austrian-ruled Venice would be the best place in which to hold the conclave. But there was no time to be lost. The Pope might die at any moment and republican France would stop at nothing to prevent the election of another Pope.

So in February 1799 the undaunted old Cardinal and his colleagues set out for Venice. They sailed from Reggio in typically Stuart weather. On reaching Venice after a tempestuous voyage, Henry was so ill and so destitute that he was forced to seek shelter in a monastery. But he had been right to insist on coming. Pope Pius VI died in a little room in Valence that August and the various cardinals were able to assemble in Venice to elect his successor. The island monastery of San Giorgio was chosen as the site of the conclave.

Of considerable comfort to the old Cardinal was the fact that his beloved friend, Ercole Consalvi, had been released from his captivity and was able to attend the conclave. In fact, he was nominated Secretary. And one of the first acts of the newly elected Pope, who took the name of Pius VII, was to make Consalvi a cardinal and to appoint him to the office of Secretary of State. The appointment brought great joy to Henry. Amid the turbulent gloom of the last few years, here was at least one ray of sunshine.

It seemed almost like a sign that better times were on the way.

4

And so they were. During the time that Henry had been attending the conclave on the island of San Giorgio, his plight was brought to the attention of George III. The kind-hearted King was upset to hear about the Cardinal's condition. Time, and circumstances, had narrowed the gap between the Houses of Hanover and Stuart. Not only did George III and the Cardinal now share a common enemy in revolutionary France but the British monarch had never harboured any resentment towards his rival. 'They were very much mistaken,' it was once reported, 'who imagined he did not very sincerely regard the family of Stuart, who were worthy of all good men's attention, were it only for their misfortune.'

Henry's present misfortune—his penury—was a state that George III could do something about. With the full approval of his Government, he granted the aged Cardinal a pension of four thousand pounds a year. The King was probably quite unaware of the fact that his Government owed the House of Stuart a great deal more than that. Well over a century before, James II had, on his accession, arranged for his wife, Mary Beatrice, to be paid a jointure of £15,000 on his death. Neither William III nor Queen Anne had denied the widowed Mary Beatrice's right to the money but neither of them had done anything about paying it. Nor had the Hanoverians made good the lapse. At one stage Charles's daughter, the bustling Charlotte, had approached the British Government about the payment of the debt but her request had been ignored. By now, therefore, the Government owed the exiled Stuarts well over a million pounds. Seen in this light, George III's offer to pay the Cardinal four thousand pounds a year was not overly generous.

But the money was very welcome. On the Continent it was worth twice that amount. When the letter announcing the granting of the royal pension reached Venice, the conclave was interrupted so that the Cardinal could be told the glad news. He was overjoyed. Far from denying, as has been claimed,

King George's kindness in the matter, Henry paid tribute to 'the noble way of thinking of the generous and benificent Sovereign'. Now that he was assured of this annual income, Henry could live out the rest of his life in something of his old style.

Coinciding with this improvement in the Cardinal's finances, came an improvement in his ecclesiastical position. For by now Napoleon Bonaparte, who was already thinking in terms of joining the charmed circle of sovereigns whom he had so recently helped overthrow, began courting Europe's established powers. Chief amongst these was the Holy See. This meant that the newly elected Pope, Pius VII, could return to Rome. And that Henry could return to Frascati.

The Cardinal set out from Venice in the spring of 1800. Travelling in easy stages, he reached Rome towards the end of June. He was rapturously welcomed. The heart of the Roman crowd had been touched by the idea of this frail, limping, seventy-five-year-old Cardinal returning home after his many misfortunes, and he was lustily cheered as he entered the Cancelleria. But it was to Frascati that Henry was most anxious to return. Remaining in the Cancelleria only long enough for a meal and a short rest, he drove on to Frascati.

In the golden light of sunset, his coach wound its way through the narrow streets of the little town towards the Palace of La Rocca. Bells clashed, bands blared, crowds cheered, banners rippled in the summer breeze as the popular old Cardinal-Bishop once more crossed the threshold of his home. On his instructions, and with the money granted to him by George III, his recently plundered palace had already been restored and refurnished, so that it was in at least something of the old comfort that the Cardinal was able to take up the threads of his life once more.

5

If the Cardinal King was to live out his last days in relative peace and prosperity, his brother's discarded mistress, Clementina Walkinshaw, Countess of Albestroff, was to spend hers in even more miserable circumstances than ever. The Revolution had driven her from Paris to Fribourg on the Swiss border and it was here that Clementina, now in her late seventies, tried to eke out a living on her small allowance. Although Charlotte had left her mother an annual pension, the bulk of Charlotte's estate, including her jewellery, had been left to the Cardinal. And Henry, of course, had been obliged to hand almost everything over to the conquering French. In any case, it is unlikely that Henry, who could be so generous to the poor of his parish, would have given anything more to Clementina. He had always disapproved strongly of Charles's liaison with her.

In 1800 an approach was made to the British Government on Clementina's behalf but no help was forthcoming. Whatever obligations George III's Government might have felt towards the last Stuart Pretender, they apparently felt none towards the last Stuart mistress.

Clementina Walkinshaw died in 1802. She must, by then, have been over eighty. Her estate, at the time of her death, consisted of twelve pounds, six silver spoons, four books—three of them devotional works—and a small gold box. For a woman who had been the mistress of one of the most glamorous figures of his day, it was not much of a legacy.

6

The other woman in Charles's life, his wife Louise, was faring rather better. But then Louise had always known how to look after herself. The years before the Revolution had found her living with Count Alfieri in a house in the Rue de Bourgogne in Paris. Sir Horace Mann's prediction that she would 'marry the Count a week after she becomes a widow' was not fulfilled. Louise knew better than that. Why should she give up her pensions for the sake of marriage to a man with whom she was living quite happily? Louise had always fancied herself as a bohemian, artistic, daringly modern creature: why bow to stuffy convention? But she also relished her role as the last Stuart Queen. Alfieri agreed. He saw no point, he argued, 'in having a simple Countess for a wife when he had a Queen for a lover.'

Louise's salon in the Hotel de Bourgogne certainly emphasised her royal status. Her rooms boasted several pieces of furniture that had once belonged to her late husband's grandmother, Mary

Beatrice, and Louise was often to be found seated in a canopied chair of state, beneath the Royal Arms of Great Britain. 'Every piece of plate,' noted one visitor, 'down to the very teaspoons, was ornamented in a similar manner.' To her servants, Louise was always 'Your Majesty'.

The year 1791 saw the celebrated couple in England where the soidisant Stuart Queen was presented to the Hanoverian sovereigns, George III and Queen Charlotte. Times had indeed changed when the widow of the once-feared Young Pretender could be received at the Hanoverian court. 'The King talked to her a great deal,' wrote one observer, 'but always about her passage, the sea, and general topics; the Queen in the same way but less.'

By now in her late thirties, Louise seems to have lost most of the bewitching beauty that had sent all those young poets into raptures. 'Well!' reported the ageing Horace Walpole on meeting Louise in London, 'I have seen Madame d'Albany who has not a rag of royalty about her. She has good eyes and teeth; but I think can have no more beauty than remains except youth. She is civil and easy, but German and ordinary.'

No more impressed by England than England was by them, Louise and Alfieri returned to Paris. But they did not stay long. The arrest of Louis XVI convinced them that they must get out of the city as soon as possible. Only after a frightening encounter with a mob at one of the barriers were they able to get away. They made for the city that had seen the dawn of their romance—Florence. By now the once liberal Alfieri, whose plays had been banned by the Holy See for their subversive content, wanted no truck with the revolutionary ideas he had once so poetically propagated. In Florence he applied his energies to less inflamatory projects: to studying Greek and to designing the insignia of the Order of Homer, of which he was the only member.

Whether at this or any stage, the love affair between Louise and Alfieri was quite the grand romantic passion they both declared it to be, is doubtful. Louise had always had a roving eye and Stendhal claimed that by now Alfieri 'bored her to death'. In any case, the playwright seems to have found himself another mistress, a less intellectually demanding French beauty whom he visited at nine o'clock most evenings. But the erstwhile lovers were too conscious of their place in history to put an end to the affair and they continued to live their self-consciously bohemian life in their palazzo on the Lung'Arno in Florence.

When Alfieri died, aged fifty-four, in October 1803, Louise's reaction was typically histrionic. 'I am now alone in the world,' she wailed. 'I have lost all, consolation, support, society, all—all.'

But not quite all. During the last years of Alfieri's life Louise had taken up a young painter by the name of François Xavier Fabre. Even at that time her interest in him was said to range beyond an appreciation of his artistic talents, and within months of Alfieri's death, Fabre had been installed in Louise's palazzo. Fabre was then in his thirties, Louise in her fifties; and not even her fashionably cropped and curled hair nor the neo-Grecian simplicity of her clothes could hide the difference in their ages nor the matronliness of her figure. But Fabre knew on which side his bread was buttered and he remained with Louise until she died.

With her brother-in-law, the Cardinal, Louise had very little contact. Quick enough to accept his pension, she was equally quick to poke fun at him. 'He is very whimsical and very dull, for he bores everyone he meets,' she told a friend. 'He belongs to a race of amphibious creatures who are intended to be seen from a distance, but whom an evil chance has brought close to our eyes.'

Yet when it seemed as though this whimsical creature was about to be removed from before her eyes—when, in 1804, Henry fell seriously ill—Louise went dashing off to Rome. It was not the possibility of Henry's death that was bothering her; it was the possibility that her allowance might end with his death. Henry recovered, but by then Louise had arranged for the continued payment of her pension.

At about this time the old rumour—that Louise had once borne Charles a son—came to the ears of the Emperor Napoleon. He sent for Louise and asked her if it were true. Perhaps the Bonaparte Emperor was hoping to continue the Bourbon tradition of making use of a Stuart pretender to stir up trouble in Britain. He was even known to have once said that if a Stuart prince had existed, he would have placed him on the British throne. In any event, Louise denied ever having had a son.

The last Stuart Queen lived long enough to see the fall of Napoleon, the restoration of the Bourbons and—on the accession of King Charles X of France—a short-lived attempt to revive the doctrine of the Divine Right of Kings. As the nineteenth century unfolded, the fat and ageing Louise became one of the sights of Florence. In her palazzo on the Lung'Arno she received, not only all of Florentine society but most of the celebrated visitors to the city. Guests, expecting to meet some free-ranging spirit, were astonished to be confronted by this imperious old lady. Like so many women who had at one stage been considered very modern, Louise now seemed strangely old-fashioned.

'I like the old customs, the old manners, the old feelings, the old atmosphere,' she now declared, 'therefore I do not receive people who do not think as I do.'

An old admirer from the days when Louise had presided over her artistic circle in the Palazzo Muti was appalled at the change in her. 'The Queen of Hearts whom I had seen in Rome was of middle height, fair, with dark blue eyes, a slightly retroussé nose, a fair, English-looking skin, and a gay, mischievous air likely to turn all heads. Thirty years later I saw again the woman whom I had left as a rosebud ... Fortunately evening was falling; the voice was hers, the expression was a little like hers, everything else was an old woman whom I accused in my heart of enclosing, as though by magic, the young woman whom I had seen in Rome.'

In Rome, he said, 'the Queen of England behaved like a shepherdess, in Florence the Countess of Albany made herself a queen as far as she could.' This was true. Guests were left in no doubt that they were in the presence of royalty. Not only would their hostess be sitting on her canopied, throne-like chair but she would expect them to bow themselves out of her presence.

Yet Louise was always careful not to offend the British royal family by making too much of her position as the last Stuart Queen. She 'spoke in terms of respect and gratitude of the royal family,' noted one of her guests, 'and felt (or affected) an absolute passion for his present Majesty, whose picture she had.'

On the day that the news of George III's death reached Florence, an acquaintance, hoping to ingratiate herself with Louise, cried out: ' Princess, I announce the death of the Usurper!'

'What usurper?' asked Louise.

Louise died, at the age of seventy-one, in 1824. She was buried, in a grandiose tomb, in that Westminster Abbey of Italy—the Church of Santa Croce in Florence. Alone out of those women whose lives had been bound up with the wreck of the Stuart fortunes, Louise of Stolberg had been able to salvage some sort of life for herself.

7

Henry, the Cardinal King, turned eighty in the year 1805. By now this last Stuart Pretender had become an almost legendary figure in Rome. He was living, once more, in great splendour. With his restored ecclesiastical benefices added to his British pension, the Cardinal could indulge his taste for gracious surroundings and good living. Guests always spoke of the 'royal state' of the Cardinal's lifestyle: the regal ceremonial at La Rocca, the way in which no one spoke until spoken to, how the Cardinal always kept his visitors standing in his presence. No one was allowed to forget who he was, or what he claimed to be. When a visiting nun, Sister Louise, spoke to the Cardinal about her meeting with George III, Henry turned to his chaplain to say, 'She means the Elector of Hanover.' And when Sister Louise took her leave, he blessed her and said, 'You have been received by Henry of England.' His only reaction to the Emperor Napoleon's invitation to attend the Coronation in Notre-Dame was an objection to being addressed as 'Cousin'. Fellow sovereigns, he explained solemnly, addressed each other as 'Brother'.

Even his dog—a mongrel that had once attached itself to him—had to be a reflection of his royal status. 'This is a King Charles dog,' he would say to his sceptical English listeners.

To the end, the aged Cardinal delighted in the great ceremonies of the Church. He might have been frail and lame but no one, not even the Pope, could dissuade him from playing his part on these colourful occasions. 'I only saw him once again, and that was at a grand procession held at St Peter's at Rome when the Pope entered, surrounded by his cardinals,' wrote one observer. 'First and foremost among them, with a far-away look in his eyes, was Henry of York. He was much loved and respected in Rome ... with the exception of the martyr King, Charles I, he seems to have been the most refined looking of all that line of Princes.'

In the summer of 1807 Henry caught a feverish chill. He was ill for a fortnight and on 13 July, at the age of eighty-two, he died in his palace of La Rocca. Three days later his body was taken to Rome to lie in state in the Palace of the Cancelleria. Unlike his father James and his brother Charles, Henry was not dressed in royal robes: he was buried as a cardinal, not a king. The funeral service was held in the Church of St Andrea della Valle and the Cardinal's body was buried, beside those of his parents, in the crypt—the Grotte Vecchie—of St Peter's. Not long afterwards, the body of Charles was brought from the Cathedral in Frascati to lie beside those of his parents and his brother. Each of the tombs of the three Stuart princes was inscribed with a royal title: James III, Charles III, Henry IX. Later still, the bodies were to be reinterred in a single tomb. They lie there to this day.

'Were it not better,' one historian had thundered during Charles's lifetime, 'for the God-cursed dynasty to die out and cease provoking the divine wrath?

What are its annals but the history of bloodshed and oppression, failure and intrigue?'

Now that the God-cursed dynasty had indeed died out, was its record really so black? Whatever the faults of the reigning Stuarts might have been, those of the exiled Stuarts could hardly include oppression. They were undoubtedly guilty of causing bloodshed, of fostering intrigue and of inviting failure but they had been in no position to oppress anyone. Nor had they any wish to do so; on the contrary, these Stuart Kings had always seen themselves in the opposite light—as deliverers from oppression. They might have been naïve, anachronistic, irrelevant even, but these exiled Stuarts had none the less been well-intentioned men. They were motivated, not by greed or ruthless ambition, but by an unshakable sense of duty. For one thing, they believed that they were kings by Divine Right: that their mission to regain the throne was a God-given one. For another, they felt compelled to release their countrymen from the foreign kings who reigned in their stead. It was for the sake of this doubly righteous cause that they were prepared to set out, time and again, to reconquer their kingdom. That they failed so dismally was in no small measure due to the fact that the majority of Englishmen had not the slightest desire to be delivered. In the Great Britain of the second half of the eighteenth century, there was simply no room for the sort of kingship which the Stuarts represented. The times had changed; it was the Kings over the Water that had stayed the same.

Yet the lure of their story remains all but irresistible. With its trail of missed opportunities, betrayals, mistakes and bad luck, their story has what one of their biographers has called 'the fascination of failure'. Of all royal lost causes, not one has a stronger allure. To stand in the shadowy crypt of St Peter's, beside the tomb of these star-crossed Kings, is to be transported to a world of high romance and bitter disillusion.

Part Eight

Stuart Twilight

Chapter Twenty-One

1

For those who like to wander in the idle but tantalising world of might-have-been, the present Stuart claimant to the throne of Great Britain is Prince Albrecht, Duke of Bavaria. He is also, for good measure, the claimant to the throne of Bavaria. As seems only fitting for the scion of two of Europe's most romantic dynasties, Prince Albrecht has a country home set in what is probably the most picturesque spot on earth: the Swan country of the Bavarian highlands. The caramel-coloured castle of Hohenschwangau crowns a wooded hill-top above the blue-green waters of the Alpsee; on a neighbouring hillside rise the turrets of King Ludwig II's fairy-tale castle of Neuschwanstein. Beyond, and stretching as far as the eye can see, lie the sparkling, snow-covered Alps. No setting could capture, more successfully, the atmosphere of fantasy that enfolds the world of pretenders to thrones.

How did this Bavarian Prince come to inherit his claim to the British throne? The process was a highly complicated one. From the Cardinal King the line of succession passed through three royal families; the Savoys of Sardinia, the Estes of Modena and the Wittelsbachs of Bavaria.

Contrary to what has sometimes been maintained, the Cardinal King did not 'bequeath' his rights to George III. It would never have occurred to him that these God-given rights of succession could pass to anyone other than the nearest legitimate Stuart heir. To establish this heir, Jacobite genealogists had had to go back several generations (but not, they were at pains to point out, as far back as the Hanoverians had been obliged to go) until they reached Princess Henrietta, or Minette, the enchanting sister of Charles II and James II. Minette had married the Duke of Orleans and it was through their daughter Anne Marie, by her marriage into the House of Savoy, that the succession had passed to the Kings of Sardinia.

So, at the time of the Cardinal King's death, his rights devolved on Charles Emmanuel IV, King of Sardinia.

Charles Emmanuel—or, by Stuart reckoning, King Charles IV of Great Britain—was of no more value to the frail Stuart line of succession than the Cardinal King had been. For, like the Cardinal King, Charles Emmanuel was a man of exceptional piety who had set more store by his religious faith than his royal blood. In 1802 he abdicated in favour of his brother, Victor Emmanuel, and was ordained to the priesthood. His rights to the Stuart succession, however, he maintained until his death in 1819. Only then did his brother, Victor Emmanuel I of Sardinia become, in Stuart eyes, King Victor I of Great Britain.

This King, Victor Emmanuel I, was only too ready to embrace the absolutist and legitimist convictions of the House of Stuart. He was a reactionary of the deepest dye. Arriving back in his capital of Turin after years of exile during the Revolutionary and Napoleonic upheavals, Victor Emmanuel had been determined to put back the clock to the days of the *ancien régime*. 'Disregarding all other laws whatsoever,' ran his edict, 'the public will, from this date, observe the royal ordinances of 1770 ...' All new-fangled liberal notions were to be firmly stamped out. Anyone reading a foreign newspaper had to have special permission from the King; University students had to attend Mass regularly and confess at least once a month; any clerk found writing the letter R in the French fashion was instantly dismissed.

As this autocratic old monarch had no sons, his right to the Stuart throne passed, on his death in 1824, to his daughter Princess Maria Beatrice. (By then he had already abdicated the Sardinian throne in favour of his brother.) Blithely disregarding the joint reign of William and Mary, the dwindling band of Jacobites hailed their new sovereign as Queen Mary II. Raised at her father's pious and reactionary court, Maria Beatrice had married into an even more pious and reactionary one: her husband was Francis IV, the reigning Duke of Modena. This meant that the Duchy of Modena, which had already supplied the House of Stuart with one Queen in the person of James II's admirable consort, Mary Beatrice, could now boast another Stuart Queen.

Whether or not this latest Stuart Queen was as admirable as her predecessor is open to question but there can be no doubt that her husband, Duke Francis, could far outstrip James II when it came to highhandedness. 'A terrible conspiracy has broken out against me tonight,' ran a typical command from Francis IV to one of his subordinates. 'The conspirators are in my hands. Send me the hangman.'

On Maria Beatrice's death in 1840 her Stuart rights passed to her eldest son, Duke Francis V of Modena. For the following thirty-five years, until his death in 1875, this Modenese Duke, as the Stuart King Francis I, was the Pretender to the British throne.

A more hidebound, narrow-minded autocratic man than this latest Stuart Pretender would have been difficult to find. The little ducal court at Modena was notorious for its formality and its piety. One of Duke Francis V's brothers-in-law (it was Don Juan, himself the Carlist Pretender to the throne of Spain) complained that the court was dedicated to religion 'to the point of madness'. Don Juan's wife even denied him her bed. She was so pious, he grumbled, that when he did once glimpse a man's shoe protruding from the tapestries surrounding her bed, the foot was found to belong to no one more exciting than an aged priest, who was hearing her confession: Whether Duke Francis V was equally chaste is uncertain but he certainly died without issue. In 1875 the Stuart rights passed to his niece, Maria Theresa.

And here the aura of bigotry surrounding the Stuart line of succession is dispersed. By the time the unassuming Maria Theresa became, somewhat to her embarrassment, the Stuart Queen Mary III, she had already exchanged the claustrophobic air of Modena for the homelier atmosphere of Bavaria. For she had married, in 1868, Prince Ludwig, who was afterwards to become King Ludwig III of Bavaria.

The strain of madness which darkened the lives of her husband's cousins, Ludwig II and Otto I, had not affected her husband's branch of the family, and Ludwig and Maria Theresa lived an old-fashioneel, comfortable, thoroughly bourgeois life. With his squat build, his open face and his baggy trousers, Ludwig looked like nothing so much as a well-meaning country squire. Known as the Milk-Peasant or the Farmer-King, his passion was for dairy farming and canals. And almost the only thing to remind the motherly Maria Theresa of her claim to the romantic throne of the Stuarts was the bouquet of white roses which arrived, mysteriously, from England on each anniversary of the execution of Charles I.

In 1913, Prince Ludwig assumed the crown of his mad cousin Otto I. But the reign of Ludwig III and Maria Theresa lasted a mere five years. At the end of the First World War they had to flee their palace in the face of a revolution. Maria Theresa died, aged seventy, early in 1919.

Her son, Crown Prince Rupprecht of Bavaria, now became the Stuart Pretender. In this tall, handsome and soldierly Prince, the House of Stuart at last had a representative with something of the glamour of Bonnie Prince Charlie during the Forty-Five. A highly trained professional soldier, Prince Rupprecht had commanded the Sixth German Army with great distinction during the First World War. On the death of his father, in 1921, Prince Rupprecht became the Pretender to the Bavarian as well as the Stuart crown but, for the most part, he lived the quiet life of a country gentleman. Artistic, athletic, intelligent, Rupprecht was extremely popular with his Bavarian countrymen: one could almost believe that he was a reigning sovereign. Strongly opposed to Hitler, both Rupprecht and his wife suffered at the hands of the Nazi dictator. The Crown Princess was actually imprisoned in Buchenwald.

In spite of occasional Jacobite demonstrations in his favour, Prince Rupprecht confined his interest in the Stuart cause to dressing his children in kilts of Royal Stuart tartan, to filling the rooms of his home with white roses on the anniversary of Charles I's death, and to making wry jokes about his claim whenever he met members of the British royal family. The fact that he had attended the Coronation of the Hanoverian-descended King George V in 1911, seemed to imply that Rupprecht had officially recognised the validity of the rival claim. Prince Rupprecht died, at the great age of eighty-six, in 1955. In London, his Requiem Mass was attended by members of the Royal Stuart Society.

Since 1955 the Stuart claimant has been Rupprecht's eldest son, Prince Albrecht, Duke of Bavaria. Now in his mid-seventies Prince Albrecht, with less of his father's knightly qualities, is more like his grandfather, the Farmer King Ludwig III. Impatient of royal protocol, he is happiest among the peasants in the forests and mountains of his native Bavaria. Hunting is said to be his passion. Twice married, Prince Albrecht has two sons and twin daughters. His eldest son, Prince Francis, born in 1933, will inherit both the Bavarian and the Stuart claims. But it is unlikely that either father or son waste much time yearning for the throne left empty, on that wild December night almost three centuries ago, by their relation, James II.

2

While the Stuart line of succession was snaking its way through various Continental royal families, others were claiming a more direct descent from James II. The old rumour—that Charles and Louise had had a son—was revived. In the year 1847 a book entitled "The Tales of the Century' was published in London. Its authors called themselves John Sobieski Stuart and Charles Edward Stuart. Their fanciful book implies that they were the grandsons of Charles and

Louise. Their father, hints their breathless account, was the baby whom Dr Beaton had seen being smuggled out of Italy in 1773. This child had grown up to become a colourful figure in the Western Highlands of Scotland. He had been known, by the admiring locals, as 'The Red Eagle'. The authors of the book were his two eaglets, the so-called Sobieski Stuarts.

'That a number of people have been found to accept this contention,' wrote Sir Charles Petrie, 'is proof of the hold which the House of Stuart has never ceased to exercise upon popular imagination in the British Isles, so that it is no exaggeration to say that while, if a man were to declare himself the heir of the Yorkist or Tudor dynasty, he will attract little attention, yet if he claim to be a Stuart he will find hundreds ready to believe him.'

And if hundreds would be ready to belieye him, thousands upon thousands would be fascinated by the possibility.

Another couple, (or possibly the same couple), were the Stuart Hay brothers. This strange pair, with their ringletted, shoulder-length hair and their 'curious, antiquated Tartan costume' were much in evidence in the Highlands during the middle years of the nineteenth century. Proud, if impoverished, they moved from one Jacobite household to another. Lady St Helier, writing half a century later, remembered being told, as a little girl, to curtsey to them and to walk backwards out of their presence. But for all that, the claim of the Stuart Hay brothers to be legitimate

Stuart descendants was not generally recognised. Yet they did command a certain respect. They were so dignified, so independent, so well-spoken. And no one could deny that they looked like Stuarts. Perhaps James III's wife, the neurotic Clementina, had not been so wide of the mark when she accused her husband of infidelity with the wife of John Hay, Earl of Inverness.

On the death of the elder brother, the younger laid claim to the title of Count of Albany. For years this bizarre creature was one of the sights of the reading rooms in the British Museum. With his studied air of melancholy, his romantically flowing hair and his threadbare costume, all furred and frogged, the Count of Albany always maintained that, as the legitimate son of Charles III and Louise of Stolberg, he was the rightful King of Great Britain. One wonders what Queen Victoria's views on the matter would have been.

A much stronger claim to be a direct descendant came from the so-called Chevalier de Roehanstart. His Germanic-sounding name gave a hint of his true identity, for Roehanstart was obviously a phonetic combination of Rohan and Stuart. In fact, the Chevalier was none other than Charles Edward, the illegitimate son of Bonnie Prince Charlie's daughter Charlotte, and the Prince de Rohan.

It appears that the boy, at the age of about nine, had been taken to Germany during the Reign of Terror in Paris and that his father, the Archbishop, who was by then also in Germany, had paid for his education. Roehanstart had spent his young manhood in the service of Prince Alexander of Württemberg fighting against Napoleon. In 1816 he had gone to Scotland. Making no secret of his origins, he explained to the students to whom he had been obliged to give French lessons in order to make ends meet, that he had come to Scotland 'to make acquaintance of the brave people who had fought so well for his grandfather'. Those who met the Chevalier at the time found him to be a studious, gentlemanly, somewhat unimpressive figure, resembling, in both looks and personality, his grandmother Clementina Walkinshaw.

He seems to have inherited too, her perenially impecunious state. So, in the hope of getting his hands on his mothet's estate, which she had willed to the late Cardinal King, Roehanstart travelled from Edinburgh to London in order to petition the Prince Regent. The Prince was all ears. The story of the ill-starred Stuart dynasty held a strong fascination for the Prince Regent; he had not long ago read Sir Walter Scott's stirring Jacobite novel, *Waverley*. But interest was one thing, active assistance another. For various reasons, the Prince Regent felt himself unable to help Roehanstart.

With his royal petition having failed, Roehanstart turned to that other remedy for a man without money—marriage. He first married the daughter of a French émigré and, after her death in 1821, married an Englishwoman. By neither of these wives did the Chevalier have any children. And as both Roehanstart's sisters, Aglaë and Marie, died unmarried during the 1820s, Bonnie Prince Charlie's illegitimate line had narrowed to the childless Chevalier de Roehanstart.

But not only had Roehanstart's marriages brought him no children, they had brought him no lasting financial relief. So, sometime during the late 1820s the Chevalier returned to the Continent to enlist as a mercenary in the Austrian army. For the following twenty-five years he served as a soldier attaining, if he is to be believed, the rank of general. But, through all these years, the pull of Scotland remained, and in 1854, at the age of seventy, Bonnie Prince Charlie's grandson returned to the land of his ancestors. But not for long. On 28 October he was killed in a carriage accident in Perthshire. He was buried in the churchyard of Dunkeld Cathedral.

On his tombstone he is described as General Charles Edward Stuart, Count Roehanstart, and beneath his name and dates is inscribed the singularly appropriate comment: *Sic transit gloria mundi.*

3

With Stuart descendants, true, false, legitimate and illegitimate, flourishing in the most unlikely places, the Stuart cause itself was withering away in Great Britain. Jacobitism, by the time of the Cardinal King's death, was very largely a spent force.

But it was not entirely spent. Odd Jacobite Clubs flourished here and there in the British Isles until well into the nineteenth century: a Jacobite Club in North Wales, known as the Cycle of the White Rose, was active until the late 1850s. For the most part, though, the activities of these clubs were confined to nothing more subversive than the raising of long-stemmed glasses, exquisitely engraved with a white rose, to drink the health of whoever the current *de jure* sovereign happened to be. When a certain Jacobite peer was pressed to say whether he 'really and truly' believed that Duke Francis V of Modena was his legitimate sovereign, he replied that he did. But only, he explained, 'after dinner'.

By the mid-nineteenth century the champions of the Stuart cause had been narrowed down, very largely, to the upholders of Europe's other dethroned Legitimist dynasties—the Bourbons of France, the Carlists of Spain, the Miguelists of Portugal. A Stuart Society, the Order of the White Rose, was based on the defiantly anachronistic principle that 'All Authority has a divine sanction and that the Sovereign power does not exist merely by the will of the people or the consent of the governed.' One of the leading Companions of the Order was the artist, James McNeill Whistler.

The hundredth anniversary of the death of Bonnie Prince Charlie—31 January 1888—brought a little flutter of Jacobite activity. Cardinal Manning's prohibition of a special Requiem Mass to mark the occasion (he was dismissed as a 'Whig') merely heightened public interest, and the hitherto little-known Order of the White Rose suddenly found itself in the limelight. Applications for membership came streaming in. Revitalised, the Order organised a Stuart Exhibition. This was held in 1889 and, in the catalogue, the last three Stuart princes were unequivocally referred to as King James III and VIII, King Charles HI and King Henry IX.

It was in Scotland, of course, that the spirit of Jacobitism lingered longest. Both Robert Burns, that self-styled 'sentimental Jacobite' and Sir Walter Scott felt themselves drawn to the bitter-sweet saga of the Stuarts; and in poems, prose, songs and paintings the legend lived on. When the famous international hostess, Roma Lister, visited Scotland in the years before the First World War, she was astonished at the undiminished loyalty of certain Scots towards the House of Stuart. 'There is no house, rich or poor, of large farmer or poor farm hand, where is not placed in some conspicuous spot in the living room the picture of Queen Mary's execution at Fotheringhay Castle.' And not only pictures of Mary Queen of Scots but of the latest Stuart Queen, Mary III, the consort of King Ludwig III of Bavaria. Some unremitting Jacobites even went so far as to make a point of placing postage stamps, bearing the head of George V, upside down on their envelopes.

'I suppose I answered thirty times, if I answered once,' claims Roma Lister, then fresh from a visit to Munich, 'their enquiries about Prince Rupert of Bavaria, and when he was coming to take his realm in Scotland. I tried to parry these questions and humbly suggested that Prince Rupert was much inclined to his Bavarian kingdom, and held Munich dear.'

One old farmer was especially puzzled by this answer. 'And where would Prince Rupert find himself so well as in his ain town of Edinburgh and his ain kingdom of Scotland?' he demanded.

But if the spirit of Jacobitism lives on in Scotland today, it is not through deep affection for the House of Stuart. It is because of the continuing coolness between Scotland and England. The Stuarts might long since have ceased to symbolise Scotland's antipathy towards England but that same antipathy remains; the echoes of the battles of the Fifteen and the Forty-Five reverberate still. Scottish nationalism, which the Stuarts were able to harness in their fight for the British throne, is hardly less clamorous today.

4

Throughout all these years of Stuart turbulence, the Hanoverian royal family had remained firmly seated on the British throne. Only after the Cardinal King had been safely buried, however, did they feel free to assuage their -feelings of guilt towards the exiled Stuarts. George III's interest in the family had not gone much beyond his granting of a pension to the aged Cardinal, but his son, the erratic Prince Regent, afterwards George IV, admitted to having Jacobite sympathies. A dozen or so years after Henry's death, George IV gave Pope Pius VII a contribution towards the cost of Canova's monument to James III and his sons in St Peter's in Rome.

Then, in 1824, the King was very interested to hear that the workmen rebuilding the parish church of St Germain had discovered three leaden boxes, each containing parts of the remains of King james II, Queen Mary Beatrice and their daughter, Princess Louise Marie. He ordered that the remains be re-interred (the Catholic Bishop of Edinburgh officiated at the reburial ceremony) and he erected marble tablets in their honour. But his attempts to find the body of James II, which had disappeared from the chapel of the English Benedictines in the Rue St Jacques during the Revolution, was unsuccessful.

Queen Victoria was equally attracted by the saga of the exiled Stuarts. When, in 1855, she paid a state visit to the Emperor Napoleon III, she drove out to the Palace of St Germain to see the rooms in which James II and Mary Beatrice had lived. Although she admired the position of the palace, she was depressed by the neglected state of the building. "The Emperor has lately recovered the property and intends to do something with it,' she wrote, 'but he was much disgusted when he saw the state of ruin and filth in which it is.' The Queen arranged for a 'modest but decent monument' to be erected in the parish church in honour of James II.

But it was by her enthusiasm for the way of life in the Scottish Highlands that Queen Victoria did most towards laying the ghost of the Stuarts. In her appreciation of her dear, good, loyal, brave, honest Highlanders she outdid even Bonnie Prince Charlie. Balmoral Castle, close to Braemar where, in 1715, the Earl of Mar had raised the standard of King James III and VIII, became the Queen's favourite home. With Victoria in a Royal Stuart tartan crinoline sitting beside Albert in a Royal Stuart tartan kilt on a settee made of stags' antlers in a room hung with yet more Royal Stuart tartan, no one could doubt that the Queen had decided to forgive, if not forget. She took, it was said, 'the keenest pride and interest' in the history of the royal House of Stuart. After all, by her direct descent through the daughter of King James I and VI, Victoria felt herself as much a Stuart as any of the Italian princes and princesses to whom that dwindling band of Jacobites still raised their glasses.

Visiting Loch Arkaig, beside which Bonnie Prince Charlie had once 'skulked,' Victoria's always emotional heart swelled with pride at the thought that she was related to this romantic dynasty. 'I feel a sort of reverence in going over these scenes in this most beautiful country, which I am proud to call my own,' she enthused, 'where there was such devoted loyalty to the family of my ancestors—for Stuart blood is in my veins, and I am *now* their representative, and the people are as devoted and loyal to me as they were to that unhappy race.'

Queen Victoria's descendants kept up the tradition of close identification with the Scottish Highlands. The British monarchs continued to spend certain periods of each year at Balmoral. A minister in attendance on Edward VII during a cruise up the British coast was once very amused to hear the always correctly dressed King say to his valet, as they approached the shores of Scotland, 'Something a little more Scottish tomorrow.'

And on one occasion, when George V was staying at Blair Castle with the Duke of Atholl, the two men discussed the Forty-Five during which one of the Duke's ancestors, Lord George Murray, had invariably been at loggerheads with Prince Charles. It had, of course, been Lord George who had insisted that the Prince turn back at Derby. 'Your ancestor was wrong,' claimed King George. 'Had Charles Edward gone on from Derby, I should not have been the King of England today.'

But it was left to George V's second son, the future King George VI, to take the step which most closely linked the British royal family to Scotland. In 1923 he married Lady Elizabeth Bowes-Lyon, a descendant of the ancient Stuart Kings of Scotland and of that Earl of Strathmore who had once entertained James III and VIII in his castle at Glamis. Into the overwhelmingly Germanic royal family the new bride introduced an almost Stuart-like panache. And it is fitting that, in later years, it should be the Scottish-born Queen Elizabeth the Queen Mother who, after visiting the remains of the Stuarts in St Peter's in Rome, paid for the restoration of the tomb.

Queen Elizabeth II has given the unmistakably Stuart names of Charles and Anne to her two eldest children. The next King of Great Britain will be King Charles III. One can only hope that when that day comes, Bonnie Prince Charlie will not turn in his newly restored grave.

5

Throughout Europe today there are numerous reminders of the exiled Stuarts. In statuary, on canvas and in monuments, in houses and palaces and castles, on battlefields, in churches and in crypts, memories of this star-crossed dynasty live on. The Palace of St Germain, although greatly altered since the days of James II, still rises high above the River Seine. If anything, it looks even more immense and forbidding than it did during the Stuart exile. From its terraces, where once Mary Beatrice and her daughter Louise Marie used to stroll, one can still see the distant domes and spires of Paris. In the formal, classically-proportioned parish church is the monument to James II. Rising white in the sunshine that shafts through a sky-light, the Grecian-styled memorial is set against the richly-patterned walls of a semi-circular alcove, on the right as one faces the altar.

In Paris, behind a fish shop in the Rue St Jacques, are the decaying remains of the Convent of the Visitation in which Clementina and her daughter

Charlotte lived out so many years of their impecunious lives.

The Palazzo Muti, where so much Stuart family drama was set, still stands in the Piazza dei Santi Apostoli, off the Via del Corso in Rome. It is now a shabby, dust-coloured, sadly sub-divided building, its sunless courtyard full of the smells of cooking. Its façade has been defaced by the large sign: *Instituti Riuniti Meschini ENSE.* A plaque set in the wall carries, in Italian, this inscription: 'There lived in this building Henry, Duke later Cardinal of York, who, surviving son of James III of England, took the name Henry IX. In him in the year 1807 the Stuart dynasty became extinct.'

For some obscure reason, no mention is made of the fact that the palazzo had also housed those other Stuarts—the melancholy James III, the neurotic Maria Clementina, the dissipated Prince Charles, the self-obsessed Princess Louise or the bustling Charlotte, Duchess of Albany.

Across from the Palazzo Muti stands the magnificent baroque Church of Sand Apostoli. A pillar on the right of the aisle carries an inscription to the effect that the heart of Maria Clementina, Queen of Great Britain, is buried in the marble urn above.

Scotland, not unnaturally, is full of reminders of those stirring Jacobite days. Numberless cairns and plaques and monuments mark the places where men gathered or fought or died for the sake of the House of Stuart. At Braemar, the lounge of the Invercauld Arms

Hotel covers the. spot where the Earl of Mar raised the standard in 1715. At Glenfinnan where, on a blustery day thirty years later the standard was again unfurled, a massive column, topped by a statue of a kilted Highlander, stands in lonely silhouette against the silver waters of Loch Shiel. A mournful wind still ripples the rough grasses on the battlefield of Culloden. A cairn on the rocky shore of Loch nam Uamh marks the spot where Charles left Scotland, forever, on 19 September 1746.

In Florence one can still see, in the Via San Sebastiano, the weather vane carrying the figures CR 1777 above the roof of the palazzo in which the drunken Charles and the frustrated Louise lived their discordant married life. A fresco in the entrance hall of the palazzo proudly displays the royal coat of arms. On the Lung'Arno is yet another Stuart palazzo, the one in which the last Stuart Queen, the ageing, imperious Louise, held her court. Her magnificent tomb, sporting the royal arms in a frame of mourning cherubs, is in the Church of Sante Croce.

In the Corso Vittorio Emanuele II in Rome stands the massive Renaissance Palace of the Cancelleria in which Henry, the Cardinal King, carried out his duties as Vice-Chancellor of the Holy Roman Church and in which Louise entertained and inspired the fiery-eyed Alfieri. The little biscuit-coloured town of Frascati still crowns its hilltop outside Rome. Both the Cathedral and the Cardinal King's palace of La Rocca suffered bombing during the Second World War, but the tablet to Charles, surmounted by the royal coat of arms, can be seen on the left of the main door. A street beside the restored palace is named the Via Duca di York.

But it is in St Peter's in Rome that one finds the final epitaph to the story of the Stuart dynasty. On the left as one enters the Bascilica, above the doorway leading to the Dome, swirls the riotously rococo monument to the unhappy Clementina Sobieska Stuart. Below are inscribed the words: Maria Clementina, Queen of Great Britain, France and Ireland. Opposite, between two marble pillars, is the impressive Canova monument to James III and his two sons. The monument, with its royal coat of arms, its laurel wreaths, its floral swags, its angels weeping beside a closed portal and its finely executed bas-reliefs of the three men, carries, in Latin, the inscription:

JAMES III
SON OF KING JAMES II OF GREAT BRITAIN
CHARLES EDWARD
AND HENRY, DEAN OF THE CARDINAL FATHERS
SONS OF JAMES III
THE LAST OF THE ROYAL HOUSE OF STUART

In the gloom of the crypt, in a simple tomb surmounted by a crown on a cushion, lie the three bodies. The long road, taken by James II when he was converted to the Roman Catholic faith ends, appropriately enough, here beneath the massive Dome of St Peter's in Rome.

Bibliography

ADDINGTON, A. C: *The Royal House of Stuart.* Charles Skilton, London, 1969

AILESBURY, Earl of: *Memoirs. 2* vols., Roxburghe Club, London, 1890

ALFIERI, Vittorio: *Memoirs of the Life and Writings of Vittorio Alfieri. 2* vols., Henry Colburn, London, 1810

ASHLEY, Maurice: *The Stuarts in Love.* Hodder and Stoughton, London, 1963

ASHLEY, Maurice *James II.* Dent, London, 1978

BAXTER, Stephen B.: *William III.* Longmans, London, 1966

BELLOC, Hilaire:.*James the Second.* Faber and Gwyer, London, 1928

BERWICK, Duke of: *Memoirs.* 2 vols., Moutard, Paris, 1779

BEVAN, Bryan: *I was James II's Queen.* Heinemann, London, 1963

BEVAN, Bryan: *King James the Third of England.* Robert Hale, London, 1967

BEVERIDGE, H.: *The Sobieski Stuarts.* R. Carruthers and Sons, Inverness, 1909

BLAIKIE, W. B.: *Itinerary of Prince Charles Edward Stuart.* University Press, Edinburgh, 1897

BLAIKIE, W. B.: *Origins of the '45.* Scottish Historical Society, 1916

BOCCA, Geoffrey: *The Uneasy Heads.* Weidenfeld and Nicolson, London, 1959

BOSQ DE BEAUMONT, G. de: *La Cour des Stuarts à Saint Germain-en-Laye, 1698–1718.* Emile Paul, Paris, 1912

BROWN, Beatrice Curtis (Editor): *The Letters of Queen Anne, 1686–1714.* Geoffrey Bles, London, 1935

BURNET, Gilbert: *History of His Own Times.* J. Nunn and R. Priestley, 1838

CAMPANA DI CAVELI, Marchioness Emilia: *Les Derniers Stuarts à Saint Germain-en-Laye.* Didier, Paris, 1871.

CASSAVETTI, Eileen: *The Lion and the Lilies.* Macdonald and Jane's, London,1977

CHANNON, Henry: *The Ludwigs of Bavaria.* John Lehmann, London, 1933

CHAPMAN, Hester W.: *Mary II, Queen of England.* Jonathan Cape, London,1953

CHAPMAN, Hester W.: *Privileged Persons.* Jonathan Cape, London, 1966

CLARENDON, Edward Hyde, 1st Earl of: *Life of Clarendon.* New ed., 3 vols., Clarendon Press, Oxford, 1827

CROSLAND, Margaret: *Louise of Stolberg.* Oliverand Boyd, London, 1962

CURLEY, WalterJ. P.: *Monarchs in Waiting.* Hutchinson, London, 1975

DAICHES, David: *Charles Edward Stuart.* Thames and Hudson, London, 1973

DANGEAU, Marquis de: *Journal de la Cour de Louis XIV.* Deterville, Paris, 1807

DANIEL, F. H. Blackburne (Editor): *Calendar of the Stuart Papers belonging to H. M. the King preserved at Windsor Castle.* H. M. Stationery Office, London, 1902–1923

DORAN, John: *'Mann' and Manners at the Court of Florence, 1740–86. 2* vols., London, 1876

DOUGLAS, Hugh: *Charles Edward Stuart,* Roben Hale, 1975

DUKE, Winifred: *Prince Charles Edward and the Forty-Five.* Robert Hale, London,1938

DUKE, Winifred: *The Rash Adventurer.* Roben Hale, London, 1952

DUKE, Winifred: *In the Steps of Bonnie Prince Charlie.* Rich and Cowan, London,1953

EARLE, Peter: *Life and Times of James II.* Weidenfeld and Nicolson, London,1972

ELCHO, David Wemyss, Lord: *A Short Account of the Affairs of Scotland, 1744–6.* (Ed. Hon. Evan Charteris) David Douglas, Edinburgh, 1907

EVELYN, John: *Diary.* 6 vols., Clarendon Press, Oxford, 1955

EWALD, Alexander Charles: *Life and Times of Charles Stuart, the Young Pretender. 2* vols., Chapman and Hall, London, 1875

FLOOD, J. M.: *The Life of Chevalier Charles Wogan.* Talbot Press, Dublin, 1922

FORBES, Robert: *The Lyon in Mourning.* (Ed. H. Paton) 3 vols., Scottish Historical Society, Edinburgh, 1895–6

FORBIN, Claude, Comte de: *Memoirs.* Amsterdam, 1730

FORSTER, Margaret: *The Rash Adventurer.* Secker and Warburg, London, 1973

FOTHERGILL, Brian: *The Cardinal King.* Faber and Faber, London, 1958

FRANCILLION, Robert Edward: *Mid-Victorian Memories.* Hodder and Stoughton, London, 1913

FRASER, Antonia (Editor) : *The Lives of the Kings and Queens of England.* Weidenfeld and Nicolson, London, 1971

GILBERT, Sir John Thomas: *Narratives of the Detention, Liberation, Marriage of Maria Clementina Stuart, styled Queen of Great Britain and Ireland.* Joseph Dollard, Dublin, 1894

GREEN, David: *Queen Anne.* Collins, London, 1970

GREW, E. and M. Sharpe: *The English Court in Exile: James II at Saint Germain.* Mills and Boon, London, 1911

HAILE, Martin: *Queen Mary of Modena.* Dent, London, 1905

HAILE, Martin: *James Francis Edward, the Old Pretender.* Dent, London, 1907

HAMILTON, Elizabeth: *William's Mary: Mary II.* Hamish Hamilton, London,1972

HASWELL, Jock: *James II.* Hamish Hamilton, London, 1972

HEAD, Frederick Waldegrave: *The Fallen Stuarts.* Cambridge University Press, Cambridge, 1901

HERVEY, John, Lord: *Memoirs of the Reign of George II, to the death of Queen Caroline.* 2 vols., Eyre and Spottiswoode, London, 1848

HOPKIRK, Mary: *Queen over the Water.* John Murray, London, 1953

ISAACSON, Charles S.: *The Story of the English Cardinals.* Elliot Stock, London,1907

JAMES II, King: *Memoirs.* (Ed. A. L. Sells) Chatto and Windus, London, 1962

JOHNSTONE, Chevalier James de: *Memoirs of the Rebellion in 1745 and 1746.* Folio Society, London, 1958

JONES, G. H.: *The Main Stream of Jacobitism.* Harvard University Press, 1954

KELLY, Bernard W.: *Life of Henry Benedict Stuart, Cardinal of York.* R. and T. Wasbourne, London, 1899

KENYON, J. P.: *The Stuarts.* Batsford, London, 1958

LANG, Andrew: *Prince Charles Edward Stuart, The Young Chevalier.* Longmans, London, 1903

LANG, Andrew: *Pickle the Spy.* Longmans, London, 1897

LANG, Andrew: *The Companions of Pickle.* Longmans, London, 1898

LANG, Andrew and SHIELD A.: *The King Over the Water.* Longmans, London, 1907

LEE, Vernon: *The Countess of Albany.* London, 1884

LINKLATER, Eric: *The Royal House of Scotland.* Macmillan, London, 1970

LISTER, Roma: *Reminiscences.* Hutchinson, London, n.d.

MACKENZIE, Agnes Mure: *The Passing of the Stuarts.* Oliver and Boyd, Edinburgh, 1937

MACKENZIE, Compton: *Prince Charlie.* Peter Davies, London, 1932

MACKENZIE, Compton: *Prince Charlie and His Ladies.* Cassell, London, 1934

MCLAREN, Moray: *Bonnie Prince Charlie.* Rupert Hart-Davis, London, 1972

MADAN, Falconer .(Editor): *Stuart Papers.* Roxburghe Club, London, 1889

MASSON, Georgina: *The Companion Guide to Rome.* Collins, London, 1965

MILLER, Peggy: *A Wife for the Pretender.* Allen and Unwin, London, 1965

MILLER, *Peggy: James: Old Pretender.* Allen and Unwin, London, 1971

MORTON, H. V.: *A Traveller in Rome.* Methuen, London, 1957

MURRAY, Sir John, of Broughton: *Memoirs of Murray, secretary to Prince Charles Edward, 1740–7.* (Ed. R. F. Bell) Scottish Historical Society, Edinburgh, 1898

NEVILL, Ralph Henry: *The World of Fashion, 1837–1922.* Methuen, London,1923

NOBILI-VITELLESCHI, Amy, Marchesa: *A Court in Exile.* 2 vols., Hutchinson, London,1903

NOBILI-VITELLESCHI, Amy, Marchesa: *The Romance of Savoy: Victor Amadeus II and his Stuart Bride.* 2 vols., Hutchinson, London, 1905

OMAN, Carola: *Mary of Modena.* Hodder and Stoughton, London, 1962

PEPYS, Samuel: *Diary of Samuel Pepys.* Allen and Unwin, London, 1914

PETRIE, Sir Charles: *The Jacobite Movement, The First Phase 1688–1716.* Eyre and Spottiswoode, London, 1948

PÉTRIE, Sir Charles: *The Jacobite Movement, The Last Phase 1716–1807.* Eyre and Spottiswoode, London, 1950

PÉTRIE. Sir Charles: *The Duke of Berwick and His Son.* Eyre and Spottiswoode, London, 1951

PÉTRIE, Sir Charles: *The Stuarts.* Eyre and Spottiswoode, London, 1958

PLUMB, J. H.: *The First Four Georges.* Batsford, London, 1956

POLNAY, Peter de: *Death of a Legend.* Hamish Hamilton, London, 1952

PORCELLI, Baron: *The White Cockade.* Hutchinson, London, 1949

RANKINE, Alexander: *Memoirs of the Chevalier St George.* London, 1702 REDMAN, Alvin: *The House of Hanover.* Alvin Redman, London, 1960

ROBERTS, Cecil: *And So To Rome.* Hodder and Stoughton, London, 1950.

ROWE, Vivian: *Royal Chateaux of Paris.* Putnam, London, 1957

STHELIER, Lady: *Memories of Fifty Years.* Edward Arnold, London, 1909

SAINT-SIMON, Duc de: *Mémoires.* Libraire Hachette, Paris, 1886

SELBY, John: *Over the Sea to Skye.* Hamish Hamilton, London, 1973

SETON, Walter: *Relations of Henry, Cardinal of York, with the British Government.* Aberdeen, 1920

SETON, Walter: *Some Unpublished Letters of Henry, Cardinal of York.* Glasgow, 1919

SÊVIGNÉ, Madame de: *Lettres.* Editions Lefèvre, Paris, 1843

SHIELD, Alice: *Henry Stuart, Cardinal York, and His Times.* London, 1908

SKEET, F. J. A.: *H. R. H. Charlotte Stuart, Duchess of Albany.* Eyre and Spottiswoode, London, 1932

STEVENSON, Christopher Sinclair-: *Inglorious Revolution: The Jacobite Risings of 1708, 1715, 1719.* Hamish Hamilton, London, 1971

STRICKLAND, Agnes: *Lives of the Queens of England.* 12 vols., Henry Colburn, London, 1840–8

TAYLER, A. and H.: *The Old Chevalier: James Francis Stuart.* Cassell, London, 1934

TAYLER, A. and H.: *Jacobite Exile. A.* Maclehose, London, 1937

TAYLER, A. and H.: *1745 and After.* T. Nelson, London, 1938

TAYLER, A. and H.: *The Stuart Papers at Windsor.* John Murray, London, 1939

TAYLER, H.: *The Jacobite Court at Rome in 1719.* Scottish Historical Society, Edinburgh, 1938

TAYLER, H.: *Jacobite Epilogue.* T. Nelson, London, 1941

TAYLER, H.: *Prince Charlie's Daughter.* Batsworth, London, 1950

TURNER, F. C.: *James II.* Eyre and Spottiswoode, London, 1948

VAUGHAN, Herbert M.: *The Last of the Royal Stuarts: Henry Stuart, Cardinal Duke of York.* Methuen, London, 1906

VAUGHAN, Herbert M.: *The Last Stuart Queen: Louise, Countess of Albany.* Duckworth, London, 1910

VICTORIA, Queen: *Leaves from the Journal of Our Life in the Highlands, 1848–61.* Smith, Elder and Co., London, 1868

VICTORIA. Queen: *Leaves from a Journal.* André Deutsch, London, 1961

VINING, Elizabeth Grey: *Flora Macdonald.* Geoffrey Bles, London, 1967

WALPOLE, Horace: *Memoirs of the Reign of George II.* 3 vols., Richard Bentley, London, 1846

WALPOLE, Horace: *Letters to the Countess of Ossory, 1769–97.* 2 vols., Richard Bentley, London, 1848

WALPOLE, Horace: *Letters to Sir Horace Mann.* 3 vols., Richard Bendey, London,1833

ZEE, B. and H. A Van Der: *William and Mary.* Macmillan, London, 1973

Made in the USA
Middletown, DE
14 January 2018